In Quest of the Self
Masquerade and Travel in the Eighteenth-Century Novel

D1824315

General Editor:
Daniel Meyer-Dinkgräfe

In Quest of the Self
Masquerade and Travel in the Eighteenth-Century Novel

Fielding, Smollett, Sterne

Jakub Lipski

Amsterdam - New York, NY 2014

Cover illustration: Pietro Longhi, Detail from *The Painter in His Studio,*
about 1741-1744, oil on canvas, 41 x 53.3 cm.
The J. Paul Getty Museum, Los Angeles, purchased in part with funds realized
from the sale of paintings donated by Burton Fredericksen and William
Garred.

Cover design by Aart Jan Bergshoeff.

The paper on which this book is printed meets the requirements of "ISO
9706:1994, Information and documentation - Paper for documents -
Requirements for permanence".

ISBN: 978-90-420-3889-9
ISSN: 1573-2193
E-Book ISBN: 978-94-012-1172-7
E-book ISSN: 1879-6044
© Editions Rodopi B.V., Amsterdam - New York, NY 2014
Printed in the Netherlands

Acknowledgements

This book would not have been written without the support and expertise of Prof. Grażyna Bystydzieńska, who encouraged the project from the very beginning, and who was always willing to share her knowledge and experience. The final shape of the book is the product of her many insightful remarks and watchful eye. I also wish to thank Prof. Daniel Meyer-Dinkgräfe for accepting the book for publication in the Rodopi CLA series and for his assistance ever since.

My sincere thanks go to Prof. Wojciech Nowicki and Prof. Marek Błaszak, the readers of the early draft, and to Prof. Gregory Tague, the reader of the revised book, all of whom drew my attention to what would have otherwise escaped me. I am also grateful to Katarzyna Dudek, Ewa Młynarczyk, Przemysław Uściński and Dr Magdalena Ożarska, who read parts of the manuscript and were kind enough to comment on its shortcomings. I am deeply indebted to Dr Stuart McWilliams, the scrupulous proof-reader of the text, who was always there to clear up my linguistic doubts.

At different stages of the writing process I consulted with various experts in the field. Prof. Christoph Heyl shared and reinforced my fascination with the masquerade, Prof. John Barrell and Prof. Anthony Johnson shed light on those aspects of the Smollettian world which I would have inevitably failed to notice, while Prof. Judith Hawley helped clarify my thoughts on Sterne. Needless to say, the responsibility for any errors and weaknesses in this book is entirely my own.

For the last five years my interest in the eighteenth-century novel has been generously supported by Kazimierz Wielki University in Bydgoszcz. I am grateful to the Faculty of Humanities for funding my research in the British Library in the years 2012 and 2014, and my participation in international conferences, most importantly in the conference Discourse of Identity (Santiago de Compostela, 2012) and in the tercentenary conference on Laurence Sterne (London, 2013), where I presented early versions of Chapter 3 and Chapter 8 respectively. My thanks are also due to the staff of the Department of English, especially to Dr Ewa Wełnic, who was the first one to encourage my enthusiasm for eighteenth-century literature.

Finally, and most importantly, my heartfelt thanks go to my family. My greatest debt is to my wife Aneta for her continuing support and forbearance, and for keeping a hold on our everyday life when the writing process was particularly absorbing. Our darling son Tadeusz also played a part in the publication of this work, as his expected date of birth was the best deadline and motivation possible for the writer who was about to become a father. This book is dedicated to them.

Contents

Abbreviations

References to the works by Fielding, Smollett and Sterne which I quote with frequency use the following abbreviations:

ASJ   Laurence Sterne. *A Sentimental Journey through France and Italy*

BJ   Laurence Sterne. *Continuation of the Bramine's Journal*

JA   Henry Fielding. *Joseph Andrews*

Letters   Laurence Sterne. *The Letters*

PP   Tobias Smollett. *The Adventures of Peregrine Pickle*

RR   Tobias Smollett. *The Adventures of Roderick Random*

Sermons   Laurence Sterne. *The Sermons of Laurence Sterne*

TJ   Henry Fielding. *Tom Jones*

TS   Laurence Sterne. *The Life and Opinions of Tristram Shandy, Gentleman*

Preface

There has recently been a tendency in literary criticism to turn to the eighteenth century for two reasons – to undermine its alleged rationality as a cultural formation and to seek affinities between the period and a time labelled by some as post- or even post-postmodern. One of the eighteenth-century socio-cultural institutions which has come to the fore as a symptom of the irrational trends permeating the Age of Reason, as well as of its instability and arbitrariness, is the masquerade – an institution which has been referred to in attempts to deconstruct the reasonableness of the Enlightenment and to argue that the contemporary concerns about the non-essentiality of identity in terms of such categories as personhood, gender, race or class were shared by the Enlightened.

This book, however, studies not only the masquerade as such but also the way in which it was transposed into the realm of literature. I treat it as a dominant trope governing the poetics and the ideological dimensions of the selected eighteenth-century novels. Consequently, throughout the study I pay special attention to the protagonists of the selected novels, who, metaphorically speaking, take part in the masquerade of the world and thus struggle to determine who they really are. The eponymous quest for identity, inherent in the masquerade metaphor, finds its most accurate realisation, as it always has, in the narrative of the road. Hence the journey, understood literally and metaphorically, does not serve as an arbitrary category narrowing the scope of the book but principally as a paradigm akin to the masquerade in its concern with identity. My approach is based on the conviction that both of these two paradigms constitute the discourse of the self underpinning a number of eighteenth-century novels. I will argue that the travelling protagonists, taking part in the masquerade of the world, find themselves in quest of their self, a process which, as I will show, rarely leads to definite and unambiguous conclusions. Thus, I will maintain, the novelistic characters testify to the contemporary concerns about personal identity, addressed explicitly in empiricist philosophy of the time and implicitly in the institution of masked assemblies.

My understanding of *self* will be consequently grounded in the eighteenth-century tradition, which, I believe, will add more credibility to my analyses. For the most part, *self* will be tantamount to the Lockean personal identity, understood as unity of consciousness, with all reservations and disruptive implications which follow (these I will discuss in the Introduction). As far as literary characterisation is concerned, treating *self* as continuing consciousness corresponds with the Aristotelian precept known as the conservation of character, which implies that literary characters should not act contrary to their established personalities. This idea stems from the core of Aristotelian ethics – the belief in the inextricable connection between *ēthos* (character) and *ethos* (habit, custom), and in a stable and deeply ingrained *hexis* (disposition). In psychological terms, my focus will be on the personality of the selected protagonists, which I will understand as a set of character traits predisposing them to act in a particular way in a variety of contexts. I will also adopt a social perspective, assuming that consciousness and personality become at times outwardly oriented, inasmuch as they are interrelated with the process of identification; that is, imitation of socially established character types, such as a gentleman, a *beau* or a fop, to name but a few. The following analyses of the selected eighteenth-century protagonists will reveal the way in which the ideas of continuing consciousness, conservation of character as well as social identification were negotiated, and also destabilised, in the novel genre.

The material which comes into focus dates from 1742 to 1768 and thus covers the three decades which were, perhaps, most productive in terms of the novelistic output in the eighteenth century. My choice of Henry Fielding, Tobias Smollett and Laurence Sterne has been motivated by several factors. Firstly, the three authors ensure that the material is as versatile as possible, ranging from the neo-classicised novel (or the novelised neo-classicism), through the picaresque novel, to the sentimental novel, with all doubts and reservations such definite categories must raise. Secondly, there certainly was some continuity between the works of the three novelists, with Smollett writing in Fielding's shadow, and Sterne ridiculing "the learned Smelfungus". The authors belonged to the same generation, even though the novels selected come from different stages of their careers (mature Fielding, early Smollett and late Sterne). Finally, all three authors were deeply concerned with the masquerade and travel, to which they testify not only through their literary work but also through their lives. As regards the choice of their novels – Fielding's *Joseph Andrews* and *Tom Jones*, Smollett's *Roderick Random* and

Peregrine Pickle, and Sterne's *A Sentimental Journey* – it has been motivated not only by the texts' preoccupation with the masquerade and travel but also by their representative nature in terms of the authors' approach to the two categories, with Fielding's mythical quest for self-discovery, Smollett's episodic and fragmented proteanism and Sterne's seemingly anti-masquerade journey of the heart.

What may raise doubts is the exclusion of other novels by the authors, especially by Fielding and Smollett, which might be regarded as natural choices. By no means can it be denied that the two paradigms in question are important aspects of such texts as Fielding's *Amelia* or Smollett's *Ferdinand Count Fathom* and *Humphry Clinker*. However, two reasons lie behind their omission. Firstly, some selection is always necessary in order to ensure integrity and a coherent line of argument. For these purposes, I believe that 22 books of *Joseph Andrews* and *Tom Jones*, as well as 183 chapters of *Roderick Random* and *Peregrine Pickle*, are sufficient material to be analysed. This does not mean, of course, that I will make no references to other works of the authors. Secondly, my choice has been based on the conviction that the pairs of novels display a rather unified approach to the two categories. Fielding's *Amelia* is not a travel novel proper, and its juxtaposition with the previous two novels would be problematic. Smollett's *Ferdinand Count Fathom,* in turn, is a rather schematic villain narrative, and the protagonist's masquerades do not correspond with changes of character (with the exception of the highly improbable reformation concluding the novel) – his changes are more about imposture than about proteanism. *Humphry Clinker,* on the other hand, represents a rather Fieldingesque quest for one's origins and journey home. Finally, my decision to limit the scope of the final chapter to *A Sentimental Journey* exclusively has been made on the grounds that Sterne's *opus magnum – Tristram Shandy –* is not a travel narrative proper, despite Tristram's Continental tour in Volume VII (which I will refer to), and thus would not serve the purpose of illustrating the ambiguities and paradoxes of Sterne's idea of the journey of the heart.

What, perhaps, also deserves an explanation is the omission of Daniel Defoe's and Samuel Richardson's narratives. The former's *Moll Flanders* and *Roxana* are undoubtedly governed by the paradigms of the masquerade and travel. Their absence in this book is related to the fact that recent criticism has already extensively elaborated on the notions of mask, disguise and role-playing in the two texts, and further attempts at analyses from this perspective could yield diminishing returns. Furthermore, I consider Defoe's representation of the picaresque road as a spatio-temporal universe demanding personal and social metamorphoses to be very much in line with Smollett's world. In this case, the choice of Smollett at the cost of Defoe seems natural to me, given the former's connections with Fielding and Sterne. Richardson's *Pamela* and *Sir Charles Grandison*, in turn, would certainly merit attention in a study of the masquerade, given the vivid accounts of masked assemblies in the two novels, but I have decided not to include them as they are not travel narratives and could not possibly illustrate the relationship between travel and the masquerade, which is my concern here.

For the sake of clarity, I analyse the three authors in separate parts, ordered chronologically. First, however, I introduce the following analyses by providing insight into the eighteenth-century understandings of identity, masquerade and travel, and their relationship with the early novel. I focus on the category of identity in eighteenth-century thought, introduce the institution of masked assemblies arguing for a metaphorical understanding of the phenomenon and outline selected forms of eighteenth-century travel narratives and their socio-cultural background. My aim is to demonstrate that the topoi of the masquerade and travel are central in the formation of the novelistic discourse of the self.

Part One is a reading of Henry Fielding's *Joseph Andrews* and *Tom Jones*. My basic assumption is that the anti-masquerade poetics of the novels reveals itself in the dichotomous organisation of the texts; good natured protagonists are juxtaposed with masquerading hypocrites, whereas friendly country seats stand in opposition to London – the corrupted capital and epitome of the masquerading world. I argue that the principle behind Fielding's discourse of identity is the belief in an unchanging, substantial self, which is reflected in Joseph's and Tom's search for their origins and true selves. I also demonstrate, however, that the didactic line of argument, advocating self-definition by means of differentiation from the world of masquerade, is disrupted by the masked assembly Tom Jones attends, which precipitates a momentary metamorphosis on the part of the so far self-consistent character.

Part Two concentrates on two early novels by Tobias Smollett – *Roderick Random* and *Peregrine Pickle*. I argue that in contrast to predetermined characters in Fielding's texts, Roderick and Peregrine do not search for any personal and social essence but find themselves in a universe which welcomes, or at times even requires, subsequent transformations and changes of roles. Consequently, I do not treat the masquerade as a metaphor of corruption, as is the case in the previous part, but as a pattern of behaviour valued positively, taking the forms of consecutive changes of roles as well as of carnivalesque pranks and stratagems.

Part Three studies Sterne's *"Work of Redemption"* – *A Sentimental Journey through France and Italy*. I point out that the author's renewal of the genre of travel writing centres around the figure of the sentimental traveller searching for natural experience. My analysis, however, reveals ambiguities and self-contradictions in the advocated return to naturalness through sentimentalism. The masquerade, which is seemingly set in opposition to sentimentalism, is at times indiscernible from the advocated disposition, just as naturalness is interwoven with artificiality. In the final chapter, I concentrate on the figure of the sentimental traveller – Mr Yorick – arguing for his polyphonic and fragmented self.

As may be clear from the outline above, my work does not rely on a single set of methodological principles. My starting point is always the literary text and its contexts – philosophical, social and cultural. Nevertheless, the following readings of eighteenth-century novels rely on those theoretical constructs which, I believe, seem to be welcomed by the studied texts. Thus, Yuri Lotman's semiotics is a logical choice for reading Fielding's dichotomous poetics, whereas Northrop Frye's archetypal criticism can shed light on the same author's conception of the hero's journey as well as on the alternate symbolic deaths and rebirths in Smollett's novels. A significant point of reference is Mikhail Bakhtin, whose ideas of the carnivalesque, dialogue and polyphony are invoked throughout the whole study and constitute the basic critical perspective for my readings of Smollett (the carnivalesque) and Sterne (dialogue and polyphony). Apart from these methodologies, generic criticism, intertextuality and Erving Goffman's theory of social performance also provide theoretical background for my analyses and interpretations of particular aspects of the texts.

I am, of course, indebted to the extensive corpus of criticism of the eighteenth-century novel, even though my perspective differs from that of recent critical trends. The novelty, I believe, lies in my understanding of the masquerade and travel as complementary paradigms, central in the construction of self in the selected novels. Nevertheless, the three categories I invoke in the work – that is, self, masquerade and travel – and their importance for our understanding of eighteenth-century fiction, have been given relatively close critical attention, even though it would be an exaggeration to say that they all have been dominant areas of interest for critics working on the period.

The category of identity in the study of the eighteenth-century novel and culture has gained in popularity ever since the publication of Ian Watt's seminal *The Rise of the Novel: Studies in Defoe, Richardson and Fielding* (1957). In his attempt at investigating the origins of the early English novel, Watt put forward the theory of "formal realism" as "the lowest common denominator of the novel genre as a whole" (Watt 2001: 34). Central to Watt's understanding of "formal realism" was the representation of individual experience, whose form, the critic maintained, was very much indebted to contemporary epistemological reflections. Consequently, the author argued for the legitimacy of applying, for example, John Locke's philosophy (the reflection on personal identity being one of its most important aspects) to the study of the eighteenth-century novel. Watt's study thus gave way to identity-oriented readings of eighteenth-century fiction, in which relationships were established between literature and contemporary philosophy.

There have been several works in this group which deserve mention. In 1976, Patricia Meyer Spacks published *Imaging a Self: Autobiography and Novel in Eighteenth-Century England*. Taking the philosophy of Locke and Hume, among others, as her starting point, Spacks continues to argue that literature, "imagining" the self as stable, played a compensatory role in a time when philosophy was doing her best to destabilise the category. This argument is taken up by Lisa A. Freeman, who in her *Character's Theater: Genre and Identity on the Eighteenth-Century English Stage* (2002) maintains that eighteenth-century novels provided the reader with "the illusion of continuity of self" (Freeman 2002: 15). She continues that "the novel displaced the reigning sense of identity as theatrically constituted and replaced it with the illusion of a 'materially constituted self', a self of substance" (Freeman 2002: 16). One of the aims I will pursue in this work is to show the limits of this understanding of the eighteenth-century novel.

At the opposite extreme there are studies regarding the novel as a form of expression complementary to the contemporary philosophical discourse. For example, John A. Dussinger in *The Discourse of the Mind in Eighteenth-Century Fiction* (1974) focuses on the Lockean and Humean understanding of self as consciousness and argues that this "radical" philosophical reflection "is rendered fictionally in the act of writing" (Dussinger 1974: 39). The importance of Dussinger's work for my approach lies especially in the author's analysis of Sterne's *A Sentimental Journey* (Dussinger 1974: 173-200), in which the author is concerned with Yorick's "sophisticated role-playing". The category of consciousness, central to the eighteenth-century understanding of personal identity, is also taken up by Christopher Fox in *Locke and the Scriblerians: Identity and Consciousness in Early Eighteenth-Century Britain* (1988), which, however, deals mainly with Alexander Pope and Jonathan Swift (treating the novel only cursorily), and by Elizabeth Kraft in her *Character and Consciousness in Eighteenth-Century Comic Fiction* (1992). The latter work, having first accounted for the complexity of the eponymous categories in eighteenth-century thought, offers analyses of several novels, including *Tom Jones* and *Peregrine Pickle*. Importantly, Kraft distinguishes between Fielding's creation of a "controlling consciousness" in the figure of the narrator and Smollett's elaboration on the momentary nature of the category. Another text of importance is *"The Stranger Within Thee": Concepts of the Self in Late Eighteenth-Century Literature* by Stephen Cox (1980), which focuses predominantly on the poetry of sensibility but also discusses Richardson's *Clarissa*. As is suggested by the title, referring to Edward Young's 1759 "Conjectures on Original Composition", literature is treated as an illustration of the eighteenth-century turmoil over the category of self. This turmoil, as Cox writes, "did make it easy for writers of the eighteenth century not only to develop anxieties about the self, but also to surround it with an aura of mystery and power" (Cox 1980: 12). The critic defines "the search for the 'true self'" the most common motif in both eighteenth-century philosophy and literature, adding, however, that "this essential self proves difficult to discover and express" (Cox 1980: 7). Cox's arguments are taken up by Marie-Paule Laden, whose *Self-Imitation in the Eighteenth-Century Novel* (1987) focuses on both French and English fiction. Her study, apart from scrutinising the eighteenth-century context, relies heavily on more recent critique, arguing, for example, that Derrida's deconstruction destabilises the category of self "much as eighteenth-century empiricism once did", and that Hume's theory of personal identity "seems to anticipate key ideas" of the French scholar (Laden 1987: 20).

Recently, a few notable works have been published offering a more general insight into the category of identity in the eighteenth century. *Rewriting the Self: Histories from the Renaissance to the Present* – a 1997 collection of essays edited by Roy Porter – includes five chapters devoted to the subject matter in question, focusing on such diverse aspects as religious introspection, social performance, theatricality, hypocrisy or gender, among others. The general impression one gains is that of instability affecting all the aspects of identity under scrutiny. This impression is also to be gained from Dror Wahrman's seminal *The Making of the Modern Self" Identity and Culture in*

Eighteenth-Century England (2004). I will treat Wahrman's conception of what he calls the *ancien régime* of identity as an accurate rendition of the time which gave birth to the novels by Fielding, Smollett and Sterne, and I will refer to the idea in the following chapters. Wahrman's comprehensive study discusses such categories of identity as gender, race and class but also addresses the philosophical background of the time. Importantly, Wahrman does not fail to account for the popularity of masked assemblies, underlining the metaphorical dimension of the phenomenon. Finally, the most recent work addressing the complexities of eighteenth-century identities is a collection of essays edited by Isabel Karremann and Anja Müller, entitled *Mediating Identities in Eighteenth-Century England: Public Negotiations, Literary Discourses, Topography* (2011), the starting point of which is the eighteenth-century dialogue between "an essential, inner self and the notion of a self as a bundle of perceptions retrospectively labelled 'I'" (Karremann 2011: 3). The eponymous categories of mediation and identity narrow the scope of the work to examining the ways in which the self "is produced and communicated socially" being "constituted, implemented, negotiated, and validated through the conduit of media", including, for example, literature (Karremann 2011: 2). The eighteenth-century novel, however, is given here a rather scant attention.

Critical literature on the masquerade can be divided into works focusing on the phenomenon as such and those examining its metaphorical implications, referring, for example, to the process of writing, the motif of disguise or changeable identity. As Maximilian E. Novak, the editor of *English Literature in the Age of Disguise* (1977), explains, the emergence of the category of mask in eighteenth-century studies dates back to the 1950s when "the concept was used so loosely as to involve a confusion with the notion of the persona and, ultimately, with the personality of the author" (Novak 1977: 5). It appears, then, that before comprehensive studies of masked balls as such were published, the masquerade had been present in eighteenth-century criticism as a metaphor of writing and the roles the writer could assume. For example, the eponymous mask in Andrew Wright's *Henry Fielding: Mask and Feast* (1966) refers to "the narrator masquerading as an author" (Wright 1966: 15).

The masquerade as such was extensively addressed in the 1970s and 1980s, when the two most important studies of the phenomenon to date were published. The first of these is Aileen Ribeiro's monumental *The Dress Worn at Masquerades in England, 1730 to 1790, and its Relation to Fancy Dress in*

Portraiture, first presented as a doctoral dissertation in 1975 and then published in 1984. Even though the book deals mainly with art history and material culture, its first chapter is of utmost importance for literary studies, too. It consists of three parts – the first deals with the background against which masked balls emerged, the second accounts for the conventions governing the balls and their social implications, whereas the third, most importantly perhaps, is a collection of contemporary literary accounts of masquerades, including excerpts of correspondence, newspapers, periodicals, travel writing and diaries. The chapter treats the eighteenth-century novel as a valuable source of information and thus refers to fictional masquerade scenes in, for example, Fielding's *Tom Jones* and *Amelia*, Richardson's *Pamela* and *Sir Charles Grandison*, or Burney's *Cecilia* and *Evelina*.

The second study is Terry Castle's *Masquerade and Civilisation: The Carnivalesque in Eighteenth-Century English Culture and Fiction* (1986). Ever since the work was published, it has served as a basic point of reference for any critic touching upon the subject matter in question. The monograph not only meticulously accounts for the historical, social and cultural background of eighteenth-century masquerades, but also, drawing on Bakhtin's theory of the carnivalesque, offers a detailed examination of the masquerade topos in eighteenth-century fiction, focusing on Richardson's *Pamela*, Fielding's *Amelia*, Burney's *Cecilia* and Inchbald's *A Simple Story*, and arguing that the disruptive powers of the masquerade as a socio-cultural phenomenon are transposed into the realm of literature.

One of the aspects on which Castle concentrates is gender, and it is this category that is elaborated on in 1990s studies of the masquerade. The three notable works published in the decade examine the phenomenon from a feminist perspective (radical at times) and instead of focusing on literary masquerades as such, treat them as metaphors for gender constructions and reversals. Mary Anne Schofield, in her *Masking and Unmasking the Female Mind: Disguising Romances in Feminine Fiction, 1713-1799* (1990), coins the term "disguising romance" or "masquerading romance" and argues that for women writers the novel served as a kind of masquerade thanks to which they could subvert the received and patriarchal marriage plot. Catherine Craft-Fairchild's *Masquerade and Gender: Disguise and Female Identity in Eighteenth-Century Fictions by Women* (1993), in turn, is thought of as a corrective to Terry Castle's positive evaluation of the masquerade in women's fiction. Craft-Fairchild, studying the works by Aphra Behn, Mary Davys, Eliza Haywood, Elizabeth Inchbald and Frances Burney, argues that the masquerade can be tantamount to both subordination and defiance. Finally, Jill Campbell's *Natural Masques: Gender and Identity in Fielding's Plays and Novels* (1995) takes as its starting point a passage from Henry Fielding's poem *The Masquerade*, in which the novelist expresses anxiety about gender reversals taking place at masked balls. Studying both Fielding's dramatic and novelistic output, Campbell focuses on the author's constructions of femininity and masculinity – the eponymous natural masques.

The decade's interest in the masquerade is concluded by the work of Janusz Ryba, a Polish literary historian, whose *Maskarady oświeconych: Próba opisu zjawiska* [Masquerades of the Enlightened: An Account of the Phenomenon] (1998), as well as his recent *Oświeceniowe tutti frutti: Maskarady – Konwersacja – Literatura* [Tutti frutti of the Enlightenment: Masquerades – Conversation – Literature] (2009), provide detailed examination of the eighteenth-century obsession with masquerades and masquerading. Even though the studies are concerned mainly with Polish and French literature and culture, the critic's broad understanding of the masquerade as a variety of patterns of behaviour is very much in line with the perspective I adopt in this book.

Recently, no monograph has been devoted to the phenomenon. Apart from Janusz Ryba's 2009 compilation of sketches, there have been two collections of essays centring on the masquerade – *Masquerade and Identities: Essays on Gender, Sexuality, and Marginality* (2001) edited by Efrat Tseëlon and *Masquerades: Disguise in Literature in English from the Middle Ages to the Present* (2004) edited by Jesús López-Peláez Casellas, David Malcolm and Pilar Sánchez Calle. Both collections give the masquerade a rather broad and metaphorical treatment, not necessarily situating it in the eighteenth-century context.

The category of travel is the one which has given rise to a substantial number of critical studies. It would be too tedious a task, and most probably impossible, to account for all significant publications in this area, and what follows is thus a brief acknowledgement of the texts to which my perspective is most indebted.

A work which I should mention in the first place is *Travel Literature and the Evolution of the Novel* (1983) by Percy G. Adams. Adams's importance lies in his examination of the affinities between factual travel writing and the early English novel. The critic argues that both travel writing and the early novel rely on the quest motif and share common features, such as the figure of the narrator, linear action, episodic encounters or scenes in coaches and inns. Adams also notices that both genres are concerned with the troublesome distinction between fact and fiction, as well as between realism and fantasy. This seminal work gave way to a number of studies focusing on the relationships between travel writing and the novel. These include, among others, John McVeagh's collection *All Before Them, 1660-1780* (1990), containing essays on Smollett and Sterne, and Jean Viviès' *English Travel Narratives in the Eighteenth Century: Exploring Genres* (2002), in which there are studies of Smollet, Sterne and the picaresque. The examination of this generic provenance of the novel is also carried out in two important studies of the origins of the early novel; namely, in Michael McKeaon's *The Origins of the English Novel, 1600-1740* (1987) and J. Paul Hunter's *Before Novels: The Cultural Contexts of Eighteenth-Century English Fiction* (1990). All the works surveyed here are concerned with the novel's indebtedness to travel in terms of its generic status. I will also adopt this perspective when discussing the travel writing conventions in the novels by Smollett and Sterne.

Apart from the works focusing on the implications of travel for the generic status of the eighteenth-century novel, there have been studies paying attention to the journey motif as such, highlighting its structural and metaphorical importance. Ronald Paulson's 1976 essay "Life as Journey and as Theater: Two Eighteenth-Century Narrative Structures", which inspired my juxtaposition of masquerades and travels in this book, considers the journey motif to be one of the two dominant structures governing the novelistic output of the time. The journey metaphor has also come under scrutiny in some of the studies of Fielding, Smollett and Sterne. The mythical road in Fielding's novels is examined, for example, in Henry Knight Miller's *Henry Fielding's* Tom Jones *and the Romance Tradition* (1976) and in Evans Lansing Smith's *The Hero Journey in Literature: Parables of Poesis* (1997: 194-210); Smollett's road of many roles is dealt with in Wojciech Nowicki's *The Picaresque Hero in a Sordid World: A Study of the Early Novels of Tobias Smollett* (1986), whereas the author's dialogue with the quest motif is accounted for by John Skinner's *Constructions of Smollett: A Study of Genre and Gender* (1996); finally, Sterne's idea of the journey of the heart is touched upon in practically any work on the author, and its impact on the genre of travel writing is discussed in Charles Batten's *Pleasurable Instruction: Form and Convention in Eighteenth-Century Travel Literature* (1978) and Carl Thompson's *Travel Writing* (2011).

As I have already mentioned, my idea to understand the categories of masquerade and travel as complementary paradigms constituting the discourse of identity has not yet been undertaken in eighteenth-century studies. Given the versatility of the three novelists, my perspective will be a comprehensive one, in accord with the outlined variety of critical literature. Thus, identity will be seen as both stable and destabilised, the masquerade will be studied literally as well as metaphorically, whereas travelling will be regarded not only as a generic necessity but also as an archetype of human condition.

Introduction

The Discourse of Identity
in Eighteenth-Century Fiction

> —My good friend, quoth I—as sure as I am
> I—and you are you—
> —And who are you? said he.—Don't puzzle
> me; said I.
>
> Laurence Sterne, *Tristram Shandy*

1. Personal identity and the eighteenth-century novel

From cultural and historical perspectives the period which witnessed the emergence of the works by Fielding, Smollett and Sterne may be referred to as the *ancien régime* of identity. The term, introduced by Dror Wahrman in *The Making of the Modern Self* (2004), points to the period of instability, mutability and changeability of identity in its every aspect. The historian highlights the "two important characteristics" of the time addressed by the term: "malleability" – that is, "the sense that one's 'personal identity' [...] could be imagined as unfixed and potentially changeable" – and the absence of "a sense of a stable inner core of selfhood" (Wahrman 2004: 168). These concerns were expressed by eighteenth-century philosophy and moral thought and found their realisations in the institutions of masked assembly and travel.

The eighteenth-century anti-substantialism with regard to personal identity was the consequence of a fundamental transformation in the meaning of self in early modern thought. As Barresi and Martin argue, "the self as immaterial soul was replaced with the self as mind [...] [which] involved movement away from substance accounts of personal identity [...] toward relational accounts of personal identity" (Barresi and Martin 2004: ix). This would imply, then, that self-formation was understood to be one of the processes of the mind and thus depended on cognition and perception. This assumption questioned the traditional Christian substantialist understanding of self, according to which it was unchangeable, permanent and distinct (see Gilson 1936: 201-204). Eighteenth-century philosophical reflection about the identity of person acknowledged this shift from soul to mind. What Locke asserted in his *Essay Concerning Human Understanding* (1689) was that formations of ideas (including the idea of one's self) are subject to impressions and perceptions, the former being dependant on sensual perception, the latter conditioned by reasoning (Locke 1975: 105). It logically follows, then, that personal identity, shaped through the processes of perception and reasoning (cognition), is a mutable construct.

Attempting, in a sense, to bring back stability, Locke put forward his theory of self-in-consciousness. The philosopher argued in the second edition of his *Essay* that what holds together all the impressions and perceptions contributing to the formation of the self – what constitutes the sameness of a person – is consciousness (*"personal Identity* consists, not in the identity of Substance, but [...] in the Identity of *consciousness*" [Locke 1975: 342]). Thus, remaining within the paradigm of self as mind, Locke pointed to consciousness, and indirectly to memory, as the states or mechanisms of mind which are responsible for self-conception:

> as far as this consciousness can be extended backwards to any past Action or Thought, so far reaches the Identity of that *Person*; it is the same *self* now it was then; and 'tis by the same *self* with this present one that now reflects on it, that that Action was done. (Locke 1975: 335)

However, it was Locke himself who was the first to realise that his attempt to bring back stability with regard to identity was not entirely successful. The somewhat disruptive implication of his theory was that "if it be possible for the same Man to have distinct incommunicable consciousness at different times, it is past doubt the same Man would at different times make different Persons" (Locke 1975: 342). Locke continued that the possibility for a man to make different persons is reflected in language, in such phrases as *to be not oneself* or *to be beside oneself* (Locke 1975: 343). Thus – perhaps contrary to his original intentions – Locke founded the philosophical and intellectual background of the *ancien régime* of identity.

The subsequent turmoil which was sparked by Locke's arguments only proves how complex the problem of identity was in the first half of the eighteenth century. Of the many voices concerned with the nature of personal identity there are some which deserve special attention. One of those is Shaftesbury's ironic remark in his *Characteristics*:

> What you Philosophers are [...] may be hard perhaps to determine: But for the rest of Mankind, I dare affirm, that few are so long themselves as *half* seven Years. 'Tis good fortune if a Man be *one and the same* only for a day or two: A Year makes more Revolutions than can be number'd. (Shaftesbury 1999: 300)

Furthermore, this time referring strictly to himself, the Earl wrote in his journal, "let me lose self every hour, and be twenty successive selfs, or new selfs, 'tis all one to me" (quoted in Barresi and Martin 2004: 64).

The controversy over personal identity was also present in the works of Anglican thinkers. One of them was Joseph Butler, who attempted to reinstate the prevalence of the identity of substance in his "Of Personal Identity" (1736). More interesting than this somewhat anachronistic endeavour was his commentary on the two-year-long (1706-1708) dispute between Anthony Collins and Samuel Clarke. His criticism of Collins's arguments constitutes, in fact, a cogent elucidation of the philosophical basis for the destabilisation of the category of identity:

> some of those hasty observations [by Locke] have been carried to a strange length by others [i.e. Collins]; whose notion, when traced and examined to the bottom, amounts, I think, to this: "That personality is not a permanent, but a transient thing: that it lives and dies, begins and ends, continually: that no one can any more remain one and the same person two moments together, than two successive moments can be one and the same moment: that our substance is indeed continually changing; but whether this be so or not, is, it seems, nothing to the purpose; since it is not substance, but consciousness alone, which constitutes personality; which consciousness, being successive, cannot be the same in any two moments, nor consequently the personality constituted by it." (Butler 2008: 102)[1]

What accurately concluded the whole debate concerning the identity of person were the observations of David Hume. His remarks may be seen as "the abandonment of personal identity" (Perry 2008: 157), as they point to

---

[1] To read more on the Anglican reaction, see Tennant 1982: 73-90.

the futility of any attempts to establish its nature. In his *Treatise of Human Nature* (1739) the philosopher argues:

> THERE are some philosophers, who imagine we are every moment intimately conscious of what we call our SELF; [...]
> Unluckily all these positive assertions are contrary to that very experience, which is pleaded for them, nor have we any idea of *self*, after the manner it is here explain'd. For from what impression cou'd this idea be deriv'd? [...] 'tis a question, which must necessarily be answer'd, if we wou'd have the idea of self pass for clear and intelligible. It must be some one impression, that gives rise to every real idea. But self or person is not any one impression, but that to which our several impressions and ideas are suppos'd to have a reference. If any impression gives rise to the idea of self, that impression must continue invariably the same, thro' the whole course of our lives; since self is suppos'd to exist after that manner. But there is no impression constant and invariable. Pain and pleasure, grief and joy, passions and sensations succeed each other, and never all exist at the same time. It cannot, therefore, be from any of these impressions, or from any other, that the idea of self is deriv'd; and consequently there is no such idea. (Hume 1975: 251-252)

Hume's argument that there is no idea of an invariable and persistent self is very much in line with Butler's statement that according to some "personality is not a permanent, but a transient thing". Such observations tell a lot about the time and were definitely made with regard to and under the influence of the cultural context of the first half of the eighteenth century. The background against which these philosophical works emerged was that of a considerable confusion over social and cultural categories of identity. Up until its closing decades, the eighteenth century was a destabilising period for such categories of identity as gender, race and class (see Wahrman 2004), and these destabilising forces had to affect the philosophical investigation into the notion of self.

Literature, naturally, reflected both the destabilisation of socio-cultural categories and the complex nature of personal identity. The genre that was inherently related to these issues was the novel. On the one hand, as McKeon argues in his theory of its origins, the novel's development coincided with or stemmed from the destabilisation of generic, social and moral categories (McKeon 2002); on the other hand, according to Watt's *The Rise of the Novel*, what constituted the new genre was preoccupation with individual experience. An individual, emerging from a particular environment, was to be in the centre of the novel; consequently, frequently in the centre was the individual's search for identity. This idea is, in a sense, supported by Hunter (1990: 303-355). The critic discusses several forms of prose narrative which made up the generic background from which the novel emerged. Some of these forms, such as private histories (diaries), autobiographies, biographies, spiritual biographies, memoirs and travel accounts, were in fact explicit discourses of identity and are purposefully classified by Hunter under such chapter headings as "The Self and the World", "The Self Observed" and "The Self in the World".

The eighteenth-century novel, preoccupied with the notion of self, was to a large extent influenced by two metaphorical topoi reflecting this preoccupation: life as journey and as theatre (Paulson 1976: 43-58). These two narrative structures by nature revolved around and were interrelated with the paradigms of one's search for or construction of identity. The causality and linearity of the narratives of the road made them centre "on the problem of the self and the process of an individual's defining and redefining himself in time" (Paulson 1976: 45). On the other hand, works based on the *theatrum mundi* topos comprised characters' constant changes of roles and disguises. Epitomising this idea were the life and writings of James Boswell, "a life long addict of the theatre" (Sherman 2005: 665), who wrote in his *London Journal*: "I have discovered that we may be in some degree whatever character we choose" (Boswell 1991: 47). Some years later, in the second essay of the series *On the Profession of a Player*, Boswell asserted: "a man is able at a certain hour to change himself into a different kind of being from what he really is" (Boswell 1929: 12).

In spite of the prominence of the theatrical metaphor, it is another, though one closely bound up with the former, that seems to have been of equal importance with the theatrical metaphor in the eighteenth century – the metaphor of the world as a masquerade. This argument can be supported by a number of quotations taken from various pieces of eighteenth-century writing, testifying to this shift from the theatrical to the masquerade metaphor. An extensive list of such quotations can be found in Wahrman's book, and they range from Charles Gildon's "the World being a Masquerade, where borrow'd Vizors so disguised e'ry one, that none knew ev'n his own acquaintance" to Hannah Cowley's "'tis one universal masquerade, all disguised in the same habits and manners" (quoted in Wahrman 2004: 167). The masquerade metaphor preserves all the implications of the theatrical metaphor but emphasises the motif of identity play and elaborates on such notions as concealment, artifice, affectation or social fluctuation. Thus, life was not

only viewed as a constant change of roles but also as a series of masked performances.

2. The journey metaphor and the eighteenth-century novel

Eric Leed, commenting on the relationship of travel and experience, exam-
ines the etymology of the two words only to find out that the Indo-European
root of the latter – *per* – was later transformed into *fer* in Germanic languages, which in turn became the root of e.g. *irfaran* in Old High German,
meaning "to travel" (Leed 1991: 5). Assuming that language reflects the
mind, it may be stated that these two phenomena have always been associated. No wonder, then, that the preoccupation of the eighteenth-century novel
with an individual's experience more often than not demanded that this individual should be depicted when on the road. And just as experience was
thought to constitute identity in early modern philosophy, adopting the journey metaphor was one of the ways of depicting the process in literature in
general and in eighteenth-century novels in particular.

According to Cirlot, "[p]rimarily, to travel is to seek" (Cirlot 2002: 165).
What was sought by eighteenth-century fictional travellers was their identity.
Thus, they seem to have followed Montaigne's precept: "This great world
[…] is the mirror in which we must look in order to recognize ourselves from
the proper angle" (Montaigne 1958: 116). Eighteenth-century literature as a
whole was largely concerned with "this great world" both in fiction and in
fact (though this distinction was at the time not so clear-cut), depicting "the
accrual of knowledge through the physical movement through space" (Hunter
1990: 351). Even if travel accounts were not a direct source of the novel's
development, they constituted a background against which this development
occurred, being, as Hunter terms it, "an enabling presence for the novel"
(Hunter 1990: 351). The novels under scrutiny do not share travel accounts'
curiosity of otherness; instead, they expose individuals who search for or
shape their identity when on the road. As such, however, they do relate to the
tradition of travel literature, which accounts for both material and spiritual,
external and internal journeys (Todorov 1995: 62). The spiritual and internal
dimensions of travelling are, in fact, present in any narrative of the road because, as Leed observes, when travelling, "the self may be changed with
change of the place" (Leed 1991: 11).

Eighteenth-century literary travels, as representations of the search for
identity, took various forms. The forms which, I believe, deserve special

attention in the context of this study include literary pilgrimages (or allegorical journeys), picaresque rambles and grand tours.

The first pattern is definitely well grounded in English literary tradition. Pilgrimages, or allegorical journeys, were organising principles of a number of influential works; most notably, for the eighteenth-century context, Bunyan's *Pilgrim's Progress* (1678) and Johnson's *Rasselas* (1759). Literary pilgrimages most transparently display the union of internal and external travelling, which means that the self on a pilgrimage is subject to both physical and spiritual motion. What is significant, however, is that both these journeys are teleological. The traveller moves towards a predetermined place and must undergo some inner development towards perfection before reaching the place. The inner journey takes precedence over the external journey when the latter is circular, ending at the point of departure. Circular pilgrimages put emphasis on the spiritual progress of the travelling self; it is not the final destination that matters most but the changed self that reaches it. M.H. Abrams indicates that it is the parable of the Prodigal Son that may be understood as the archetypal circular journey, figuring the "spiritual history of humanity" (Abrams 1994: 2). As such, it gives way to the Augustinian topos of *peregrinatio vitae*, which, in turn, is one of the key paradigms adopted in eighteenth-century fiction, as Ronald Paulson (1976) explains.

In the seventeenth and early eighteenth centuries, the topos of *peregrinatio vitae* was one of the prevailing ones in Puritan and latitudinarian homiletic traditions.[2] The former, according to William Haller, depicted man's soul as "a traveller through a strange country [...] who must adhere through peril and hardship to the way that leads home" (Haller 1957: 142). This idea, epitomised in Bunyan's *The Pilgrim's Progress*, was taken up by latitudinarian divines. Isaac Barrow (1630-77) in his sermon "On the Consideration of our latter End" teaches:

> The scripture aptly resembles our life to a wayfaring, a condition of travel and pilgrimage; how he that hath a long journey to make, and but a little time of day to pass it in, must in reason strive to set out soon, and then to make good speed; [...] so we must, in our course toward heaven and happiness take care that we set out soon [...], then proceed on speedily, and persist constantly; nowhere staying or loitering, shunning all impediments and avocations from our progress, lest we never arrive near, or come too late unto the gate of heaven. (Barrow 1798: 238)

---

[2] Studies on the relationship between eighteenth-century fiction and Puritan and latitudinarian doctrines include, among others: Müller 2009, Steward 2010.

Another latitudinarian clergyman, Bishop Benjamin Hoadly (1676-1761), in the sermon entitled "No continuing City here", preaches:

> Heaven, that Seat of established Happiness above, is our Home; [...] Thither all our Steps ought to be tending: and through this World must we go, as through a Road, before we come to it. In our Journey, We have all the Unhappinesses of Travellers. We meet with an inconvenient Lodging, and ordinary Entertainment, for some time. [...] The little Rest we have, if we have any, is, as in a strange Place, disturbed and interrupted with much Noise, and Hurry, and Disorder; and, like that of Travellers, to be left, perhaps, with the next Morning's Light; and ourselves to be called Home to a more fixt and durable State. (Hoadly 1755: 149-50)

Naturally, it is the didactic dimension of eighteenth-century fiction that translates the Christian topos. The moral lesson taken by the Prodigal Son is, in a sense, re-taught to the wayfaring characters of Defoe, Fielding or Goldsmith. They all reach their true home changed, having completed an internal pilgrimage alongside the external one. Thus understood pilgrimage pattern will be important for my reading of Fielding's *Joseph Andrews* and *Tom Jones* in Part One.

As for the second form of literary travels in eighteenth-century literature – picaresque rambles – I would claim that no other epoch in literary and cultural history would have been more appropriate for the rebirth of picaresque fiction than the *ancien régime* of identity. In his seminal article defining the modal status of picaresque narratives, Ulrich Wicks thus comments on the role-playing motif: "Metamorphoses and changing roles are part of the picaro's survival kit – as the world is in a flux, so he can change roles to face it. Picaresque life is a constant change of masks on the world-as-stage", or world-as-masquerade, as one could add (Wicks 1974: 247). Wicks continues that the picaro's abilities to perform versatile jobs or to serve numerous masters testify to his having a "large repertoire of many masks" at his disposal, which in turn makes it justifiable to call him "the master of many masks" (Wicks 1974: 247). This idea is taken up by Anna Wieczorkiewicz, who argues that the role-playing motif is what defines the picaresque as a genre (Wieczorkiewicz 1996: 124). In a similar vein, Stuart Miller comments on the protean form of the picaro:

> In his protean guises, the picaro's character becomes, once more, radically undefined. [...] The picaro is every man he has to be, and therefore no man. [...] As the infinitely adaptable man, however, the picaro sits on the pole furthest from integ-

rity. [...] Now we have only the impression of complete plasticity. (Miller 1967: 70-73)

The lack of integrity in the protean picaro reflects the general instability and chaos of the depicted world, which is also indicated by the episodic nature and the fragmentation of the narrative (Miller 1967: 9).

It is also the picaro's journey that becomes an accurate manifestation of this sense of chaos, instability and disintegration. On the one hand, it does not have any clear destination and is full of interruptions and abrupt reversals; on the other, it contributes to the layer of the narrative focusing on identity play, for, as Wieczorkiewicz suggests, the time spent on the road is "the time when one can play many roles" (Wieczorkiewicz 1996: 145, my translation). Thus, the picaro's journey is the one that perfectly combines the two patterns discussed by Paulson and as such becomes "a series of roles adopted". The masquerade, theatre and identity play are then inherent in the chronotope[3] of the picaresque road. I will refer to these ideas throughout the whole book, but especially in the second part, focusing on *Roderick Random* and *Peregrine Pickle* by Tobias Smollett.

The third pattern, the grand tour, was originally a socio-cultural paradigm which came into existence somewhere in the seventeenth century and was immediately transposed into the realm of literature. Naturally, the initial literary grand tours took the form of non-fictional travel writings giving a detailed account of the continental journey undergone by the narrator. These grand tour accounts belonged to the rapidly developing tradition of travel writing, which corresponded with global expansion and geographical discoveries of the time. The prototypes of the genre in English were *Coryat's Crudities* (1611) by Thomas Coryat and *An Italian Voyage* (1670) by Richard Lassels, the latter of which introduced the term "grand tour" into English. Henceforth, it referred to a "social ritual" the purpose of which "was to round out the education of young men of the ruling classes by exposing them to the treasured artifacts and ennobling society of the Continent" (Buzard 2002: 38). The custom flourished in the eighteenth century, having worked out a rather rigid convention dictating what a well-mannered gentleman was supposed to see. What helped to establish the convention was Joseph Addison's *Remarks on Several Parts of Italy* (1705); an indispensable handbook for

---

[3] I understand the term chronotope in accord with Bakhtin's definition, as "the intrinsic connectedness of temporal and spatial relationships that are artistically expressed in literature" (Bakhtin 1981: 84).

subsequent generations of eighteenth-century grand tourists. The standard itinerary that was followed included crossing the Channel to Calais, visiting Paris and the South of France, crossing the Alps, touring Italy (Turin or Milan, Florence, Venice, Rome and optionally Naples), and returning home via Austria and Germany. On the road, the grand tourist was supposed to familiarise himself with the classical tradition, about which he had hitherto been taught, and had the opportunity to marvel at and to obtain modern works of art of the Mediterranean and thus to develop fine aesthetic judgement. Moreover, the traveller cultivated good manners coming into contact with the elite of the societies he visited, so that he would be prepared to perform some appropriate social or political function back in England. Last but not least, having been freed from social restriction and control, the young traveller was likely to enjoy numerous morally dubious relationships with women of diverse social backgrounds.

As such, the grand tour could be seen as a plot model of the *Bildungsroman* (Bohls 2009: 106), in which the traveller's identity is being shaped on various levels. The continental tour was conducive not only to the traveller's growth as a person in the Lockean sense (the accumulation of experience) but also to the development of a sense of national, social and cultural identity. I will study the transposition of the grand tour into the realm of fiction in Part Two (Smollett's *Roderick Random* and *Peregrine Pickle*) and in Part Three (Sterne's *A Sentimental Journey*).

3. The masquerade metaphor and the eighteenth-century novel

As a mass and democratic socio-cultural phenomenon,[4] the masquerade first appeared on British soil sometime in the early eighteenth century, and its emergence is traditionally attributed to the arrival of John James Heidegger (1659-1749), a Swiss impresario, who came to England in 1708. Shortly after, this *arbiter elegantiarum*, as he was later called, transformed contemporary elitist masked assemblies into popular mass entertainments, having recognised their potential to become profitable enterprise (Castle 1986: 11). In 1713 Heidegger became manager of the Haymarket Opera House, and it was there that he organised his masquerades. Other popular venues throughout the eighteenth century included Vauxhall Gardens, Ranelagh Gardens and

---

[4] The eighteenth-century masquerade should not be seen as a direct continuation of the tradition of Tudor, Stuart and Restoration masked balls, which were exclusively an aristocratic diversion. In its eighteenth-century form, masquerades were mass entertainments welcoming participants from various social backgrounds.

Carlisle House, which hosted masked balls organised by another foreigner, Theresa Cornelys (1723-97), an Italian opera singer, who settled in London in 1759.

What makes it possible to visualise an eighteenth-century London masquerade are numerous written and pictorial accounts, including texts published in the *Spectator*, the *Weekly Journal* and the *Gentleman's Magazine* as well as graphic works by William Hogarth, Remigius Parr and Thomas Rowlandson. What follows is an excerpt from a detailed report of the masquerade organised by Theresa Cornelys on February 26, 1770, published in the *Gentleman's Magazine*:

> It was held at Mrs Cornely's house in Soho Square, which was illuminated in the most splendid and picturesque masquerade manner imaginable with between three and four thousand wax-lights. About one hundred musicians were dispersed in various parts. The following is the list of the principal masques. – The figure of Nobody, the Duke of Buccleugh, who after entertaining himself and his friends some time in that character, withdrew, new dressed himself, and appeared in a most elegant dress of a Hungarian Hussar. – The figure of Somebody, his companion, Colonel Fitzroy who also afterwards appeared in another character. – Cherokee Chief, Mr Meadows, a new and very striking masque. – Cyrus, Sir William Wrottesley. – A Double Man, half Miller and half Chimney-sweeper, Sir Richard Philips: this dress was so admirably contrived that it required some observation to discover which was his real front; and this not only when standing, but also when walking; Sir Richard sometimes walking with one front forwards, and sometimes the other. (*The Gentleman's Magazine* 1770: 98)

Apart from the indicators of luxury and glamour, what draws attention in the quoted passage is the enumeration of masked characters who took part in the assembly. The names given to the disguised participants – Nobody, Somebody and A Double Man – suggest that identity play and the negotiable nature of the category of person were very much in question at a masked ball. As Wahrman puts it, a masked assembly was an "exploration of the possibilities inherent in the *ancien régime* of identity" (Wahrman 2004: 164).

Naturally, what constitutes the masquerade and what is indispensible for a masked ball to take place is the very act of putting on a mask. Ronald L. Grimes in his article devoted to the phenomenology of masking distinguishes four modes of the act: concretion, concealment, embodiment and expression (Grimes 1975: 508); of the four types, the first two are especially relevant for the study of eighteenth-century masked balls. The first mode, masking as concretion, is constituted by "concretizing of *dynamis* in a fixed form"

(Grimes 1975: 511). As the anthropologist explains, concretion as a mode of masking can be exemplified by the character-types of *commedia dell'arte*, who cannot exist without their masks, which, in a sense, bring them to life as stereotypical stock-characters. Concealment, in turn, refers to the mode of masking as "an act of concealing identity", in which a person "don[s] an other and doff[s] a selfhood" (Grimes 1975: 511). As Grimes continues, this "masked identity-suspension" leads to a situation in which "[w]ho one is not becomes more important than who one is" (Grimes 1975: 512-513). At an eighteenth-century masquerade these two modes seem to have been combined in a very peculiar way. On the one hand, masqueraders sought identity-suspension, which was guaranteed by the masks and disguises they wore, and which lifted social and cultural restrictions they were subject to; on the other, the roles they typically chose as substitutes for their suspended selves were usually selected from a range of stock masks and dresses which were then at their disposal (see Ribeiro 1984). Suspending their identity, masquerades provided participants with new, typified selves valid only during the assembly and concretised by masks and costumes they wore.

The masquerade, however, may be understood more broadly and its meaning does not necessarily have to be limited to masked assemblies. This broader understanding is advocated by Janusz Ryba, who defines the masquerade as "a rather extensive sphere of human gestures and behaviours, aiming at changing one's appearance or identity, pretending and misleading others by means of false 'creations'" (Ryba 1998: 19, my translation). Before offering this definition, Ryba comments on selected eighteenth-century customs and argues that, in fact, it would not be an exaggeration to talk about an eighteenth-century obsession with masquerading (Ryba 1998: 18). This more comprehensive approach towards the phenomenon brings to mind the metaphor of the world as a masquerade, which emerged as a consequence of the transposition of masquerading behaviours into diverse spheres of social life.

Eighteenth-century masquerades almost immediately found their place in fiction. On the one hand, as Terry Castle demonstrates, novels and masquerades were by nature related, as both were democratic and expressed tensions between morality and transgression (Castle 1986: 114-5); on the other, as Ryba notices, novelistic realism, the prevailing mode of eighteenth-century fiction, simply demanded that all significant spheres of contemporary life, masked assemblies being one of these, were exposed in literature of the time (Ryba 1998: 50). As was the case with the understanding of the masquerade as a socio-cultural phenomenon, its exposition in the novel was twofold, taking the form of masquerade scenes, which literally transposed masked balls into the realm of literature, and masquerade poetics, which testified to the eighteenth-century obsession with masquerading. The former appeared in the works of almost every notable eighteenth-century author; most memorably perhaps in Defoe's *Roxana* (1724), Richardson's *Pamela* (1741), Fielding's *Tom Jones* (1749) or Cleland's *Fanny Hill* (1749). As Castle explains, their function was mainly that of "plot catalysts" (Castle 1986: 127), precipitating consequent shifts of fortune, discoveries, major social and moral reversals and transformations. At the same time, they constituted a cultural emblem of the *beau monde*, which was to be discovered by the wayfaring protagonists who had left their home. As such, Castle continues, masquerade scenes were typical of the picaresque tradition, in which the picaro "journey[s] out of ordinary existence, away from the patterns of everyday life, into a world of strangeness, transformation, and mystery" (Castle 1986: 116).

I put forward the idea of masquerade poetics, on the other hand, as a literary rendition of the masquerade broadly understood, which can be discerned in those works in which the masquerade metaphor becomes the organising principle. This transposition is parallel to what Mikhail Bakhtin called the "carnivalization of literature"; that is, the "transposition of carnival into the language of literature" (Bakhtin 1984a: 122).[5] Drawing on Bakhtin, I would like to formulate the definition of masquerade poetics as the transposition of the masquerade into the language of literature. Works relying on this poetics feature all the forms of masquerading included by Janusz Ryba in the excerpt I have quoted, and the key concepts for the study of this poetics are mask and disguise, both literally and metaphorically understood, and identity play, all of which are going to be central considerations in my readings of the selected eighteenth-century novels.

The overview of the forms taken by the discourse of identity in eighteenth-century fiction proves that, in fact, they were all interrelated and well-grounded in contemporary social, cultural and intellectual reality. The philo-

---

[5] Terry Castle in her *Masquerade and Civilization* (1986) treats eighteenth-century literary masquerades as yet another manifestation of the carnivalisation of literature, highlighting in her analyses the motif of role reversal, central to carnival and also typical of the masquerade. It cannot be denied that the carnivalesque and the masquerade are strictly related, and that the latter is, in fact, a feast of the carnival type; yet still, in the context of the *ancien régime* of identity, it is the masquerade alone that is suitable for "the historically specific understanding of self" at the time (Wahrman 2004: 164), and I believe the category of masquerade poetics to be more appropriate against the eighteenth-century background.

sophical reflection about the identity of person provided a background sanctioning the self-oriented dimensions of the socio-cultural institutions of travel and masquerade. As such, in the literary form of the journey and the masquerade metaphors, they became organising principles of a substantial number of novels, which by their nature were preoccupied with the category of self. The following chapters will trace the development and the metamorphoses of the discourse patterns I have presented.

PART ONE

JOSEPH ANDREWS AND *TOM JONES*: TRAVELLERS IN THE MASQUERADING WORLD

> The whole World becomes a vast Masquerade, where the greatest Part appear disguised under false Vizors and Habits; a very few only shewing their true Faces, who become, by so doing, the Astonishment and Ridicule of the rest.
>
> Henry Fielding, "An Essay on the Knowledge of the Characters of Men"

Chapter One

Fielding's Travellers

Fielding's two best-known novels, *The Adventures of Joseph Andrews* (1742) and *The History of Tom Jones* (1749), both revolve around the notions of masquerade, travel and identity. The travelling protagonists expose the masquerading world and comply with the ancient precept "know then thyself" by differentiating themselves from the world of hypocrisy and affectation. This dichotomous organisation of the novels is well paralleled by the epigraph to this part, in which those who show "their true faces" are in opposition to the masquerading world (Fielding 1972a: 155). In fact, as the narrator of *Tom Jones* explains, the idea of contrast "runs through all the Works of the Creation, and may probably have a large Share in constituting in us the Idea of all Beauty, as well natural as artificial: For what demonstrates the Beauty and Excellence of any thing, but its Reverse?" (*TJ*, 212) It is not only beauty, naturally, that is defined through its reverse throughout Fielding's narratives; nature is best exposed when confronted with artifice, benevolence when juxtaposed with corruption, whereas the pastoral utopia can be enjoyed to the fullest only after the experience of the city.

What can shed some light on Fielding's dichotomous poetics is the theory of the semiosphere put forward by Yuri Lotman (1990). According to the semiologist, one of the "laws binding on any real semiotic system" is binarism (Lotman 1990: 124). Its basic implication for Fielding's novels is that, to use Hourihan's words, "[t]he conceptual centre of a hero story consists of a set of binary oppositions: the qualities ascribed to the hero on the one hand and to his 'wild' opponents on the other" (Hourihan 1997: 15). This accords with the general rule governing the semiosphere – its composition of "conflicting structures" in the form of spaces which are "'ours', 'my own' [...] 'cultured', 'safe', 'harmoniously organized'" and those which appear as "'other', 'hostile', 'dangerous', 'chaotic'" (Lotman 1990: 131). In Fielding's novels these are "meaningful contrasts" and as such are indispensable for "the production of meaning" (Culler 1975: 14-15). Naturally, it is not only the arrangement of characters that is subject to the law of binarism but the author's entire ideological discourse, throughout which the advocated qualities are juxtaposed with their opposites, and the spatial organisation of the narratives. I will thus treat the idea of contrast as the principle that lies behind the poetics of the two novels, and as such it will govern the organisation of this part.

The titles of the two novels themselves indicate that special emphasis is to be placed on the eponymous characters. I find it therefore natural to focus on the two protagonists first, as one of the two extremes of Fielding's binary system. Both Joseph and Tom for the most part of the narratives are travelling. Their journeys, however different, follow a similar route; one of them being the reversed version of the other. Joseph Andrews, being dissatisfied with the London high life, sets back to the countryside to be reunited with his Fanny. Tom, conversely, travels to London in search of his beloved Sophia but also becomes involved in the *beau monde*. Characteristically of Fielding, who explicitly emphasised the literariness of his work (see Nowicki 1994), Joseph and Tom as travellers are in constant dialogue with archetypal wayfarers from the literary tradition, especially with those emerging from the genres Fielding found relevant for his own theory of the novel as the comic epic in prose. These include the epic, the romance, the picaresque and allegory.

1. Joseph, Tom and the literary tradition

Joseph and Tom at first glance do not appear to bear any resemblance to traditional epic heroes – they are by no means extraordinary and do not possess any superhuman qualities. In fact, they both could be called quintessentially ordinary, which, in the case of Tom, is signalled by his name and surname – the two most common names in English (Watt 1949: 335).[1] On the other hand, both protagonists demonstrate a great deal of heroism, though it is far from the Homeric ideal. As Nancy Mace observes, even though Homer's and Virgil's epics were widely valued and imitated in the first half

---

[1] In his article, Watt discusses the lowness and unheroic nature of the name in greater detail, referring to Fielding's ironic commentary on the name Thomas in the *Champion* and invoking well known criminals of the time known by the name of Tom Jones (Watt 1949: 335-336).

of the eighteenth century, their heroic code of honour was questioned and largely renounced as non-Christian (Mace 1996: 72). This is implicitly addressed in the London section of *Tom Jones*, in which the protagonist, for the sake of honour, maintains a morally dubious relationship with Lady Bellaston and fights in a duel. In his criticism and finally abandonment of the Homeric ideal, Fielding affiliated himself with others who, in Mace's words, "were uncomfortable with the epic hero" (Mace 1996: 72). The author then situated himself in the middle of the famous Battle of the Books – the Quarrel of the Ancients and the Moderns – advocating the modern epic which features the modern epic hero.

The heroism of Joseph and Tom is to be found in the constancy in virtue they both manifest, even though in Tom's case this is rather unorthodox given his weaknesses. Constancy as such is a character trait that was, in fact, put forward already in antiquity, when the principle of the conservation of character was formulated. Thus, Fielding's modernised, or Christianised, understanding of heroism is embodied in Joseph's perseverance in chastity[2] and Tom's unchanging devotion to charity. Endowed with these character traits, defining their selves throughout the narratives, Joseph and Tom both find themselves on the road, which, as it appears, parallels the roads gone down by three archetypal travellers – Telemachus, Odysseus and Aeneas. This parallelism is both literal and metaphorical and for the most part revolves around the nature of the quest pursued by the three epic heroes. What makes Fielding's travellers analogues of Telemachus, whose quest was to search for his father, is that their peregrinations are concluded by the scenes of recognition in which Joseph and Tom learn who their parents are. Even though this aim was never explicitly articulated by either of the protagonists (Joseph thought he knew his parents, whereas Tom accepted his status as a foundling), their journeys, given their culmination, are both metaphors of the search for the knowledge of one's origins.

---

[2] After Lady Booby's designs are made apparent, the narrator starts, "for a good Reason" (*JA*, 29), to call the protagonist Joseph instead of Joey. Joseph's Biblical predecessor and namesake was likewise able to reject the seductions of a woman who was higher on the social ladder (Potiphar's wife), thanks to which he became the archetypal model of chastity. The character of Joseph enjoyed a substantial popularity at the time, especially in the homiletic tradition (e.g. I. Barrow, L. Sterne) but also in the visual arts (e.g. a number of prints after the Italian Masters, including R. Strange's 1769 print *Joseph and Potiphar's Wife* after Guido Reni, or W. Blake's 1785 cycle *The Story of Joseph*). For a detailed study of the Biblical provenance of characters in *Joseph Andrews*, see Battestin 1959: 26-43.

Joseph's and Tom's affinity with the other two epic travellers seems to be of a more literal nature and as such has been recognised and commented on by critics.[3] What they share with both Odysseus and Aeneas is that their journeys are brought to an end when the protagonists find their true home.[4] Joseph's firm resolution to travel back from London to the country, where he could be reunited with his Fanny, corresponds with Odysseus' journey back to Ithaca and his faithful wife Penelope. Tom's true home, on the other hand, is not clearly defined and thus is not something towards which he is heading from the outset, as was the case with Joseph and Odysseus. It is something he must find the way to recognise, just as he must recognise his true self and heritage. This makes him an analogue of Aeneas, who similarly found himself on a journey culminating in the recognition of his true home and his true self.

The defined nature of the quests Fielding's travellers pursue and the recognition scenes at the end of their journeys are qualities that relate the two novels to the romance tradition; something Fielding himself most probably wished he had avoided. This relationship occurs in spite of several declarations to the contrary made by the narrator.[5] In fact, both Joseph and Tom fit perfectly into the standard romance plot, as defined by Northrop Frye in his *The Secular Scripture* (1976). According to the critic, what comes into focus in a romance is the development of the hero whose ultimate objective is to win the heroine. The quest is thwarted by antagonists, who exist in antithetic relation to the idealistic protagonists. The hero's adventures, journeys to "otherworlds" and obstacles met along the road are all combined with the shaping of identity and, ultimately, self-realisation (Frye 1976: 55). In Frye's archetypal terms, the pattern of romance plot, as the *mythos* of summer, begins with a disruption of a state of order, which leads through winter and death to a new order (a rebirth) and maturity (Frye 1957: 198-202). Both Joseph and Tom, at the moment of their departure, disrupt the state of order the reader was familiarised with at the beginning of the narrative and set out

---

[3] See, for example, Thornbury 1931: 108, Ehrenpreis 1964: 63, Maresca 1974: 203-216, Stovel 1989: 263-279.

[4] Apart from the journey home motif, what the two novels share with the *Odyssey* and the *Aeneid* are Didoesque female figures who thwart the protagonists in accomplishing their quest.

[5] In *Joseph Andrews*, for instance, we read that "those voluminous Works commonly called *Romances*" contain "very little Instruction or Entertainment" (*JA*, 4). Elsewhere, Fielding declares that he will "cautiously avoid the Term Romance" so as not to be accused of introducing unrealistic characters (*TJ*, 489).

on a journey which, in ritual terms (as a rite of passage), stands for the phase of winter and death. They create the new order (are reborn) when they return home to be united with their loved ones and settle in the countryside, which in Fielding's worldview is interrelated with ultimate self-realisation and personal maturity. As such, the journey taken by Fielding's travellers follows the pattern of the so-called Hero's Journey, or the monomyth, which according to Joseph Campbell is constituted by Departure, Initiation and Return (Miller 1976: 23).

The conception of the journey as a rite of passage is also a structural pattern that relates Fielding's texts to the picaresque novel, and indeed, both *Joseph Andrews* and *Tom Jones* abound in qualities that testify to their author's indebtedness to narratives belonging to this tradition. The two young protagonists, accompanied by comrades functioning as character-foils, find themselves in a travel milieu whose literary rendition relies on such typically picaresque material as scenes in coaches, inns, prisons or bedrooms, as well as vivid fisticuffs, scatological humour and encounters with villagers and criminals.

The picaresque chronotope of the two novels, a "road that winds through one's native territory" (Bakhtin 1981: 165), constructs a spatial dichotomy that is typical of the genre – the home and the world. This, however, is by no means an exclusively picaresque peculiarity. In her article devoted to literary travels, Janina Abramowska distinguishes four modes of travelling with regard to this dichotomy. Her typology, which seems to follow from Lotman's assertion that places in journey narratives are subject to ethical evaluations (Lotman 1990: 172), is best rendered in the scheme she proposes:

	Home	World
1.	+	−
2.	−	+
3.	+	+
4.	−	−

The mode that defines picaresque rambles is the one in which both extremes of the dichotomy bear negative connotations. The picaroon roaming the world of hostility and constant danger is at the same time a homeless being who will never find a place of secure retirement. This, however, could not be said about either of Fielding's travellers, who will eventually restore the primordial state of blissful existence, however troubled they are by the sordid world they have to traverse. Therefore, I believe it is more appropriate to categorise the two travellers as those following the first pattern, in which positive qualities are ascribed to the home and negative to the world. Within this mode, as Abramowska explains, the home "represents highest values and is a place that is sought and longed for" (Abramowska 1978: 296, my translation), whereas the world stands for a hostile but transitory phase. This, in turn, once again relates Fielding's novels to the tradition of romance writing, in which the home is a spatio-temporal construct valued positively, and even though it is lost or abandoned at the beginning of the narrative, it will be regained towards its end.

This positive evaluation of the place lost by the two travellers is explicitly articulated in both texts. When Joseph becomes aware that he might soon lose his post as Lady Booby's servant, he writes a letter to his sister Pamela, in which he informs her about the resolution he will most probably make:

> I fancy, I shall be discharged very soon; and the Moment I am, unless I hear from you, I shall return to my old Master's Country Seat, if it be only to see Parson *Adams*, who is the best Man in the World. *London* is a bad Place, and there is so little good Fellowship, that the next-door Neighbours don't know one another. (*JA*, 32)

His "old Master's Country Seat", the place he was forced to abandon when his professional obligations made him settle in London, is set in strong opposition to the capital, "a bad Place" he cannot wait to leave. The state of longing for the lost home, amplified by the hostility of the world (London and the road), is combined with the protagonist's eagerness to start a new life back at home: "*Joseph* and *Fanny* were impatient to get home and begin those previous Ceremonies to their Happiness which *Adams* had insisted on" (*JA*, 229). Thus, in Joseph's travel milieu the home is both a space of lost peace and order and a promised land where his maturity (as the husband of Fanny) can be achieved. In this respect, Joseph's home bears close resemblance to Tom's, which is addressed throughout the narrative in terms of the paradise lost and the paradise regained. These two categories bring to mind the titles of Milton's two epic poems, and, indeed, this relationship is explicitly established.[6] The very name of Mr Allworthy's mansion, Paradise Hall, lends

---

[6] Milton's *Paradise Lost* was clearly one of the plot models for *Tom Jones*, which is visible not only in the pilgrimage pattern but also in Blifil's diabolical stratagems leading to Tom's expulsion from Paradise Hall (these I will address later on). To read

credence to this intertextual link – Paradise Hall is lost and can be regained only after the penance (the pilgrimage) is performed. At its beginning, after being forced to leave Mr Allworthy's country seat, Tom could realise that

> *The World*, as *Milton* phrases it, *lay all before him*; and *Jones*, no more than *Adam*, had any Man to whom he might resort for Comfort or Assistance. All his Acquaintance were the Acquaintance of Mr. *Allworthy*, and he had no reason to expect any Countenance from them, as that Gentleman had with-drawn his Favour from him. (*TJ*, 331)

The positive evaluation of the home and the negative of the world is constructed here in a vein similar to that of Joseph's letter to his sister. The home is perceived as a friendly space due to its welcoming social atmosphere, whereas the hostility of the world is directly related to the feeling of loneliness it provokes.

This contrast would again support the argument of Fielding's reliance on the romance tradition, in which the home functions as the state of order disrupted at the beginning of the narrative and restored at its end. However, this antithetic organisation of space also relates the two narratives to the Christian allegorical tradition, which, in turn, would be far more acceptable for the author, who wished to "avoid the Term Romance", and who openly addressed Christian thought and ideology throughout his work. As Martin Battestin argues:

> Fielding rejected the methods of "formal realism" for a mode which verges on the symbolic and the allegorical: his characters and actions [...] frequently demand to be read as tokens of a reality larger than themselves; his novels may be seen as artful and highly schematic paradigms of the human condition. (Battestin 1989: 151)

The "paradigms of the human condition" that Fielding's travellers represent are well grounded in the Biblical tradition. The journeys of both Joseph and Tom refer to the two fundamental scriptural paradigms – exile and pilgrimage. What lies at their core is the conviction that the man, who once lost the paradise, is a constant wayfarer in this world in search of the true home. Sim-

---

more on Milton's contribution to the development of eighteenth-century fiction, see Erickson 2005.

ilarly to John Bunyan's *The Pilgrim's Progress*,[7] *Joseph Andrews* and *Tom Jones* offer plots built around the hero's road to his true home, which, if allegorically understood, refers directly to the Augustinian topos of *peregrinatio vitae*. A key Biblical text worth mentioning in this context is the parable of the Prodigal Son, a model circular journey to which the history of Tom bears close resemblance. In both the parable and the novel the destination (which was at the same time the point of departure) is a stable construct, and it is only the peregrinating protagonist that is changed, having found his true self.

Concluding this survey, I will point out that the three traditions on which Fielding either explicitly or implicitly relied – that is, the epic, romance and allegorical traditions – all advocate a specific understanding of the wayfaring self. According to this understanding, man's predestination is a quest which sooner or later will have to be performed. This, in turn, finds its resolution in the achievement of a new order, or in the reinstatement of an order that was once lost. The characters embarking on the quest move both horizontally, approaching their spatial destination, and vertically (inwardly), coming to understand the essence of their being. The search for essence is a quality that distances the two narratives from the picaresque tradition, in which fluidity and chaos supersede essence. Fielding's reliance on the picaresque paradigm can only be observed at a surface level, whereas the deeper level of his work displays a diametrically-opposed ideological system.

2. In search of the true self

If Joseph's and Tom's quest culminates in the travellers' discovery of their essence – in both social and personal terms – the pattern of the discourse of the self emerging from Fielding's texts should be called *searching for* rather than *shaping of* identity. These two paradigms are both grounded in the seventeenth- and eighteenth-century philosophical reflection about the category of self, which is the background against which the two novels emerged. As I pointed out in the Introduction, there was, on the one hand, the Christian tradition advocating the substantialist understanding of a unique, permanent and unchangeable self, and, on the other, the empiricist tradition of Locke and Hume undermining the idea of stability and substantiality. Whenever a hero or heroine *searches for* his or her identity, it is implied that there is

---

[7] The text is one of the key examples in attempts to draw parallels between the tradition of seventeenth-century spiritual biographies and the rise of the modern novel (see e.g. Preus 1991, McKeon 2002).

something permanent and unchanging which can be searched for; conversely, the *shaping of* identity suggests that there is no such thing, and that one's person is subject to constant becoming; an idea manifested by the Lockean assertion that a newly born is "white Paper, void of all Characters, without any *Ideas*" (Locke 1975: 104).

The plots of the two narratives both follow the paradigm of the heroes' search for their true selves – who they really are is discovered at the end of their adventures. By following the convention of resolving the plot with an *anagnorisis*, Fielding, in fact, situated his work within the substantialist reflection about identity – there was some essence to be discovered, especially in social terms. I will now trace the process of Joseph's and Tom's discovering and coming to understand their social and personal identity.

One of the forms into which the picaresque novel transformed in the eighteenth century was the novel of social ascension. Such narratives, written usually in accord with the conventions of fictional biographies or autobiographies, build their plots around the motif of the protagonist's climbing the social ladder. Among Fielding's contemporaries, the authors exploiting the motif included, most notably, Daniel Defoe and Samuel Richardson. Texts such as *Roxana* (1724) or *Pamela* (1740), whose heroines ascend the social hierarchy, constitute, in fact, fictionalisations of a quality inherent in the *ancien régime* of identity – that is, the arbitrariness of social roles. What both these texts imply is that one is not born into a given social status but can modify it throughout life. The traditionally-understood social hierarchy is depicted as an artificial construct, which can easily be deconstructed.

On the surface, the histories of Joseph and Tom could be regarded as some further variations on the motif in question – Joseph, a poor servant, and Tom, a foundling (thus nobody), both end up as respected gentlemen, which most appropriately concludes their adventures. However, what distinguishes Fielding's narratives from the two I have mentioned previously is that neither Joseph nor Tom, in fact, improves his social status; instead, towards the end of the novels, they both discover who they really are in social terms, which is diametrically opposed to what they have seemingly been so far.

At the beginning of the two texts, both protagonists are socially misplaced. Joseph, as the reader is informed, is "esteemed to be the only Son of Gaffar and Gammer *Andrews*, and Brother to the illustrious *Pamela*, whose Virtue is at present so famous" (*JA*, 20), whereas Tom, introduced as "an Infant, wrapt up in some coarse Linnen" (*TJ*, 39) found in Mr Allworthy's bed, is after some investigation regarded as the bastard son of Jenny Jones and Mr Partridge. According to traditional reasoning, social identity was largely formed by one's antecedents. In fact, one of the meanings of the word *person*, as Marcel Mauss explains, is the ancestral mask used during family rituals (Mauss 1985: 13). These masks testified to the widespread belief among traditional societies that just because individuals should be seen as reincarnations of forefathers, they inherit particular names and particular social functions. This conviction, as Riley points out, governs aristocratic societies, in which one is "born into a title and its properties and functions" and where "[t]he title and the kind of identity it indexes precede and survive the individuals who bear them" (Riley 2007: 79). Accordingly, when one's origins are low, there is literally nothing to be born into, and the individual is supposed to assume one of the appropriate social roles, such as a servant, a gamester, a whore, a vagrant, etc, irrespective of his or her character traits and qualities.

Generally speaking, as I mentioned in the Introduction, the idea of inheriting one's social identity was largely questioned in the literature of the time, and its deconstruction was a quality that constituted the novel of social ascension as a genre. Frequently, these novels featured bastards of unknown parents as their protagonists, which literarily criticised the aristocratic ideology of linear inheritance (McKeon 2002: 159). The case of Fielding's texts is, however, different. Even though it is possible for the reader to come across statements which openly question the ideology (e.g. "Would it not be hard, that a Man who hath no Ancestors should therefore be render'd incapable of acquiring Honour, when we see so many who have no Virtues, enjoying the Honour of their Forefathers?" [*JA*, 21]), the resolutions strengthen it nonetheless. The scenes of discovery at the end of the narratives do not lift the protagonists up on the social ladder but reinstate them in the positions they should have attained from the very beginning. That is why, as a way of foreshadowing their reinstatement, the narratives both contain various figural and narratorial commentaries contradicting the characters' seemingly low social standing and exposing their true nobility and gentility.

When Joseph is first introduced as a ten-year-old apprentice to Sir Thomas Booby, we learn that his voice is so "extremely musical" and displays such a "sweetness" that he is not able to perform the roles given to him – that is, of a bird keeper and a whipper-in (*JA*, 21-22) – which otherwise would be entirely appropriate for a basely born apprentice. Some time later, being "in one and twentieth Year of his Age" (*JA*, 38), Joseph arouses feelings of love in Lady Booby by his idealised appearance:

He was of the highest Degree of middle Stature. His Limbs were put together with great Elegance and no less Strength. His Legs and Thighs were formed in the exactest Proportion. His Shoulders were broad and brawny, but yet his Arms hung so easily, that he had all the Symptoms of Strength without the least clumsiness. His Hair was of a nut-brown Colour, and was displayed in wanton Ringlets down his Back. His Forehead was high, his Eyes dark, and as full of Sweetness as of Fire. His Nose a little inclined to the Roman. His Teeth white and even. His lips full, red, and soft. His Beard was only rough on his Chin and upper Lip; but his Cheeks, in which his Blood glowed, were overspread with a thick Down. His Countenance had a Tenderness joined with a Sensibility inexpressible. Add to this the most perfect Neatness in his Dress, and an Air, which to those who have not seen many Noblemen, would give an Idea of Nobility. (*JA*, 38-39)

As Sean Shesgreen convincingly explains, such anatomical character renditions are grounded in at least five literary traditions: ancient Greek love poetry, Italian pre-Renaissance love poetry, Provençal poetry, English Renaissance poetry and French romance prose, the last of these being the one with which the correspondence is most transparent (Shesgreen 1972: 23). Thus idealised presentations of the protagonist's looks can easily "give an idea of nobility" and as such were as a rule reserved for personages of a relatively high social status, belonging "to a long tradition of portraiture that was used to depict nobility" (Shesgreen 1972: 37). Shesgreen's argument that the portrait of Joseph bears striking resemblance to the presentation of Don Alvares, a nobleman from Scudéry's romance *Almahide* (Shesgreen 1972: 33), only proves the point. Later on, the contrast between Joseph's appearance and his social standing is noted by Betty, the servant taking care of the injured Joseph after his encounter with rogues. After seeing Joseph for the first time, she proclaims that he is a gentleman, "for she never saw a finer Skin in her Life" (*JA*, 61), and when he starts to recover, she returns to her initial observation claiming that the protagonist is "a greater Man then they took him for", which manifests itself in "the extreme Whiteness of his Skin, and the Softness of his Hands" (*JA*, 66).

At one point in the final book of the novel, Fielding perversely embraces the convention of the novel of social ascension. He introduces the characters of Pamela and Squire Booby, the agents of the most famous literary social ascension in the mid-eighteenth-century novel, which results in Joseph's vindication, thus accounted for by Pamela's husband to Lady Booby:

Madam, as I have married a virtuous and worthy Woman, I am resolved to own her Relations, and shew them all a proper Respect; I shall think myself therefore

infinitely obliged to all mine, who will do the same. It is true, her Brother hath
been your Servant; but he is now become my Brother; and I have one Happiness,
that neither his Character, his Behaviour or Appearance give me any reason to be
ashamed of calling him so. In short, he is now below, drest like a Gentleman, in
which Light I intend he shall hereafter be seen; (*JA*, 292)

Joseph is indeed "drest like a Gentleman", and the act of his donning the new
social self, constructed out of the pieces of clothing he receives from his
brother-in-law, is related just before the Squire's conversation with his aunt:

Joseph was soon drest in the plainest Dress he could find, which was a blue Coat
and Breeches, with a gold Edging, and a red Waistcoat with the same; and as this
Suit, which was rather too large for the Squire, exactly fitted him; so he became it
so well, and looked so genteel, that no Person would have doubted its being as
well adapted to his Quality as his Shape; (*JA*, 291)

Wahrman argues that what was typical of the *ancien régime* of identity was
"the literalness with which dress was taken to make identity, rather than
merely to signify its anterior existence" (Wahrman 2004: 177-178). Bernard
Mandeville, in turn, observed that people

are generally honour'd according to their Clothes and other Accoutrements they
have above them [...] which encourages every Body to wear clothes above his
rank [...] and consequently have the pleasure of being esteemed by a vast majority, not as what they are, but what they appear to be. (quoted in Hundert 1997: 75)

Such arbitrariness of social roles, however, was not something Fielding
would advocate, and this leads to the resolution of the narrative – the discovery of Joseph's true social self.

The discovery makes Joseph's gentleman-like appearance and conduct
socially sanctioned. Mr Wilson, who turns out to be Joseph's father, was
"descended of a good Family, and was born a Gentleman", as he himself
informs his listeners at the beginning of the story of his life (*JA*, 201). A
beginning of this kind is not accidental, as it implies that one's life story
starts from the acknowledgement of one's ancestors. Such was the case with
the introduction of Joseph, who was "esteemed to be the only Son of Gaffar
and Gammer *Andrews*, and Brother to the illustrious *Pamela*". Purposely,
there was no mention of Joseph *being* the son of his alleged parents but only
of his *being esteemed* to be the one. The recognition scene reveals Joseph's
true parents; an event which is indispensably related to the discovery of his

true social self. This substantialist approach to the category of social self is strengthened by the symbolic birthmark that makes the protagonist's discovery possible. Joseph's strawberry mark has been the unchanging and permanent index of his social status throughout the whole narrative, whose true nature, however, is revealed only when it can be identified accordingly.

An analogous pattern of highlighting qualities seemingly contradicting the protagonist's social status, and thus foreshadowing the *anagnorisis* at the end of the narrative, is adopted in *Tom Jones*. Just as was the case with *Joseph Andrews*, in Fielding's second novel Tom's nobleness, gentility and some higher social pedigree are exposed both by a full-length character sketch and by numerous comments throughout the narrative. The character sketch follows the convention of depicting nobility I have just discussed,[8] but, preceding the celebrated love scene at Upton inn, the description is given a tinge of eroticism:

> Mr. *Jones*, [...] was, in reality, one of the handsomest young Fellows in the World. His Face, besides being the Picture of Health, had in it the most apparent Marks of Sweetness and Good-Nature. These Qualities were indeed so characteristical in his Countenance, that [...] so strongly was this Good-nature painted in his Look, that it was remarked by almost every one who saw him.
>
> It was, perhaps, as much owing to this, as to a very fine Complexion, that his Face had a Delicacy in it almost inexpressible, and which might have given him an Air rather too effeminate, had it not been joined to a most masculine Person and Mien; which latter had as much in them of the *Hercules*, as the former had of the *Adonis*. He was besides active, genteel, gay, and good-humoured, and had a Flow of Animal Spirits, which enlivened every Conversation where he was present. (*TJ*, 510)

Tom's comparison to Hercules and Adonis, the mythological figures standing for the ideals of an excellent warrior and a perfect lover respectively, is by no means accidental. The two characters epitomise qualities traditionally ascribed to the chivalric ideal, which is reinforced here by means of such character traits as being "active, genteel, gay, and good-humoured" and having "a Flow of Animal Spirits". All these construct the image of Tom as a sexually attractive knightly figure and undermine his seemingly low social standing.

A similar function is performed by shorter characterisational comments interlarding the narrative. When he is still just an infant, we learn about his

---

[8] Shesgreen argues that it bears close resemblance to another character rendition from Scudéry's *Almahide* – that of a knight named Abinarrays (Shesgreen 1972: 127).

"Beauty and Innocence" (*TJ*, 46); when twelve, for the sake of honour, he does not reveal the name of Black George, with whom he illegally hunted a partridge (*TJ*, 121-2); when eighteen, he is able to give "Tokens of that Gallantry of Temper which greatly recommends Men to Women" (*TJ*, 139); finally, being already in exile, he presents himself to the company of soldiers he wants to join being "very well dressed", "naturally genteel" and having "a remarkable Air of Dignity in his Look, which is rarely seen among the Vulgar" (*TJ*, 370). Tom's knightly appearance is also the reason why some of the women he encounters fall for him. Mrs Waters, for instance, is deeply impressed by Jones's looks: "I could almost conceive you to be some good Angel; and, to say the Truth, you look more like an Angel than a Man, in my Eye" (*TJ*, 496). This is followed by a short sketch of the protagonist's physical features, which, emphasising his "Health, Strength, Freshness, Spirit and Good-Nature" (*TJ*, 496), is again very much in line with presentations of knights in chivalric romances (Baker 1960: 418). The protagonist makes a similar impression on Mrs Fitzpatrick, the encounter with whom is his first contact with the high life of London:

> There is a certain Air of natural Gentility, which it is neither in the Power of Dress to give, nor to conceal. Mr. *Jones*, as hath been before hinted, was possessed of this in a very eminent Degree. He met, therefore, with a Reception from the Lady, somewhat different from what his Apparel seemed to demand; and after he had paid her his proper Respects, was desired to sit down. (*TJ*, 692)

The implication that Tom's apparel should demand a somewhat different reception refers to what was related earlier in the chapter, that is, the poor quality of his dress – "a Suit of Fustian" (*TJ*, 690). At this point, what Tom wears matches his low social status, just as was the case with Joseph for the most part of his travels.

However, similarly to what he does at one point in *Joseph Andrews*, Fielding for a while embraces the convention of the novel of social ascension, when he introduces a high life representative who seemingly lifts the protagonist up on the social ladder. In the previous novel, it was Squire Booby, who literally made Joseph a gentleman, having given him a set of his gentlemanly pieces of clothing. In *Tom Jones*, the agent of the hero's ascension is Lady Bellaston, who, making him her kept man, contributes to his becoming "one of the best dress'd Men about Town" and raises him "to a State of Affluence, beyond what he ha[s] ever known" (*TJ*, 724). Nothing at this point would make the history of Tom more in line with typical novels of social ascension – a banished bastard, a nobody, is transformed into a London *beau* kept by a powerful and affluent lady. Unlike Joseph's, Tom's social rise is not immediately sanctioned by the discovery of his true self. Instead, like in a real rite of passage, he must first experience a symbolic death and only then re-enter society, which in Tom's case is accompanied by reinstatement to his true social position. Tom's symbolic death – that is, his imprisonment, expectation of immediate execution and the burden of guilt over his alleged incest – on the one hand marks the end of his false self, which evolved from his initial misplacement as the bastard son of Jenny Jones, and on the other, suggests that the role of a London *beau*, enjoying the pleasures of the town, is not the one he was born into.

The recognition scene in *Tom Jones*, conducted in a vein reminiscent of *deus ex machina* resolutions in classical drama, is far more extensive than the one in *Joseph Andrews*. In the latter, it takes no more than several paragraphs, which are enough to identify Joseph's and Fanny's true families. In Fielding's second novel, its more extensive form results from its broader nature – it is not only about reinstating Tom to the social position he should have occupied from the very beginning but also about unmasking those characters who have done their best to maintain the status quo, resorting to "the blackest and deepest Villainy" (*TJ*, 943). Thus, before Tom finally learns about his true social self, Mr Dowling and Blifil are exposed as those who have hindered his ascension throughout the narrative.

When Tom is finally recognised to be the son of Bridget Allworthy, a nephew of Mr Allworthy and a gentleman, there still remains something ambiguous to his rise – he is still a bastard, though of parents who belonged to a higher rank of society, and consequently an illegitimate heir to Allworthy's Paradise Hall. It appears to be even more ambiguous if one, following Claude Rawson, poses the question "why Tom could not have been made a legitimate foundling like Joseph Andrews" (Rawson 1972: 7). This can be read as a threat posed to the aristocratic ideology, and it could seem logical to argue that Fielding, by vindicating a bastard, questioned traditional approaches to succession and inheritance. Such assumption stems from a belief, most notably articulated by McKeon, that bastard heroes in the eighteenth-century novel constitute "implicit criticism of aristocratic ideology" (McKeon 2002: 159). However, assuming this were the case, Fielding would have achieved a far more powerful effect if Tom had been vindicated as a bastard of either unknown parents or of parents emerging from the lower classes of society. That is why I believe it is more convincing to consider

Tom's illegitimacy as a motif organising plot structure. If he had not been conceived outside marriage, he would not have first appeared in the narrative as a foundling, as no masquerading scheme would have been necessary on Bridget's part (Sherburn 1959: 257). Apart from that, Fielding was very keen on resorting to various at times even contradictory literary conventions, and, as Lisa Zunshine demonstrates, writing the history of a bastard hero made it possible for the author to situate himself inside a versatile network on conventions governing fiction featuring illegitimate characters (Zunshine 2005: 86-100).

Taking the above into account, I do not consider Fielding's texts as novels of social ascension. Joseph's and Tom's noble and genteel looks and behaviour foreshadow their recognition as born gentlemen, which manifests Fielding's traditional belief in the unchanging substance with regard to social identity. Joseph and Tom are thus characters whose journeys lead to self-discovery in social terms – they were born gentleman, predetermined to peacefully reside in the countryside, as did their ancestors. In both novels what on the surface appears to be a road towards social ascension turns out to be a circular journey, culminating in the discovery of the travellers' origins.

Another genre of prose fiction which is brought up in casual discussions of Fielding is the *Bildungsroman* – that is, the novel of formation, which centres on the protagonist's development as a human being, depicting his or her (usually his, as Cuddon notices [1999: 82]) life from birth to the moment at which maturity is achieved. The genre flourished in the eighteenth century, which was closely related to the literary popularity of empiricist reflection about personal identity, questioning the notions of innate ideas and substance, and highlighting the role of experience in the formation of human personhood. Thus, the *Bildungsroman* as a genre is by nature anti-substantialist, and the paradigm of human development it represents is that of creation or becoming. With regard to the two patterns of the discourse of the self I put forward at the beginning of this part, the genre constitutes a variation on the *shaping of* identity paradigm. In Fielding's novels, however, as I have argued so far, the two travellers are not being shaped at any time. In social terms, they search for their true self, whereas in personal terms, they are self-consistent as characters throughout the narrative (with some reservations, though, which I will demonstrate later).

The idea of self-consistence in literary characterisation, otherwise known as the conservation of character, is a principle formulated in antiquity and advocated by such notable figures as Aristotle in Chapter XV of *Poetics*

(2000: 76) and Horace in *Ars Poetica* (2000: 101). As Coolidge notices, the principle "corresponds to the philosophical conviction that the essential reality of a person is a certain idea which is his nature and to which he has a kind of duty to conform" (Coolidge 1960: 160), and this situates it within traditional, substantialist approaches to personal identity, asserting its unchangeable and permanent nature. This is noted by Fielding himself, when he writes that

> the Actions should be such as may not only be within the Compass of human Agency, and which human Agents may probably be supposed to do; but they should be likely for the very Actors and Characters themselves to have performed: For what may be only wonderful and surprising in one Man, may become improbable, or indeed impossible, when related of another.
>
> This last Requisite is what the dramatic Critics call Conservation of Character, and it requires a very extraordinary Degree of Judgment, and a most exact Knowledge of human Nature.
>
> [...]I will venture to say, that for a Man to act in direct Contradiction to the Dictates of his Nature, is, if not impossible, as improbable and as miraculous as any Thing which can well be conceived. (*TJ*, 405)

The reason why dramatic criticism is invoked here is that the principle was one of the basic conventions governing Restoration drama, which was best manifested in the adoption of character types. As such, following Coolidge's argument, the conservation of character was "part of the equipment" Fielding, a former dramatist, brought with him into the realm of prose fiction (Coolidge 1960: 160). He was, naturally, not the only eighteenth-century novelist following the principle, which, according to Spacks, resulted in an "imagined" identity of some eighteenth-century novelistic characters, compensating for the instability of philosophical reflection over the category of personal identity (Spacks 1976: 1-27). In Fielding's case, however, Spacks argues, "the principle of consistency" is elevated "almost to one of rigor" (Spacks 1976: 7). In effect, no character formation is fictionalised in the two novels, and that is why the application of the term *Bildungsroman* to Fielding's narratives raises doubts. Instead, Joseph and Tom should rather be seen as grounded in literary traditions reliant upon the substantialist approach to the category of person, such as epic, romance and allegory. The two travellers are represented as coming to understand their predestination and the unchanging essence of their selves.

In *Joseph Andrews* the authoritative narrator endows the protagonist with permanent qualities, which from the outset are defined by means of literary allusion. Before Joseph is introduced, the narrator situates the history of his adventures against the background of two recent life writings, that is, "the Lives of Mr. *Colley Cibber*, and of Mrs. *Pamela Andrews*" (*JA*, 18-19). Both texts are ironically praised, the former for denigrating "worldly Grandeur" and exposing "the Emptiness and Vanity of that Fantom, Reputation", the latter for putting forward a model of virtuous chastity (*JA*, 19). The setting of Joseph's life against this particular background, given Fielding's true attitude towards these two texts (articulated most prominently in his *Shamela*, written under the pseudonym of Mr Conny Keyber), constitutes a clear message to the reader – the protagonist as a hero will have little in common with Cibber's hypocrisy and affectation, and Pamela's mercantilist understanding of virtue as a commodity which can be traded for social ascension.

Another text directly referred to by Fielding, and contributing to the literary construction of Joseph's character, is Cervantes' *Don Quixote*.[9] As Ardila points out, literary scholars have always had different opinions concerning Joseph's Quixotic qualities. Just as there has been a general consensus over Parson Adams being the Quixote of the narrative, the eponymous hero's status has been considered troublesome. Some believe him to be the second Quixote, some to be the Sancho of the novel, whereas Ronald Paulson, curiously enough, considers him to be the latter, arguing at the same time that his beloved Fanny performs the role of Dulcinea (Ardila 2009: 129). Ardila in his article avoids authoritative statements regarding the controversy but rightly notices that even if Joseph is not a Quixote proper, there is a Quixotic quality in his person. The quality the critic ascribes to him is the unconditional belief in the model of virtue advocated by his sister Pamela and at the same time ridiculed by society which surrounds him (Ardila 2009: 129). This, however, raises doubts. Joseph's identity as a moral paragon in Fielding's text is constituted by a rather different conception of virtue. Ardila is right in claiming that Joseph's perseverance in chastity is a Quixotic feature which results in social rejection, but he fails to notice that it is indispensably related to his faithfulness to Fanny, for whose sake "*Joseph* made such extraordinary haste out of Town" (*JA*, 48). When Joseph ultimately rejects Lady Booby's temptation, his references to his sister's virtue and to "the Chastity of his

---

[9] The full title of the novel is *The History of the Adventures of Joseph Andrews and his Friend Mr Abraham Adams. Written in Imitation of the Manner of Cervantes, Author of* Don Quixote.

Family, which is preserved in her" (*JA*, 41) constitute, in fact, only rhetorical devices employed to thwart her attempts to seduce him. Furthermore, any relation between Joseph and Pamela is symbolically dissolved in the end, following the recognition scene. Thus, Joseph's Quixotic nature is related to his steadiness, faithfulness and chastity (qualities he inherits from his biblical namesake rather than from Pamela), which all make him, as constituents of his truthfulness and moral goodness, "an Astonishment and Ridicule of the rest",[10] juxtaposed with destabilised, faithless and adulterous society.

Once endowed with these qualities, Joseph is true to them throughout the whole text. In the novel, there is no *Bildungsroman*-like formation but rather a series of episodes enabling the protagonist to manifest his constancy. The first of these is Joseph's time as a servant to Lady Booby, which I have already touched upon. The protagonist finds himself accompanying his lady in London, which would seem the best opportunity for his weaknesses, if he had any, to surface. Joseph remains, however, constant in his virtue, and even though he is "a little too forward in Riots at the Play-Houses and Assemblies" and "behave[s] with less seeming Devotion than formerly" at church, his moral principles are "entirely uncorrupted", and his acquaintances in the town are not able to "teach him to game, swear, drink, nor any other genteel Vice the Town abounded with" (*JA*, 27). It may be concluded that if London, the town which has witnessed many falls of those who have visited it, does not manage to ruin Joseph's character (as it does, for instance, with the protagonists of Hogarth's progresses and with his father, Mr Wilson), nothing ever will. Joseph's constancy in London and his insensibility to its alluring charms thus foreshadow his perseverance throughout his forthcoming adventures, which culminate in his marriage to Fanny and peaceful residence in the countryside. All this contributes to the conservation of Joseph's character and to his static constitution as a moral paragon, through the construction of which the author expresses his didactic and literary tenets.

The eponymous protagonist of *Tom Jones* is undoubtedly a more dynamic figure than his literary predecessor. Because of his "naturally sanguine" temper (*TJ*, 708), he is much more inclined to inconsistencies, at least as far as his relations with women are concerned. His more versatile nature is also related to the extent to which the narrative itself is developed. In comparison with Fielding's first novel, *Tom Jones* is in every aspect more diverse, complex and dynamic, and thus its protagonist is no longer a static moral paragon

---

[10] Nowicki argues that Joseph's Quixotism depends on his playing the role of "a tester of human goodness" (Nowicki 2008: 68, my translation).

but rather a real human being, "transcribed" from the "original Book of Nature" (*TJ*, 377), with his strengths and weaknesses. Nevertheless, even though chastity in Tom's case is by no means a permanent character trait, the hero is, similarly to Joseph, endowed with qualities that do not change throughout the narrative.

Perversely, the first character sketch of Tom (at the age of 12), shows him in a rather negative light. The general opinion about him is that he was "born to be hanged [...] having, from his earliest Years, discovered a Propensity to many Vices" (*TJ*, 118), which is even more transparent, we read, when confronted with the virtuous conduct of Master Blifil (*TJ*, 118). The presentation of Tom as a binary opposite to the seemingly virtuous Blifil follows from the general masquerading pattern adopted by the author, which I will study later. For the time being, let it be enough to remark that what is implied by this juxtaposition is that Tom's inclination to vice is as real as Blifil's perseverance in virtue.

Apart from the two basic weaknesses Tom displays – that is, impetuosity and susceptibility to female charms – his character, even if not a moral paragon or an exemplum, is nevertheless put forward by the didactically-oriented author as some rather more realistic model of behaviour worth imitating. As Battestin recognises (1959: 58-59), at the core of Fielding's understanding of human nature is the theory of passions, which is curiously explained by the author himself in his least acclaimed piece of fiction, *A Journey from This World to the Next*, published in the same year as his *opus magnum* – 1749. This moral treatise guised in the form of a travel narrative (see Lipski 2010) constitutes a very interesting context for *Tom Jones*. In fact, it appears that what is theoretically proposed in the former, is put into practice in the latter. In the *Journey* the travelling soul of the author witnesses the scene in which Fortune equips spirits for their entrance into the flesh. As the narrator reports, first, the spirit receives "THE PATHETIC POTION", which is "a Mixture of all the Passions, but in no exact Proportion, so that sometimes one predominates and sometimes another"; then, Fortune provides the spirit with a "medicine called the NOUSPHORIC DECOTION", being "an Extract from the Faculties of the Mind" (Fielding 1993: 29). In effect, the man appears to be constituted by a mixture of different, often contradictory passions, which are supposed to be, in a sense, maintained in a proper proportion by reason. This, however, is rather demanding in practice, and that is why transgression, which follows from a momentary predomination of a given passion, should not be utterly condemned. At the gates of Elysium the author's soul confesses: "I had indulged myself very freely with Wine and Women in my Youth, but I had never done an Injury to any Man living, nor avoided an Opportunity of doing good" (Fielding 1993: 36). What follows this declaration is his admittance to Paradise, which implies that weaknesses and flaws will not lead to eternal punishment if counterbalanced by a quality Fielding calls "Good-Nature", defined in his poem "Of Good-Nature" (1743) as "the glorious Lust of doing Good" (Fielding 1972b: 31). In "An Essay on the Knowledge of the Characters of Men", in turn, he refers to the basic assumptions of latitudinarian thought and calls the quality "that benevolent and amiable Temper of Mind which disposes us to feel the Misfortunes, and enjoy the Happiness of others; and consequently pushes us on to promote the latter, and prevent the former" (Fielding 1972a: 158).[11]

This permanent characteristic is what stands behind the benevolent deeds of Fielding's protagonists. In the case of Joseph, it was only one of the several virtues making up his character, whereas in the case of Tom it is a quality that outweighs his libertine tendencies. Most importantly, however, the term as such relates Fielding's idea to innatist and substantialist approaches to personal identity. Good-Nature, as the second component of the name suggests, is what the character is born with, and as such it distinguishes him till the end. The protagonist of *Tom Jones* manifests it continually throughout the whole narrative, which is best noticeable in his behaviour towards Black George and his family at the beginning of the novel (not without reason is one of the chapters entitled: "*A childish Incident, in which, however, is seen a good-natur'd Disposition in* Tom Jones" [*TJ*, 142]), and in his compassionate involvement in the affair between Nancy Miller and Mr Nightingale in the London part of the text (*TJ*, 764-770). It is also a quality Tom shares with Mr Allworthy, and when the latter first sees the foundling in his bed, the bond between them is established by means of its workings: "He stood some Time lost in Astonishment at this Sight; but, as Good-nature had always the Ascendant in his Mind, he soon began to be touched with Sentiments of Compassion for the little Wretch before him" (*TJ*, 39). Tom's good nature is also a characteristic more than approved of by Mr Allworthy, who in reaction to Tom's charitable account of the hardships undergone by the family of Black George "st[ands] silent for some Moments, and before he sp[eaks] the Tears [have] started from his Eyes" (*TJ*, 143).

---

[11] To read more on Fielding's indebtedness to latitudinarian thought, see Battestin 1959, Müller 2008: 229-280, Stewart 2010: 33-70.

In conclusion, the literary function of both Joseph and Tom is to serve as "tokens of a reality larger than themselves", to invoke Battestin's observation once again. However different they are, the former being a moral paragon constructed in response to contemporary didactic discourse, the latter being a good-natured constitution, though not deprived of faults, "transcribed" from "the book of nature", they both appear as mere puppets in the hands of the almighty narrator – the "controlling consciousness", in Kraft's terms (1992: 65) – used for transmitting his moral and anthropological observations. No formation as such is thus thematised in the two texts. What they essentially are in personal terms is confirmed when they discover their true social selves, so that the reinstated social nobility could parallel their true and natural nobility. Just as the former had to be searched for, endowing the narrative with an attractive storyline, the latter, displayed by the characters throughout the texts, was never lost.

Chapter Two

The Masquerading World

So far, I have discussed only one of the two extremes of the ideological structure of the two novels – the travellers, who, "shewing their true faces", stand as binary oppositions to the world they are forced to confront. This world, as the epigraph of this part demonstrates, is a masquerading world governed by disguise, artifice and hypocrisy, and I will be concerned with its nature in this chapter. The metaphor of the world as a masquerade was by no means Fielding's invention. The novelist, however, referred to it practically throughout his whole literary career, which, quite tellingly, started with the comedy *Love in Several Masques* (1728) and a verse satire entitled *The Masquerade* (1728). His attitude towards the phenomenon literally understood and towards its transposition into the realm of social behaviours and conventions was rather negative, and most of his works touch upon it in a vein typical of the so called anti-masquerade writing; that is, moralistic satires and pamphlets written in reaction to the disruption of social decorum at masked assemblies.

The trend flourished in the 1720s and continued till the 1780s, and its representatives published their works simultaneously with the organisation of subsequent masked balls. A text typical of the trend is *Short Remarks upon the Original and Pernicious Consequences of Masquerades* published anonymously in 1721, in which a masked ball is nothing but

> a Pastime utterly unlawful, being a Congress to an unclean end; not a Mystery of Iniquity, but an open Scene of outrageous and flaming Debauchery; where Temptation is passionately courted, the wanton Imagination indulged to the last degree, so that none who go there return from thence chaste and innocent. (*Short Remarks* ... 1721: 41)

As Castle demonstrates, anti-masquerade writings exposed the ways in which the possibilities opened up by masked assemblies threatened the received social and moral order. They offered "a paradoxical safe zone" for the sexual underworld, made it possible for women to enjoy "promiscuous freedom" and distorted social divisions and hierarchies (Castle 1986: 41-44, 79-86). The critic, in an attempt to interpret the existence of the trend, argues that its representatives manifested "a desire for firm conceptual boundaries" and "celebrated a world made up of discrete forms, of rigid categories and hygienically polarized opposites" (Castle 1986: 102). Such beliefs, as I have already argued, were close to Fielding's heart, and it comes as no surprise that many of his works make use of the conventions of anti-masquerade writings.

1. Fielding's anti-masquerade writing
Fielding's first attempt at anti-masquerade writing was his literary debut, the 1728 verse satire entitled *The Masquerade*, dedicated to "C[OUN]T H[EI]D[EG]G[E]R", for the writing of which the author himself put on a mask of the pseudonym of "Lemuel Gulliver, Poet Laureat to the King of Lilliput". The poem is a first-person account of the speaker's visit to a masked assembly organised by Heidegger at Haymarket theatre. As Craft-Fairchild sees it (1993: 1-2), it is primarily concerned with the disruptive implications of masquerades, which manifest themselves in the mingling of the classes and sexes. This is what initially strikes the visitor, who on entering the assembly is confronted with the following "heap of incoherencies":

> So here in one Confusion hurl'd,
> Seem all the Nations of the World:
> Cardinals, Quakers, Judges dance;
> Grim *Turks* are coy, and Nuns advance.
> Grave Churchmen here, at Hazard play;
> Conque-Ace ten Pound—done, Quater-tray.
> Known Prudes there, Libertines we find,
> Who masque the Face, t'unmasque the Mind.
> Here, Running Footmen guzzle tea;
> There, Milkmaids Flasks of *Burgundy*.
> I saw two Shepherdesses dr-nk
> And heard a Friar call'd a p-nk. (Fielding 2008: 17)

The passage, exuding an aura of the carnivalesque, invokes the idea of social turmoil, taking the form of national, religious and class confusion. The confusion is amplified by the participants' behaviour, which is often contradictory to the social status signified by their clothes – "Judges dance", "Nuns advance", "Churchmen here at Hazard play", "Milkmaids [guzzle] Flasks of *Burgundy*". As such, masquerades disrupt one of the received rules governing the social order of the *ancien régime* of identity – the policy of "literalness with which dress was taken to make identity", which I have referred to before.

The quoted passage, however, apart from serving as an illustration of the destabilising qualities of the masquerade, is also related to Fielding's distrustful attitude towards the outwardly manifested virtue, which is thematised, for instance, in the character of Blifil. In *The Masquerade*, the visitor reports: "Known Prudes there [...] / Who masque the Face, t'unmasque the mind"; on the other hand, on encountering a group of prostitutes, the poet asks his companion: "Madam, how from another Woman / Do you Strumpet masqu'd distinguish?", and the conclusion of her reply is: "Virtue is a Masque" (Fielding 2008: 22); a melancholic statement testifying to Fielding's concern with the masquerading world. Supporting her observation, the companion tells the story of a typical masquerade ending; that is, a scene of unmasking in which "The Lover, who has now possess'd / From unknown *Flora*, his Request; [...] / Pulls off her Masque in am'rous Fury, / And finds a gentle Nymph of *Drury*" (Fielding 2008: 27). This scene, as Castle observes, constitutes a lesson on the limits of appearances (Castle 1986: 178) and thus relates to the *fronti nulla fides* topos, present in practically every work by Fielding.

There is, however, one exception to the rule. Some reliance can certainly be placed on the appearance of the following personage:

> Hold, Madam, pray what hideous Figure
> Advances? Sir, that's C—t H—d—g—r.
> How cou'd it come into his Gizard,
> T' invent so horrible a Vizard?
> How cou'd it, Sir? (says she) I'll tell you:
> It came into his Mother's Belly;
> For you must know, that horrid Phyz is
> (*Puris naturalibus*) his Visage.
> Monstrous! that human Nature can
> Have form'd so strange Burlesque a Man.
> [...]

And that, as *Mulciber* was driv'n
Headlong, for's Ugliness from Heav'n;
So, for's Ugliness more fell,
Was H—d—g—r toss'd out of Hell.
And, in Return, by *Satan* made
First Minister of's Masquerade. (Fielding 2008: 19-20)

This far-fetched rendition of Heidegger's face, following the conventions of burlesque and caricature, introduces some polyphony into the ideological dimension of the poem. On the one hand, as proved by the argument of the poet's companion, faces cannot be trusted as they are nothing more than masks; on the other hand, as suggested by the sketch of Count Heidegger, inner corruption can be imprinted on one's countenance, which becomes, as Campbell notices, a "natural Masque" (a term introduced by the author of the poem in its dedication) which can never be taken off (Campbell 1995: 13).

The concerns articulated in *The Masquerade* remained with Fielding throughout his whole literary career, and he adopted the anti-masquerade vein quite frequently. In *The Champion* for 19 February, 1740, the author of *Tom Jones*, in response to one of the masquerade tickets issued by Heidegger, criticises those who attend his balls, especially the so called "Women of Fashion", and declares that

a pretty Creature, neatly and plainly dress'd, walking in the Park in a Morning, and giving an Instance of the Bloom and Health of her Constitution in the Face of the Sun, will be apter to make a useful Impression on a sensible young Fellow, than any Town Complexion at a Midnight Assembly, with the Assistance of Paint, Candles, or any other Aid. (Fielding 2003: 188-189)

This may be taken as yet another example of the dichotomous organisation of Fielding's thought and poetics. The juxtaposition of "Women of Fashion", resorting to artificial aid, and "pretty Creature[s]", displaying their natural charms and gentility, is a principle governing the arrangement of major female characters in his two novels, with Fanny standing in contrast to Lady Booby and Pamela, and Sophia in opposition to Lady Bellaston and Harriet Fitzpatrick.

In a similar vein, Fielding voices his anti-masquerade criticism in *Miss Lucy in Town*. In the play, in an ironic manner, the masquerade is invoked as one of the pleasures of the town in the dialogue between Lucy and the prostitute Tawdry:

WIFE. [...] But pray, madam, are there no sights for a fine lady to see?

TAWDRY. O yes, Madam; there are Ridottos, Masquerades, Court, Plays, and a thousand others, so many, that a fine Lady has never time to be at home, but when she is asleep.

[...]

WIFE. What do your fine Ladies do at these Places? what do they do at Masquerades now? for I have heard of them in the Country.

TAWDRY. Why they dress themselves in a strange Dress, and they walk up and down the Room, and they cry, *Do you know me?* and then they burst out a laughing, and then they sit down, and then they get up, and then they walk about again, and then they go home. (Fielding 2011: 480)

A typical masquerade behaviour – the quasi-ritual sequence of "Do you know me?" questions – is presented alongside other routine actions, which all together make up an image of a nonsensical performance, being nothing more than waste of time. The diversion is similarly addressed in the masquerade scene in *Tom Jones*, where Lady Bellaston declares that the participants of the masked ball "may [...] be said to kill Time in this Place, than in any other" (*TJ*, 716).

It is also Fielding's legal works that contain fragments written in the anti-masquerade convention. In "A Charge delivered to the Grand Jury" (1749), at one point the author thus addresses the legislative body:

Gentlemen, our News-Papers, from the Top of the Page to the Bottom, the Corners of our Streets up to very Eves of our Houses, present us with nothing but a view of Masquerades, Balls, and Assemblies of various Kinds, Fairs, Wells, Gardens, &c. tending to promote Idleness, Extravagance and Immorality, among all Sorts of People.

This Fury after licentious and luxurious Pleasures is grown to so enormous a Height, that it may be called the Characteristic of the present Age. And it is an Evil, Gentlemen, of which it is neither easy nor pleasant to foresee all the Consequences. [...] [T]he Rod of the Law, Gentlemen, must restrain those within the Bounds of Decency and Sobriety, who are deaf to the Voice of Reason, and superior to the Fear of Shame. (Fielding 1988a: 25)

What distinguishes the excerpt from those quoted previously is a hitherto-unarticulated call to action. This time, Fielding is not only commenting on the immorality and nonsensical nature of masked assemblies but also putting forward a legal solution to the problem. The metaphor of the "rod of law" well relates to the author's belief in social order, which is threatened by the disruptive doings of "masquerades, balls, and assemblies of various kinds", but which can be restored by means of severe legislation. In *An Enquiry into the Causes of the Late Increase of Robbers* (1751), on the other hand, the author discusses the appropriateness of various "Places of Pleasure" for specific social groups and thus concludes his argument:

> I cannot dismiss this Head, without mentioning a notorious Nuisance which hath lately arisen in this Town; I mean, those Balls where Men and Women of loose Reputation meet in disguised Habits. As to the Masquerade in the *Hay-market*, I have nothing to say; I really think it is a silly rather than vicious Entertainment: But the Case is very different with these inferior Masquerades; for these are indeed no other than the Temples of Drunkenness, Lewdness, and all Kind of Debauchery. (Fielding 1988b: 84)

As the author believes, elitist masked assemblies organised for the highest stratum of society – that is, for those who can afford wasting their time – are nothing but "silly rather than vicious Entertainment". A true threat to social order is posed by "these inferior Masquerades", belonging to the London underworld, which welcome participants of lower origin and contribute to their fall. Published in 1751, Fielding's *Enquiry*, on the one hand, testifies to some diversification within the phenomenon – "inferior Masquerades" are juxtaposed with "the Masquerade in the *Hay-market*", towards which, after the death of Heidegger in 1749, the author must have taken a more tolerant approach; on the other hand, it provides evidence for Fielding's firm belief in social hierarchy and boundaries between its sections.

2. The anti-masquerade poetics of *Joseph Andrews* and *Tom Jones*

Traces of anti-masquerade writing can also be found in *Joseph Andrews* and *Tom Jones*. In fact, their basic assumption is arguably anti-masquerade – the criticism of hypocrisy, affectation and disguise. In the Preface to *Joseph Andrews*, the reader learns that "the true Ridiculous" (*JA*, 7), the exposure of which is the ultimate objective of the comic epic in prose,[1] finds its only source in affectation. The latter, as Fielding explains,

> proceeds from one of these two Causes, Vanity, or Hypocrisy: for as Vanity puts us on affecting false Characters, in order to purchase Applause; so Hypocrisy sets

---

[1] In the Preface we read: "The Ridiculous only, as I have before said, falls within my Province in the present Work" (*JA*, 7).

us on an Endeavour to avoid Censure by concealing our Vices under an Appearance of their opposite Virtues. (*JA*, 8)

The true subject matter of Fielding's comic epic in prose thus revolves around the masquerade topos, which, in the passage above, is signalled by such keywords as "false Characters", "concealing our Vices" or "under an Appearance".

The idea of contrast introduced in the epigraph of this part is transposed into the poetics of the two novels. On the one hand, there are good-natured characters, such as the two protagonists and their beloved ones, who show their true faces to the world, but on the other, there are those who participate in the "vast Masquerade" of the world. As a result, Fielding's criticism of the masquerade voiced in *Joseph Andrews* and *Tom Jones* is of a rather metaphorical nature. There is only one literal masquerade scene in the two novels, so what is exposed instead are numerous scenes in which the characters of the second kind give metaphorical masked performances. These include those of a larger scale (one's whole life seen as a masquerade) and those of a momentary nature, such as behaviours, gestures and expressions.

The former constitute a versatile body. Lady Booby and Mrs Slipslop, the vain duo in *Joseph Andrews*, struggle to appear greater than they really are – Booby as a sophisticated aristocrat, possessing "all the Dignity of the Woman of Fashion" (*JA*, 36), and Slipslop, being "a Maiden Gentlewoman" (*JA*, 32), as her respected confidante and somebody more than just a servant. The narrator's attitude towards them takes the form of satire and caricature. This is because of their imperfection at the art of affectation – the image of themselves they would wish to create is disintegrated as a consequence of the limits of their masquerade. Lady Booby's mask of a woman of fashion is at times suspended by the workings of her emotions and thoughts which can either imprint themselves on her countenance (at one moment, for example, she displays "redness in her cheeks" [*JA*, 33]), or prompt her to violent actions, such as her hysterical conversation with Joseph before his dismissal – unfit for a proper lady of fashion, who, as Mrs Western instructs, should know how to "hide [...] Thoughts a little better" (*TJ*, 287). Mrs Slipslop, in turn, fails to fashion herself as a gentlewoman through linguistic devices – she is a "mighty Affecter of hard Words" (*JA*, 26). The mask she puts on is constituted by means of sophisticated vocabulary, in contrast to her lowly social status, but is a comic one given her frequent malapropisms, many of which, as Shesgreen notices, "are delightful Freudian slips that expose her lewdness" (Shesgreen 1972: 98). Lady Booby and Mrs Slipslop illustrate the first of the two sources of "the true Ridiculous" – vanity – manifested in their attempts to "purchase Applause" by "affecting false Characters" of a lady of fashion and a gentlewoman.

The second of the two sources – hypocrisy – is embodied by several characters but most notably by the young Blifil and his two advisors Mr Thwackum and Mr Square. Blifil, in a way, inherited a natural predisposition for the masquerade, being the son of Bridget Allworthy, whose masquerading scheme lays the foundation for the plot of *Tom Jones*, and Captain Blifil, whose hypocritical epitaph, "the Monument of / His Virtues" (*TJ*, 115), is a mask which will conceal his true character forever. The young Blifil's hypocrisy manifests itself in his relations with the three good-natured characters – Allworthy, Tom and Sophia – which is very much in line with the archetypal hypocrite discussed in "An Essay on the Knowledge of the Characters of Men", who "is a most detestable Character in Society; and [...] its Malignity is more particularly bent against the best and worthiest Men, the sincere and open-hearted" (Fielding 1972a: 168). This only amplifies his true corruption hidden behind the masks of a virtuous nephew and thus a proper heir, a morally intact half-brother and a courteous candidate for a husband. And just as he is almost instantly unmasked and seen in true light by Tom and Sophia, his hypocritical behaviour towards his uncle for the most part of the narrative remains concealed, and its final discovery at the end of the novel corresponds with the discovery of Tom's true self.

In contrast to vanity embodied by the two heroines of *Joseph Andrews*, Blifil's hypocrisy throughout *Tom Jones* never becomes an object of satire. It is rather depicted as something serious, not to be laughed at; it is not a folly but a serious vice and a source of corruption. Blifil is never caricatured but presented as a cold-blooded villain disguised in virtue, to invoke the metaphor put forward in *The Masquerade*. The other two hypocrites in *Tom Jones* are treated slightly less seriously, and their literary portraits are constructed by satirical means. They are not villains proper but rather emblematic caricatures standing for the idea of hypocrisy as articulated in "An Essay on the Knowledge of the Characters of Men" – "Sanctity [...] flows from the Lips, and shines in the Countenance", yet, like Pharisees, they "perpetrate their Villainies under this Mask" (Fielding 1972a: 167). The criticism directed against them is twofold; on the one hand, the narrator condemns their double moral standards and the discrepancy between the theory they advocate and what they put into practice, but on the other hand, the very theory itself – "the

Platonic Model" in the case of Square (*TJ*, 125) and "the *divine Power of Grace*" in Thwackum's (*TJ*, 126), which, in fact, both absolve of the responsibility to perform benevolent deeds, the core of Fielding's moral thought. In other words, both their masquerades and the very masks they wear come under criticism.

A character towards whom the narrator adopts a similarly satirical attitude is Tom's foil and companion Mr Benjamin Partridge, whose masquerade has two aspects. On the one hand, his life becomes a constant change of roles. He is introduced as a tutor, but after having been erroneously accused of being Tom's father and exiled, he appears in the character of "Mr. *Barber*, or Mr. *Surgeon*, or Mr. *Barber-Surgeon*" (*TJ*, 423), only to become Tom's Sancho Panza-like companion and valet in the London part of their adventures. On the other hand, Partridge is not free from the two sources of ridicule discussed in the Preface to *Joseph Andrews*. His vanity, similarly to Slipslop's, manifests itself in the language he uses. Partridge frequently supports his speeches and judgements with classical quotations, by the use of which he wishes to fashion himself as a learned scholar. However, this, in fact, means attempting to appear greater than he really is. As Mace demonstrates, the quotations Partridge invokes are mere "snippets", for the most part taken out of context and misused, and the majority of them come from well-known classical set texts and coursebooks of the time, being "short enough that any schoolboy with a little Latin could produce them" (Mace 1996: 92-93). Partridge's hypocrisy, in turn, lies in his rather ambiguous relationship with Tom. Despite various proclamations of friendship and dedication on the part of Benjamin, the narrator makes clear the true reason why he joined Tom:

> He concluded [...] that *Jones*, of whom he had often from his Correspondents heard the wildest Character, had in reality run away from his Father. [...] If he could by any Means, therefore, persuade the young Gentleman to return home, he doubted not but that he should again be received into the Favour of *Allworthy*, and well rewarded for his Pains; nay, and should be again restored to his native Country; a Restoration which *Ulysses* himself never wished more heartily than poor *Partridge*. (*TJ*, 427)

Thus, just as he tries to disguise his false learning in banal and wrongly used classical tags, Partridge puts on the mask of loyalty and friendship only to cover his self-interest.

Apart from these major characters, there is a group of episodic ones who also participate in the masquerade of the world, likewise functioning as emblems of vanity and hypocrisy. In *Joseph Andrews*, there is, for instance, the lady in the stage coach, whose mask of virtue and chastity, symbolically represented by "her Fan before her Eyes" (*JA*, 53), demanded that Joseph was left naked on the road and not taken inside, for she would rather be left alone "than ride with a naked Man" (*JA*, 52).[2] Later on, the reader becomes acquainted with Mrs Tow-wouse and parson Barnabas, whose doings prompt the narrator to produce a "sarcastical Panegyrick" (*JA*, 70) on vanity, "deceiv[ing] mankind under different Disguises", such as "Pity", "Generosity" or "heroick Virtue" (*JA*, 69). There are also the two Trullibers, who cover their avarice with the mask of a rather peculiar understanding of charity, which, as they hold it, is "better than to give to Vagabonds" (*JA*, 167), and cheats, such as the gentleman, whom the travellers meet in a tavern, or the huntsman, arranging a scheme to abduct Fanny. In *Tom Jones*, in turn, there is a Quaker, who despite seeming "plain" and "honest", becomes "fired with no less Indignation than a Duke would have felt" on learning about Tom's low social background (*TJ*, 362-365), and the vain and hypocritical Mrs Whitefield, who refuses to have tea with Tom "with a Manner so different from that with which she had received him at Dinner" (that is, before she became aware of his poor financial status) (*TJ*, 434).

What adds to this assembly of masquerading characters are the interpolated tales – the life stories of Leonora, "or the unfortunate jilt" (*Joseph Andrews*), Mr Wilson (*Joseph Andrews*) and the Man of the Hill (*Tom Jones*) – which, on the one hand, all illustrate the corrupting force of the pleasures of the town, masked balls being one of these, and on the other, feature vain and hypocritical characters participating in the metaphorically-understood masquerade of the world. The interpolation of seemingly irrelevant tales was not only typical of the picaresque tradition but was also extensively employed in classical epics and in romance literature, being one of the most common narrative techniques of the eighteenth century followed "by every narrator of the time" (Thornbury 1931: 109). As such, Bartolomeo points out, the technique was frequently diminished by literary critics, who regarded the interpolated tales as superfluous elements, reflecting the imperfections of plot construction in the works of the early novelists (Bartolomeo 1991: 405).

---

[2] The juxtaposition of Joseph's nakedness and the fan before the lady's eyes brings to mind the biblical representation natural innocence (the nakedness of Adam and Eve before the Fall) and negatively evaluated experience leading to civilised and thus artificial behaviour (the fig leaves after the Fall).

Fielding's interpolated tales, however, are not mere narrative embellishments and are to be recognised by the reader as thematically related to the novels' main threads and their ideological dimension. This was noticed by Cauthen, who rightly argues that the two tales incorporated in the narrative of *Joseph Andrews* are related to the theory of the ridiculous arising from vanity and hypocrisy, and that "[b]y their inclusion Fielding has doubled his emphasis on his theme" (Cauthen 1956: 382). The first tale features Leonora, whose status and emblematic function is already established at the beginning of the story: "she was an extreme Lover of Gaiety, and very rarely missed a Ball or any other public Assembly; where she had frequent Opportunities of satisfying a greedy Appetite of Vanity" (*JA*, 103). Her "Appetite of Vanity" is also satisfied when a French fop, Bellarmine, seduces her, after which she abandons her good-natured fiancée Horatio. Leonora's vanity prompts her to become a true lady of fashion, enamoured of a Parisian, whose "Clothes were as remarkably fine as his Equipage could be" (*JA*, 108), and with whom she could converse about "Balls, Operas and Ridotto's" (*JA*, 109). Bellarmine, however, turns out to be a hypocrite, a fortune hunter wearing the mask of a devoted lover, who leaves Leonora after unsuccessful negotiations with her father.

The protagonist and the narrator of the second tale, Mr Wilson, eventually recognised as Joseph's father, tells the story of his youthful corruption and absorption in the pleasures of London. What distinguishes the tale from the previous one is its first person narration and consequently its confessional mood. The story-telling "I" differs from the "I" participating in the narrated event, and this narrative distance enables Mr Wilson to adopt a critical and moralising stance towards his former self. When "[a] little under seventeen", he sets out for London in order to become a *beau*:

> The Character I was ambitious of attaining, was that of a fine Gentleman; the first Requisites to which, I apprehended were to be supplied by a Taylor, a Periwig-maker, and some few more Tradesmen, who deal in furnishing out the human Body. (*JA*, 202)

Just as was the case with the history of Leonora, the beginning of the narrative already establishes the emblematic function of the young Wilson – he is to serve as an embodiment of vanity, who wishes to fashion himself as "a fine gentlemen". He attempts to do so using sartorial means, and the process of "attaining a character" appears to be a masquerading scheme.[3] The young Wilson leads the life of an urban *beau*, taking up the roles of a seducer, a gambler, a drunkard and eventually an unsuccessful playwright, only to end up in prison having been arrested for debt. Contrary to the unhappy ending of Leonora's history, the resolution of Mr Wilson's tale is a joyful one. The good-natured Miss Harriett Hearty rescues the imprisoned and thus reformed libertine, after which they retire "from a World full of Bustle, Noise, Hatred, Envy, and Ingratitude, to Ease, Quiet, and Love" in the countryside (*JA*, 224). The narrative distance between the young Mr Wilson and the story-teller enables the latter to interlard the tale with commentaries upon the immoral doings of his previous self and upon the corruption of London. Two of the latter category are typical anti-masquerade observations, which could have been just as well articulated by Fielding himself. They are also both rather misogynistic, referring to the masquerading lives of urban women. At one point, Mr Wilson thus relates his critical stance towards London ladies of the evening: "I looked on all the Town-Harlots with a Detestation not easy to be conceived, their Persons appeared to me as painted Palaces inhabited by Disease and Death" (*JA*, 209); a remark very much in line with the anecdote in the final part of Fielding's *The Masquerade*.[4] The *fronti nulla fides* topos is similarly invoked in another observation, this time addressing the character and conduct of a coquette:

> Indeed its Characteristick is Affectation, and this led and governed by Whim only: for as Beauty, Wisdom, wit, Good-nature, Politeness and Health are sometimes affected by this Creature; so are Ugliness, Folly, Nonsense, Ill-nature, Ill-breeding

---

[3] The process of attaining a new self by sartorial means on arrival in London was a recurring motif in the eighteenth-century novel and visual arts. It is present, for example, in the first two plates of Hogarth's *A Rake's Progress* (1735), on which, as critics have recognised, Fielding based the story of Mr Wilson. To read on the correspondences between Mr Wilsons's story and *A Rake's Progress*, see Moore 1948: 124-125; Shesgreen 1972: 84-88; Nowicki 2008: 72-75. Fielding openly expressed his predilection for Hogarth's cycles in *The Champion* for 10 June 1740: "I almost dare affirm that those two Works of his, which he calls the *Rake's* and the *Harlot's Progress*, are calculated more to serve the Cause of Virtue, and for the Preservation of Mankind, than all the *Folio's* of Morality which have been ever written; and a sober Family should no more be without them, than without the *Whole Duty of Man* in their House". (Fielding 2003: 366; quoted in Voogd 1981: 42)

[4] In fact, prostitution was believed to be metonymically related to the masquerade at the time. To read more on this curious relationship, see the chapter "'This *Female Proteus*': prostitution, masquerade and the masquerading female body" in Carter 2004: 129-154.

and Sickness likewise put on by it in their Turn. Its Life is one constant Lye, and the only Rule by which you can form any Judgment of them is, that they are never what they seem. (*JA*, 209-210)

Such commentaries, along with the general presentation of his life in London, construct the image of the capital as a place governed by corrupted and corrupting masquerading schemes, which swallow up anyone who is not strong enough to oppose them.

This idea is also addressed in the life story of the Man of the Hill, which, as Schonhorn demonstrates (1968: 207-214), occupies an analogically central position in *Tom Jones* as Mr Wilson's tale in Fielding's first novel. Its basic function, despite the lack of the latter's dimension as a parallel of Joseph's adventures, is again to expose the corruption of London, the masquerading metropolis. The Man of the Hill's life story, similarly to Mr Wilson's, finds its climactic point in London, which once again appears to be the most appropriate setting for the story-teller's constant changes of roles, including that of a penniless wanderer, a drunkard, a gamester and a sharper. His immersion in the corruption of London is interrupted by the arrival of his father, who convinces him to return to his family estate, saving him from further destruction. His life story, however, is not concluded at this point but continues, following the Man of the Hill's further changes of roles, including a classical scholar, a convalescent in Bath and a soldier in the army of the Duke of Monmouth. Finally, the Man of the Hill finds his permanent residence in a solitary place, which, however, he leaves from time to time to embark on journeys to different parts of Europe.

The various experiences he has gone through, including his travels, enable him to formulate a sad but, in his view, true and universal observation concerning human nature:

those who travel in order to acquaint themselves with the different Manners of Men, might spare themselves much Pains, by going to a Carnival at *Venice*; for there they will see at once all which they can discover in the several Courts of *Europe*. The same Hypocrisy, the same Fraud; in short, the same Follies and Vices, dressed in different Habits. In *Spain* these are equipped with much Gravity; and in *Italy*, with vast Splendour. In *France*, a knave is dressed like a fop; and in the Northern Countries, like a Sloven. But Human Nature is every where the same, every where the Object of Detestation and Avoidance. (*TJ*, 482)

This Swiftian variation on the corruption of human nature, just like Mr Wilson's commentaries on the affectations of urban women, is articulated in a typically Fieldingesque anti-masquerade vein. Significantly, what stands here as an allegory of the world is the carnival of Venice; a feast indispensably related to the masquerade. Thus, the Man of the Hill's concluding remark is yet another articulation of the world as a masquerade metaphor, which, given the story-teller's melancholic mood, defines human nature as constituted by hypocrisy, fraud and disguise.

The second kind of masked performances exposed in *Joseph Andrews* and *Tom Jones* are those of momentary nature, for the most part in the form of facial expressions, in which the countenance appears to be a protean fabric which can be both controlled and modified, as if the bearer had at his or her disposal a number of masks suitable for any occasion.[5] This idea is created by a very peculiar language of the face. For the most part, it is constituted by sartorial metaphors, built around the verbs "to wear", "to dress" and "to put on", indicating that facial expressions, grimaces but also emotions can be worn like clothes. To exemplify, Parson Trulliber upbraids Adams having "put on a stern Look" (*JA*, 166); Bridget Allworthy mourns her late husband "by that Colour of Sadness in which she had dressed her Person and Countenance" (*TJ*, 114); whereas Lady Bellaston is able to hide her embarrassment having "put on an Air of Good-Humour" (*TJ*, 734) and to conceal "much Indignation against *Sophia*" by means of "all the Smiles which she wore in her Countenance" (*TJ*, 785). Apart from sartorial metaphors, there are statements testifying to an almost supernatural capacity for evoking signs of emotions in the face but also for constraining them and hiding before the presented facade. To illustrate, the squire addresses himself to Joseph and Parson Adams "summoning all the Terror he was Master of, into his Countenance" (*JA*, 242); Dr Blifil, in turn, one day approaches Mr Allworthy "with great Gravity of Aspect, and all the Concern which he could possibly affect in his Countenance" (*TJ*, 69); the young Blifil agrees on an alliance with Squire Western "having conveyed the utmost Satisfaction into his Countenance" (*TJ*, 344); Mrs Honour, having lost her post as Sophia's servant, "th[inks] fit to produce a Shower of Tears" (*TJ*, 813); whereas the doctor whom Joseph and Adams meet along with the group of huntsmen has "a perfect Command of his Muscles" and is able to "laugh inwardly without betraying the least Symptoms in his Countenance" (*JA*, 249).

---

[5] I discuss Fielding's language of the face also in my article "The Face as Mask in Fielding's *Joseph Andrews* and *Tom Jones*" (Lipski 2012).

Concluding, I will point out that the anti-masquerade poetics of Fielding's novels is constituted by criticism of the doings of vain and hypocritical characters, who belong to "the artful and cunning Part of Mankind [...] enabled to impose on the rest of the World" (Fielding 1972a: 153). What is implied through this, however, is that whatever the deceiving facade looks like, there is something unchangeable hidden behind it; Fielding's masquerade metaphor is not about creating new identities but about concealing one's true self. Castle is right to claim that what underpins various masquerading schemes in Fielding's work is the idea of *carnaval moralisé* (Castle 1986: 190-193); that is, a poetics of reversal which strengthens the essence by exposing its opposite.

Chapter Three

Joseph and Tom in the Masquerading World

Up to this point, I have discussed separately the two extremes constituting the binary poetics of Fielding's novels – the good-natured travellers and the masquerading world. Now, I believe it worthwhile to scrutinise the way in which Joseph, Tom, and the world of naturalness and benevolence they represent, are juxtaposed with the world of masquerade and its embodiments. This antithetic organisation of the two novels is a quality which determines their poetics and ideological dimension throughout, not being limited to any particular part of the narratives. In other words, the adventures of the two protagonists are a constant struggle with the world of vanity and hypocrisy, which implies that the boundaries separating the two "conflicting structures" are frequently suspended.

Despite its emblematic role throughout the two novels, the masquerade, perversely, also functions as the organising principle of the protagonists' adventures. On the one hand, in social terms their identities at the moment of departure are different from those at their return (recognition, then, appears to be a form of unmasking); on the other hand, just as they are forced into false social identities by the narrator, or, to be more precise, by their literary parents, they are continuously forced into the masquerade by others, thus becoming its passive participants.

1. Joseph's and Tom's passive masquerade

From the moment when he is first introduced to the reader, Joseph is forced to change his roles throughout the whole text. His status as the passive participant of the masquerading world is established already in the second chapter of the novel, in which Joseph's change of occupations, starting from bird keeper, through whipper-in and gamester, to Lady Bobby's footman, does not stem from any initiative on the part of the protagonist but rests solely on his superiors – Sir Thomas Booby and Lady Booby, after the former's death. Such passive changes of Joseph's social self continue after he leaves the Booby Hall. On his arrival in London, "he beg[ins] to scrape an acquaintance with his party-colour'd brethren", who make him change his appearance – "His Hair [is] cut after the newest Fashion" (*JA*, 27). He is literally made a man of fashion, and even though he enjoys some of the pleasures offered by the capital ("He applied most of his leisure Hours to Music" [*JA*, 27]), he remains largely uncorrupted, as I have already argued.

Later on, having staunchly rejected Lady Booby's advances, he is informed that "he must not stay a Moment longer in the House" and is "forced to borrow a Frock and Breeches of one of the Servants" (*JA*, 47), which transform him back into an ordinary, this time unemployed, servant, who resolves to travel home. As I explained in the Introduction, the chronotope of the road in eighteenth-century literature was seen as offering possibilities for changing one's social roles, thus being directly related to the masquerade metaphor. Yet, Joseph does not take advantage of the potential of the road and does not change himself throughout his adventures. He continues to be the same Joseph, travelling home to his beloved Fanny. On his return to the countryside, however, he undergoes the final (passive) change of social self, when his "esteemed" brother-in-law, Squire Booby, provides him with suitable garments and proclaims a gentleman (*JA*, 290-292).

In *Tom Jones*, the plot can be easily associated with that of the parable of the Prodigal Son, with Jones's disobedience towards his eventually merciful father – Mr Allworthy, the owner of Paradise Hall. Likewise, it can also be related to the expulsion from the Garden of Eden, which is sanctioned by the narrator himself through the direct invocation of Milton's epic. In actual fact, these allegorical readings are only possible due to the masquerading stratagems worked out by Tom's antagonist Blifil. It is he who forces Tom into roles which he himself would never be willing to adopt. Just as the antagonist conceals his vices with the mask of virtue, he turns Tom's benevolence and loyalty towards Allworthy against him and covers them with the mask of their opposites. Seen in this light, Blifil appears to be a diabolical figure – his masquerade and its aftermath are analogous to Satan's stratagem and the consequent expulsion from Eden. Satan's doings in the garden of Eden, as Castle demonstrates, were seen by anti-masquerade writers as the first masquerade to ever take place in human history, and Satan was credited with the title of the inventor of masked assemblies (Castle 1986: 64). This idea is expressed, for example, by Richard Steele, who in *Guardian* 142 writes that "the devil first addressed himself to Eve in a mask", adding that "we owe the loss of our first happy state to a masquerade, which that sly intriguer made in the garden" (quoted in Castle 1986: 64).[1] The second remark could just as well summarise the complication of the plot of *Tom Jones* – the eponymous hero loses his "first happy state", Paradise Hall, as a result of the intrigues of the masquerading Blifil, who, as Tom at one point reflects, "hath the Cunning of the Devil himself" (*TJ*, 657).

As an exile, Tom does not follow any clear plans regarding his future social standing. This is symbolically expressed already at the beginning of his journey, when he finds himself at a loss as to where to go:

> And now, having taken a Resolution to leave the Country, he began to debate with himself whither he should go. [...]
> What Course of Life to pursue, or to what Business to apply himself, was a second Consideration; and here the Prospect was all a melancholy Void. (*TJ*, 331)

Foreshadowed here is Tom's unwillingness to take advantage of the opportunity given him by the time he is going to spend travelling. He ends up on the road contrary to his will, as a result of Blifil's diabolical schemes.

His first resolution is expressed in figurative terms, which situate Tom in a rather passive position: "At last the Ocean, that hospital Friend to the Wretched, opened her capacious Arms to receive him; and he instantly resolved to accept her kind Invitation" (*TJ*, 331). Even if it is only a metaphor, it clearly implies that Tom is not the doer; he does not manifest a protean quality making him easily adapt to new circumstances and benefit from his newly adopted roles. Instead, at the beginning of his journey he is presented as being at a loss to decide on his future and on his future social selves. When the realisation of this resolution turns out to be impossible (with the guide being unable to lead Tom to Bristol [*TJ*, 361]), a company of soldiers come to Tom's rescue, addressing "some Heroic Ingredients in his Composition" and encouraging his decision to enlist (*TJ*, 368). Tom's transformation into a soldier, even if on the surface appearing to be in accord with the convention of picaresque fiction, differs from other seemingly similar transformations. Just as Smollett's Roderick, for instance, joins the army to survive after being

---

[1] Milton, too, presents Satan as a shape-shifter, capable of deceiving not only Eve (first as a toad, then as a serpent) but also Uriel (assuming the appearance of a cherub).

robbed by the Capuchin, thus manifesting his ability to adapt to any circumstances (*RR*, 220), Tom does so in response to the doings of his heroic disposition, which is, as I have already discussed, one of the permanent qualities defining his character.

Tom's quasi-masquerade on his journey also takes some less serious forms. Having suffered injuries in his fight against Northerton, Tom is duly taken care of, and the result of this is a very peculiar appearance:

> He had on [...] a light-coloured Coat, covered with Streams of Blood. His Face, which missed that very Blood, as well as twenty Ounces more drawn from him by the Surgeon, was pallid. Round his Head was a Quantity of Bandage, not unlike a Turban. In the right Hand he carried a Sword, and in the left a Candle. So that the bloody *Banquo* was not worthy to be compared to him. (*TJ*, 387-388)

As such, he constitutes "a more dreadful Apparition" than has ever been "raised in a Church-yard" (*TJ*, 388) and quite appropriately rises from his sickbed and attempts to pay his antagonist a visit when "the clock ha[s] [...] struck twelve" (*TJ*, 387). He has not, however, constructed this ghastly appearance himself but has been forced into the role by others.

Tom's journey finds its climactic point in London, and so does his passive masquerade. Not only is he invited to a masked assembly (being provided with a mask and a costume, as well) but also undergoes a transformation in its aftermath. By Lady Bellaston's means, he becomes "one of the best dress'd Men about Town" and is "raised to a State of Affluence" he has not experienced so far (*TJ*, 724). Thus, similarly to Joseph, Tom is not an active modifier of his constitution but rather a passive participant absorbed, contrary to his will (at least at the outset), in the masquerading world, whose representatives stand behind the transformations of his social self. The only character Tom himself aspires to assume is that of a soldier, in which, however, he does not become a masquerader but rather answers to the encouragement of his invariable heroic constitution.

2. Joseph's and Tom's false identities and the limits of character reading

What is in a sense related to this passive masquerade, in which the protagonists are involved contrary to their will, is the way in which their characters are perceived and interpreted by others. Quite often, when they come into contact with those embodying hypocrisy, vanity and affectation, they are recognised as possessing qualities which are, in fact, the reversed versions of the ones with which they are really endowed. The effect Fielding achieves is a comic one, which follows from the adopted pattern of reversal – the good-natured travellers are recognised as masquerading villains, whereas their opposites fashion themselves as embodiments of virtue. This carnivalesque aspect of Fielding's poetics is yet another one manifesting the idea of *carnaval moralisé*. Thus, villainy, falsely attributed to the characters of Joseph and Tom, in fact exposes their goodness, whereas the masks of virtue put on by those they encounter point to its opposite hidden beneath.

In *Joseph Andrews* the first instance of the protagonist's character being misread takes place in London, where Joseph accompanies Lady Booby as her gallant footman. When he happens to be having a walk with his mistress in Hyde Park, Lady Tittle and Lady Tattle do not hesitate to interpret the situation to Joseph's disadvantage and spread the rumour of their alleged affair (*JA*, 28). Joseph's false identity as Lady Booby's lover, which after "a hundred Visits [...] performed by the two Ladies" (*JA*, 28) becomes a widely known "fact", constitutes, in reality, the reversed version of his true self governed by the principles of chastity and faithfulness to his beloved Fanny. This pattern of reversal is continued throughout the early phase of the novel. Both Lady Booby and Mrs Slipslop attribute promiscuity and dishonesty to Joseph, which only reinforces the protagonist's real character qualities. For example, after her first unsuccessful attempts to seduce Joseph, Lady Booby sends him away exclaiming: "your pretended Innocence cannot impose on me" (*JA*, 30), whereas Mrs Slipslop, after her advances to the protagonist have been rejected, presents the following evaluation of his character to Lady Booby:

> To my knowledge he games, drinks, swears and fights eternally: besides, he is horribly *indicted* to Wenching [...] he is so lewd a Rascal that if your Ladyship keeps him much longer, you will not have one Virgin in your House except myself. And yet I can't conceive what the Wenches see in him, to be so foolishly fond as they are; in my Eyes he is as ugly a Scarecrow as I ever *upheld*. (*JA*, 35)

Slipslop's harangue addresses not only Joseph's alleged corruption but also his repulsive appearance, which stands in opposition to Joseph's agreeable looks. Joseph's reversed identity – that is, that of a promiscuous and loathsome young man – has no more basis in fact than Slipslop's professed virginity and as such highlights his true disposition, just as Slipslop's mask of chastity exposes her lewdness.

This topsy-turvy juxtaposition of characters is a technique Fielding also adopts in *Tom Jones*; most importantly, perhaps, at the beginning of Book III,

where the 12-year-old Tom fades in comparison, as we read, with the paragon-like Blifil:

> The Vices of this young Man were moreover heightened by the disadvantageous
> Light in which they appeared, when opposed to the Virtues of Master *Blifil*, his
> Companion: A Youth of so different a Cast from little *Jones*, that not only the
> Family, but all the Neighbourhood resounded his Praises. He was indeed a Lad of
> a remarkable Disposition; sober, discreet, and pious beyond his Age. Qualities,
> which gained him the Love of every one who knew him, while *Tom Jones* was
> universally disliked, and many expressed their Wonder that Mr. *Allworthy* would
> suffer such a Lad to be educated with his Nephew, lest the Morals of the latter
> should be corrupted by his Example. (*TJ*, 118)

Crucial here is the focus on identity outwardly, rather than inwardly, oriented. In other words, the narrator does not judge the personality of the two
characters himself but discusses the way in which they are regarded by others, with Tom appearing "in the disadvantageous Light" and being "universally disliked", and Blifil being generally "praised" and in possession of "the
Love of every one who kn[ows] him". Tom's false identity is thus twofold;
established, on the one hand, by the masquerading scheme of Bridget, and by
the limits of character reading, on the other. The final recognition scene, then,
uncovers Tom's two-sided mask and reveals the essence both in social and
personal terms. His antithetical pairing with Blifil is consequently reversed,
or, in fact, re-arranged in accord with reality, with both opposites appearing
in the true light.

Tom is endowed with false identities and has his character misread also
when out of Paradise Hall. For example, the landlady of the inn in which
Tom is recovering, referring to the precept "every Thing is not what it looks
to be", dismisses Tom's gentlemanly appearance and pronounces him to be
"an arrant Scrub" (*TJ*, 412); Partridge, in turn, as I have mentioned before,
joins Tom believing that the latter in fact "ha[s] run away from his Father" –
an assumption he makes on the basis of Tom's "wildest Character", about
which he often heard "from his Correspondents" (*TJ*, 427). When already in
London, Tom, curiously enough, is mistaken for Blifil by Harriet Fitzpatrick
(*TJ*, 692) and reaches bottom being forced to come to terms with his alleged
incest (*TJ*, 915) and being imprisoned as a "common strolling Vagabond"
(*TJ*, 930).

The motif of reversal, as adopted by Fielding, does not aim at destabilising Joseph's and Tom's identities but is yet another technique which allows

the author to express his belief in the unique essential self. Joseph's and Tom's reversed identities, especially when contrasted with the reversed identities of their antagonists, only highlight the opposite essence. The instances of their characters being misread imply that in the masquerading world hypocrisy, affectation and imposture are taken for granted. Thus, such misinterpretations and character misjudgement tell more about those who formulate them than about their objects.

3. Joseph and Tom in London

I would now like to examine Joseph's and Tom's contact with the world of masquerade from the perspective of the spaces they occupy. As I have already argued, in Fielding's literary travels the idea of home is valued positively, whereas the road bears negative connotations. The masquerade, however, is an omnipresent phenomenon, likewise affecting the pleasant spaces (*loci amoeni*), such as the country seat in *Joseph Andrews* or Paradise Hall in *Tom Jones*, and their opposites (*loci horridi*). As such, it has no boundaries and is not limited to any particular spaces. Joseph's destination, his "old Master's Country Seat", where he spent the joyous years with his beloved Fanny and Parson Adams, "the best Man in the World", is idealised throughout the narrative and constructed as a *locus amoenus* which stands in contrast to London, "a bad Place". Nevertheless, it is also where the Booby Hall is located, and as such, despite being presented as a rural ideal, the country seat is also a stage for the masked performances of Lady Booby or Mrs Slipslop. A similar dualism applies to Mr Allworthy's Paradise Hall. On the one hand, the following picturesque presentation establishes the place as a *locus amoenus* par excellence:

> It stood on the South-east Side of a Hill, but nearer the Bottom than the Top of it, so as to be sheltered from the North-east by a Grove of old Oaks, which rose above it in a gradual Ascent of near half a Mile, and yet high enough to enjoy a most charming Prospect of the Valley beneath.
>
> In the midst of the Grove was a fine Lawn sloping down towards the House, near the Summit of which rose a plentiful Spring, gushing out of a Rock covered with Firs, and forming a constant Cascade of about thirty Foot, not carried down a regular Flight of Steps, but tumbling in a natural Fall over the broken and mossy Stones, till it came to the bottom of the Rock; then running off in a pebly Channel, that with many lesser Falls winded along, till it fell into a Lake at the Foot of the Hill, about a quarter of a Mile below the House on the South Side, and which was seen from every Room in the Front. Out of this Lake, which filled the Center of a beautiful Plain, embellished with Groupes of Beeches and Elms, and fed with

Sheep, issued a River, that for several Miles was seen to meander through an amazing Variety of Meadows and Woods, till it emptied itself into the Sea, with a large Arm of which, and an Island beyond it, the Prospect was closed. (*TJ*, 42-43)

The landscape, which, had it been written a few decades later, could be seen as following to the letter Gilpin's guidelines for picturesque writing, comprises many of the typical elements of the poetics of a *locus amoenus* as listed by Curtius (1990: 195-200), which include a hillside, a grove, a valley and a river. On the other hand, however, this Edenic space is likewise affected by the doings of masquerading characters, including, as I have already mentioned, the diabolical masquerade of Blifil.

Spatial binarism, therefore, so carefully demarcated throughout both narratives and correlated with the advocated ideal of rural retirement (enjoyed not only by the protagonists at the end of their adventures but also by the narrators of interpolated tales) does not define the range of the masquerade as a social phenomenon. There are no spaces in the two novels which would be free from its influence. Nonetheless, it is London, a city expressing "a persistent popular urge toward disguise and metamorphosis" (Castle 1987: 157), which was itself addressed in terms of "a vast masquerade" (Smollett 1988: 145), that is metonymically related to the phenomenon.

The London of Fielding's two novels is a fallen city, which attempts to absorb the good-natured protagonists into its corruption. The theme is most thoroughly explored in the novelist's final piece of fiction, *Amelia* (1751), which is set "almost entirely in the seediest neighbourhood of inner London" (Varey 1990: 177). The novel's first setting is Newgate prison, which is not only the stage of Booth's and Miss Matthews' first adulterous contact but also the site of "laughing, singing" and "various kinds of Sports and Gambols" (Fielding 1983: 27). As such, Varey notices, Newgate is an analogue of London itself, since "both are dominated in the same way by greed, hypocrisy, injustice, and petty crime" (Varey 1990: 178). The image of *Amelia*'s London is also constituted by what happens at Ranelagh Gardens and the Opera House in the Haymarket, where the two masquerade scenes take place. These settings, being one of the most popular sites for masked balls in eighteenth-century London, evoke an aura of masquerade that surrounds the events in *Amelia*.[2]

---

[2] For a detailed study of the masquerade scenes and the carnivalesque in *Amelia*, see Castle 1986: 177-252.

In *Joseph Andrews* the image of London as a masquerading city is created in the early part of the narrative, when Joseph accompanies Lady Booby in her entrance into the capital's high life. As I have pointed out before, on his arrival Joseph is made to change his appearance and is introduced into the pleasures of the town offered by operas, play-houses, assemblies or public parks (*JA*, 27). These spaces, as Heyl demonstrates, were in eighteenth-century London indispensably related to the masquerade, and consequently "[m]asked women were apparently stock characters connected with certain urban localities" (Heyl 2001: 125). No wonder, then, that they are the sites for the first part of the narrative, which establishes the themes of hypocrisy and affectation as central, especially as the city itself from the very beginning of the novel is related to the masquerading characters of Lady Booby, who "was bless'd with a Town-Education" (*JA*, 25), and Mrs Slipslop, who "had been frequently at *London*" (*JA*, 25). The time spent in London is also imprinted on Joseph's looks and, to some extent, on his behaviour, which I have already commented on. The hostile spaces of London, the *loci horridi* in Fielding's antithetical spatial arrangement, are thus trying to absorb the good-natured Joseph into their corruption. Nevertheless, the argument that he "steps slightly out of the character established in chapter iii" (Sacks 1964: 85) is, I believe, a little far-fetched. He is still the same Joseph, whose principles are "entirely uncorrupted", and who takes the greatest delight in music, functioning in Fielding's works as an indicator of proper learning and as an entirely positive character attribute.[3] The new, *beau*-like dress is not enough to transform him into a fop; instead, the seeming change of his character exposes his unchangeable self. When Lady Booby decides to make advances to him, she does so being aware of "the Effects which the Town-Air hath on the soberest Constitutions" and consequently on Joseph (*JA*, 27). But what she sees in Joseph – that is, foppery, hypocrisy, lewdness and imposture – in fact only highlights his true disposition, which has little to do with these qualities. Joseph's will, therefore, is indomitable, and neither the "town-air" nor any urban pleasures can break it. A tinge of sanguine temper, something that inclines him to be "a little too forward in Riots at the Play-Houses and Assemblies", cannot be taken as detrimental to his morals or to his self-consistent character, just as was the case with the author's soul in the *Journey from this World to the Next*. Joseph's final resolution to leave London – "a

---

[3] Apart from Joseph, Sophia in *Tom Jones*, Amelia and Mrs Ellison in Fielding's final novel are all presented as musical connoisseurs.

bad Place" as he calls it – is nothing but a logical conclusion to his staunch persistence.

As I have already pointed out, Tom as a character is far more dynamic than his literary predecessor, and thus his stay in London becomes a source of ambiguity. The metropolis as a setting is much more extensive than in *Joseph Andrews*; it is a destination rather than a point of departure, its spaces are more diverse, and it is there that the climactic point of the plot takes place. It would be perfectly natural for its pleasures and charms to meet with a fa-vourable response from Tom, given his unchanging inclination towards amusements. However, the protagonist, having arrived in the capital, ex-presses a greater disinterestedness towards them than the paragon-like Joseph did. Tom does not enter London as a place offering amusement but as the one in which he would find his beloved Sophia. His intention determines the first steps he takes in the metropolis. These are not directed towards any play-houses, operas or public parks but towards the mansion of the Irish peer, who has taken Sophia and Mrs Fitzpatrick to London. The place is not easy to be found, and he takes "many a weary step" before finally reaching the house, where, regrettably, he finds Mrs Fitzpatrick alone and no trace of Sophia. He is, however, by no means disheartened and carries on with his "Pursuit of Sophia" (*TJ*, 689) the following day:

> Mr. *Jones* had walked within Sight of a certain Door during the whole Day, which, though one of the shortest, appeared to him to be one of the longest in the whole Year. At length, the Clock having struck five he returned to Mrs. *Fitzpat-rick*, who, though it was a full Hour earlier than the decent Time of visiting, re-ceiv'd him very civilly; but still persisted in her Ignorance concerning *Sophia*. (*TJ*, 696-697)

The passage above accurately illustrates Jones's disposition and his attitude towards the capital at the early phase of his stay there. There is nothing he finds attractive or alluring and can only spend hours walking aimlessly and killing time before being allowed to pay another visit to Sophia's cousin, who continues affecting her ignorance. The mansion is also where Tom first comes into contact with Lady Bellaston. Both ladies seem to belong to a different world, and the protagonist clearly sees he does not belong there. When Lady Bellaston and Mrs Fitzpatrick take delight in a vain conversation, Jones seems rather abstracted:

> Poor *Jones* was rather a Spectator of this elegant Scene, than an Actor in it; for though in the short Interval before the Peer's Arrival, Lady *Bellaston* first, and afterwards Mrs. *Fitzpatrick*, had addressed some of their Discourse to him; yet no sooner was the noble Lord entered, than he engrossed the whole Attention of the two Ladies to himself; and as he took no more Notice of *Jones* than if no such Person had been present, unless by now and then staring at him, the Ladies followed his Example. (*TJ*, 698)

The Irish peer's mansion thus establishes London as the capital of hypocrisy and affectation. It hosts Harriet Fitzpatrick who imposes on Tom, affecting ignorance about Sophia's whereabouts, as well as Lady Bellaston and the peer, who give themselves airs, conversing in a manner far too sophisticated for the "poor *Jones*". The early events in London, consequently, contribute to the reinforcement of the antithetical method of characterisation and spatial organisation. The masquerading metropolis, a *locus horridus* in comparison with the rural paradise Tom lost, is inhabited by vain and hypocritical figures, among whom the good-natured protagonist is a total stranger. The boundary, however, is to be dissolved when new urban spaces come into question.

Tom directs his steps towards Bond Street where Mrs Miller, an old friend of Mr Allworthy, provides him with accommodation. Her hospitable house functions as an enclave within the hostile spaces of London, yet it is by no means entirely isolated from its influence:

> The first Floor was inhabited by one of those young Gentlemen, who, in the last Age, were called Men of Wit and Pleasure about Town, and properly enough: For as Men are usually denominated from their Business or Profession, so Pleasure may be said to have been the only Business or Profession of those Gentlemen to whom Fortune had made all useful Occupations unnecessary. Play-Houses, Coffee-Houses and Taverns were the Scenes of their Rendezvous. (*TJ*, 700)

Tom's contact and the ensuing friendship with Mr Nightingale, as that is the young gentleman's name, marks the dissolution of the boundaries clearly separating the good-natured protagonist from the corrupted London life. Nightingale himself, however, despite being "a little too much tainted with Town Foppery", expresses "Sentiments of great Generosity and Humanity" (*TJ*, 706), which endear him to Tom. His character, then, reconciles the two opposing qualities, and his meeting with Tom foreshadows the forthcoming changes in the disposition and behaviour of the protagonist.

The turning point in the London adventures of Tom falls on the fourth day of his stay, when his pleasant conversation with Mrs Miller, her daughter

Nancy and Mr Nightingale is interrupted by the delivery of a parcel containing a mask, a domino,[4] a masquerade ticket and a card with a very peculiar invitation: *"The Queen of Fairies sends you this, / Use her Favours not amiss"* (*TJ*, 707).[5] At first, Tom is rather discomfited and his initial aloofness from the matter well corresponds with the distance he has so far maintained towards the pleasures of London and the capital's high life. Naturally, of all the characters gathered at Mrs Miller's it is Nightingale who seems most enthusiastic about the invitation and pronounces Tom "a very happy Man" who "will have the Happiness of meeting [some lady] at the Masquerade" (*TJ*, 707). This makes Jones accept the invitation, as he believes that he may have the chance to meet Sophia at the ball. In accord with convention,[6] Mrs Miller gives him a word of warning, begging that she "may hear of no more Masquerades", for when her daughter attended a masquerade a year before "it almost turned her Head, and she did not return to herself [...] in a Month afterwards" (*TJ*, 709). What, however, points to the subversive dimension of the masquerade is "a gentle Sigh, which stole from the Bosom of *Nancy*", which seemed to "argue some secret Disapprobation of these Sentiments" (*TJ*, 710). The masked ball is thus conceptualised as a destabilising force, and its impact on Nancy foreshadows the way in which it will affect Tom's person.

---

[4] The domino, a long black cloak, was probably the most popular masquerade costume in the eighteenth century. When both the costume and a mask were worn at the same time, it was impossible to recognise any physical constituents of a masquerader's identity.

[5] The following analysis of the masquerade scene in *Tom Jones* develops some of the ideas included in my article "Crossing the Boundaries of the Self: The Masquerade Scene in *Tom Jones*" (Lipski 2011). For an alternative reading of the masquerade scene and its aftermath in *Tom Jones*, see Kukkonen 2013: 167-170.

[6] A masquerade scene's placement and its poetics are subject to a set of literary conventions (Castle 1986: 118-120). Such scenes are usually prefaced with some didactic remarks on the immorality of the masked assembly, depicting the diversion as the epitome of the corruption of the town. Thus, the upcoming scene of ambiguity and subversion is to be rendered under the guise of conventionalised anti-masquerade didacticism. After introductory remarks by the narrator, or by characters, the hero hesitates over whether to go to the ball or not and finally decides to attend it. At the ball the protagonist marvels at the variety of masks, costumes and enchanting decorations, which all give them visual pleasure. Diversified images are accompanied by sounds of squeaking voices (a typical masquerade behaviour) and musical performances. Finally, masquerade scenes turn out to be "plot catalysts" (Castle 1986: 127), precipitating consequent shifts of fortune, discoveries, major social and moral reversals.

Fielding's first novelistic masquerade starts somewhat extraordinarily. Tom is entirely devoted to his search for Sophia, and nothing else seems to impress or absorb him. The character of Tom remains stable and conserved. He accosts every mask who seems to resemble his Sophia in any way, but the only answers he receives are *"Do you know me?"*, *"I don't know you, Sir"*, *"Indeed I don't know your Voice"* (*TJ*, 713); some of them are articulated "in a squeaking Voice", which is all very typical of the poetics of masquerade scenes. Finally, he encounters "a Lady in a Domino" (*TJ*, 713) – the fairy queen – who teases him with the name of Sophia. He follows her until he is satisfied with a conversation, which with time becomes a flirtation. At this point it would entirely adhere to convention if Tom betrayed Sophia, however er

> *Jones* had never less Inclination to an Amour than at present; but Gallantry to the Ladies was among his Principles of Honour; and he held it as much incumbent on him to accept a Challenge to Love, as if it had been a challenge to Fight. Nay, his very Love to *Sophia* made it necessary for him to keep well with the Lady, as he made no doubt but she was capable of bringing him into the Presence of the other. (*TJ*, 715)

There is something ambivalent in the behaviour of Jones. Apparently, he neither betrays Sophia nor remains faithful to her. Fielding seems to have been faced with the difficulty – how to conserve the character of Tom, in love with Sophia, at a masquerade? Arguably, his didactic purpose makes him challenge the disruptive force of the masquerade. Initially, he is still to some extent successful – Tom's flirtation is rendered under the guise of honour and love to Sophia. Later on, however, the remembrance of Miss Western seems to disappear, being superseded by Tom's rather violent desire to spend the night with the fairy queen. Insisting on going home with her, Jones says: "as you have taken my Heart by Surprize, the rest of my Body hath a Right to follow" (*TJ*, 716). The resolution of the scene turns out to be nothing unusual – Tom and Lady Bellaston, for it was her who hid behind the mask of the fairy queen, spend the night together having a "Conversation which consisted of very common and ordinary Occurrences, and which lasted from two till six o'Clock in the Morning" (*TJ*, 717).

Tom's "Conversation" with Lady Bellaston is his third betrayal of Sophia. The previous two, with Molly Seagrim and Mrs Waters, were committed when the protagonist was not "perfect Master of that wonderful Power of Reason" (*TJ*, 257), which was subdued by wine (*TJ*, 257) and "some bottled

Ale" (*TJ*, 512) respectively. In Lockean terms, Tom was *beside himself*, as, according to the philosopher, a man who is drunk is not the same person as when being sober (Locke 1975: 343). Locke's definition of person as "a thinking intelligent Being, that has reason and reflection" (Locke 1975: 335) implies that whenever a human being is deprived of these powers, he or she cannot be referred to as a person. At one point Fielding dismisses this idea, claiming that "nothing is more erroneous than the common Observation, That Men who are ill-natured and quarrelsome when they are drunk, are very worthy Persons when they are sober" (*TJ*, 253); however, a little later, after Tom's fornication with Molly, the narrator excuses the protagonist explaining that even though "in a Court of Justice, Drunkenness must not be an Excuse, [...] in a Court of Conscience it is greatly so" (*TJ*, 257).

It is somehow surprising that the masquerade, a scene of gallantry and fashion, is similarly destabilising to Tom's identity as the scenes of drunkenness and violent satiation of lust. The masquerade, just like, for instance, alcohol intoxication, seems to excuse transcending one's self. Contrary to the two other events, however, the masquerade affects Tom's person for a longer period of time. In fact, what is most important is not Tom's being *beside himself* during the ball and in its immediate aftermath but the fact that the event has far-reaching consequences in the remaining part of the narrative. A momentary infidelity could be accounted for by the protagonist's sanguine temper or by the specific aura the ball exudes, given its intoxicating nature. But the Tom of subsequent events does not seem to be as innocent and as good-natured as before. This is noticed by Ronald Crane, who argues from a Neo-Aristotelian perspective that the whole affair with Lady Bellaston should be regarded as one of the "faults" of the novel's plot:

> With the best will in the world [...] it is impossible not to be shocked by Tom's acceptance of fifty pounds from Lady Bellaston on the night of his first meeting with her at the masquerade and his subsequent emergence as "one of the best-dressed men about town"; it is necessary, no doubt, that he should now fall lower than ever before, but surely not so low as to make it hard for us to infer his act from our previous knowledge of his character and of the rather modest limits hitherto of his financial need; for the moment at least, a different Tom is before our eyes. (Crane 2006: 129-130)

From a slightly more modern perspective (Castle 1986: 197), what happens at the masquerade and Tom's consequent transformation are not necessarily "faults" and incongruities in Fielding's plot. They testify to the destabilising function of the masquerade, which, as Castle observes, poses a threat to "the allegorical coherence of the narrative" (Castle 1986: 198). The change in Tom's character is symbolically marked by the new clothes he starts to wear – he becomes a *beau*, "one of the best dress'd Men about Town", and thus, at least for some time, a different person. This, in turn, undermines Spack's argument about Fielding's elevation of the principle of consistency in characterisation "almost to one of rigor" (Spacks 1976: 7). The masquerade scene subverts this assertion, as what Tom does at the masquerade and afterwards is somehow unlike him.

With time, Tom's former self starts to take precedence over the newly adopted one:

> Indeed, he began to look on all the Favours he had received, rather as Wages than Benefits, which depreciated not only her [i.e. Lady Bellaston], but himself too in his own Conceit, and put him quite out of Humour with both. From this Disgust, his Mind, by a natural Transition, turned towards *Sophia*: Her Virtue, her Purity, her Love to him, her Sufferings on his Account, filled all his Thoughts, and made his Commerce with Lady *Bellaston* appear still more odious. (*TJ*, 819)

Curiously enough, when Tom resolves to end his affair with Lady Bellaston, he resorts to a method belonging rather to the world of affectation and hypocrisy than naturalness. On Nightingale's advice he comes up with a truly masquerading design – he officially proposes to the lady safe in the knowledge that the proposal will be turned down. In other words, he puts on the mask of a desperate lover and as such is rejected by the lady, who falls for the scheme. Paradoxically, he reinstates his former self by means of a scheme much more suitable for his new person. This is something the protagonist is aware of himself, for, as the narrator informs us, despite being "satisfied with his Deliverance", Tom is not "perfectly easy in his Mind", believing that his scheme has been constituted by "too much of Fallacy to satisfy one who utterly detest[s] every Species of Falsehood or Dishonesty" (*TJ*, 821).

In Frye's archetypal terms, Tom's absorption into the hostile world of masquerade, which follows from his attendance at the masked assembly, is the period of the harshest winter. This is when the character is not only at a loss about what will happen next – Tom certainly looks into the future with anxiety – but also seems to have lost some of the qualities which have so far defined his person. The period of winter leads to the character's symbolic death which will make it possible for him to be reborn. Tom becomes imprisoned and undergoes a penance he duly deserves. It is then, however, that fortune smiles on him and not only reinstates him to his proper social position but also allows to return to himself in personal terms.

Fielding's two novels, then, differ with regard to the emphasis the narrator places on the protagonist's adventures in London. What is only an emblematic representation of the corrupted world in *Joseph Andrews*, becomes a source of ambiguity and destabilisation in *Tom Jones*. What is strengthening the binary divisions in the former novel, dissolves them in the latter. Joseph, who is initially presented as considerably susceptible to the pleasures offered by the capital, turns out to be an indomitable figure leaving them all behind as he determines to leave the "bad Place". Tom, conversely, succumbs to the temptations, despite being rather uninterested initially. As a consequence of his absorption into the world of masquerade, he becomes unlike the Tom the reader has known so far. Tom in the London part of the novel appears to be beside himself and can return to his true self only after experiencing the symbolic death in prison.

Fielding's *Joseph Andrews* and *Tom Jones* feature protagonists whose constitution reflects the author's world view. As literary characters, both Joseph and Tom are derived from the traditions of epic, romance and allegorical writing, advocating the idea of a substantial and thus unique and unchanging self, which has to be searched for rather than constructed. Consequently, Fielding distances himself from the three extremely popular novel types of the eighteenth century – the picaresque novel, the novel of social ascension and the *Bildungsroman* – all of which questioned the idea of a stable social and personal identity. The two protagonists, endowed with permanent personal qualities, find themselves on journeys which culminate in the discovery of their true social selves. Both at home and in the world, Joseph and Tom are juxtaposed with the representatives of the masquerading world – the world of hypocrisy, affectation and falsehood. Throughout the novel, this world is depicted in accord with the conventions of anti-masquerade writing, which Fielding practiced himself in some of his non-fiction works. The good-natured characters attempt to distance themselves from the world of masquerade but are at times seen as its members, being wrongly interpreted by others and forced contrary to their will into new social roles. The epitome of the masquerading world is London, which absorbs both Joseph and Tom into its corrupted life. At this point, the two protagonists show different dispositions. Joseph remains almost a moral paragon by discarding the urban pleasures and thus strengthening the antithetical organisation of the novel. Tom, in turn, as a consequence of his participation in the masked ball, becomes for some time a different person and can return to himself only after performing an act of penance. The masked ball, therefore, not only precipitates a character transformation, undermining the so-far observed principle of the conservation of character, but also destabilises the carefully structured binary system of the novel.

PART TWO

RODERICK RANDOM AND *PEREGRINE PICKLE*: PROTEAN TRAVELLERS

> In a word, this metropolis is a vast masquerade, in which a man of stratagem may wear a thousand different disguises, without danger of detection.
>
> Tobias Smollett, *The Adventures of Ferdinand Count Fathom*

Chapter Four

Smollett's Travellers

Previously, I have discussed the notions of masquerade and identity with reference to the two best-known novels by Henry Fielding. I have argued that the author's approach to the two categories was a traditional one, advocating strict boundaries, hierarchies and moral evaluations. In Fielding's world identity is an essential quality individuals are born into, whereas the masquerade stands for the depravity and corruption of society. Fielding's systematic approach is reflected in the plots he constructs. Their regularity, clear design and traditional Aristotelian qualities correspond closely with the ideological dimensions of the novels. I find a similar correspondence in Tobias Smollett's *The Adventures of Roderick Random* (1748) and *The Adventures of Peregrine Pickle* (1751). This time, however, it reveals a rather different nature and does not revolve around the ideas of regularity, tradition, strict boundaries and clear evaluations. The world of Smollett's protagonists is a chaotic and fragmented world and as such finds its realisation in similarly chaotic and fragmented plots. Recent criticism has recognised this quality of Smollett's fiction to be not a defect of its poetics but a conscious choice on the part of the author. As Beasley rightly observes, the fragmented and chaotic novel enabled Smollett "to expose [...] the illogic and irregularity of actual experience" (Beasley 1998: 20), and thus his novels faithfully copy the world seen by the novelist as "a dangerous and unstable place" (Beasley 1998: 29). Arguably, just as Fielding's plots, given their ideological dimensions, perfect the reality to convey a particular message, Smollett depicts it as it really was in the eyes of the novelist.

I will thus see the two novels by Smollett as accurate representations of the *ancien régime* of identity. The chaotic, fragmented and irregular world of the novels parallels the constructions of the protagonists' identities. In the novels by Fielding the discourse of the self was conceptualised in terms of the *search for* identity, which implied that some essence, a true self, was to be discovered; approaching Smollett's texts, in turn, I will refer to the category in terms of the *shaping of* identity, which suggests an anti-substantialist approach to the self. Consequently, I will make use of the notion of protean identity; one of the indispensable aspects of the picaresque poetics to which Smollett refers.

My perspective on the masquerade will likewise differ from the one adopted previously. I will no longer treat it as a trope allowing the narrator to construct dichotomous structures within the narrative but as a strategy enabling the protagonists to exercise their protean qualities; that is, to take on whichever character they wish. Such understanding of the masquerade metaphor lies behind the epigraph of this part. It lacks the negative evaluation of the phenomenon articulated in the epigraph of the previous part and instead introduces the figure of "a man of stratagem" (Smollett 1988: 145), whose protean nature makes it possible for him to adapt to any circumstances of fragmented and unstable society.

Smollett's life was so deeply imprinted on his literary output that practically any study of his novels revolves around their autobiographical content. A thorough analysis of the traces of Smollett's autobiography in his fiction is therefore redundant, having been done so many times before, and what should suffice here is a brief outline of the correspondences between the travels on which Smollett set out himself and those made by his literary alter egos. The first of importance is the formative journey from Glasgow to London, on which both Smollett himself and his literary creation Roderick embarked with a view to a successful career. There, in 1740, they both joined the naval expedition to Cartagena, an account of which, apart from finding its place in *Roderick Random*, was published separately, in a modified, more documentary form, in the author's *Compendium* of voyage narratives (1756). In 1749 and 1750 the novelist travelled through the Continent, visiting some parts of France, Flanders and Holland, which provided him with material for Peregrine's Continental travels. Finally, his three-year-journey (1763-1765) to France and Italy in search of a healthier climate resulted in *Travels through France and Italy* (1766), being a rather unconventional epistolary account of the tour, whereas his last visit to Scotland gave rise to *The Expedition of Humphry Clinker* (1771), in which the novelist mastered the epistolary form.

Just as Smollett himself was a constant traveller, the two protagonists of the novels in question are predefined as travellers. In the Preface to *Roderick Random*, the choice of the hero's national identity is explained on the grounds of "the disposition of the Scots, addicted to travelling" (*RR*, 5). This disposition, predetermining the character of Roderick, is re-established in the first chapter of the novel, which features the protagonist's mother plagued by a dream:

> —During her pregnancy, a dream discomposed my mother [...]. She dreamed, she was delivered of a tennis-ball, which the devil (who, to her great surprize, acted the part of a midwife) struck so forcibly with a racket, that it disappeared in an instant; and she was for some time inconsolable for the lost of her off-spring; when all of a sudden, she beheld it return with equal violence, and enter the earth, beneath her feet, whence immediately sprung up a goodly tree covered with blossoms, the scent of which operated so strongly on her nerves that she awoke. (*RR*, 17)

The meaning of the dream is deciphered by a seer, who informs Roderick's parents that "their first-born [will] be a great traveller" (*RR*, 17). *Peregrine Pickle*, in turn, features a protagonist of a similar disposition even though he is not a Scot. His name, bringing to mind the idea of travel or pilgrimage, is a Latin borrowing (*peregrinus*), whose original meaning, as OED informs, is "coming from foreign parts, foreign, alien, exotic, concerned with foreigners or aliens". The Latin meaning of the word conveys the idea of displacement and alienation, both of which are central considerations also in *Roderick Random*.

1. Roderick as a dislocated Scot

Roderick's dislocation becomes one of the basic themes of the narrative already in its initial part, when the protagonist sets out for London. Instead of being a typical home tour account, providing "a form of descriptive statistics" on Britain (as was the case with Defoe's *A Tour through the Whole Island of Great Britain* [1724-7], a model home tour narrative of the first half of the eighteenth century [Hulme and Youngs 2002: 6]), Roderick's relation of his tour constitutes an opportunity to constantly emphasise the traveller's Scottishness. What logically follows is that Roderick's travel narrative is also far from offering any "constructions of Britishness" by presenting the nation as a "homogenous community", which was undertaken by domestic travel writing in the aftermath of the union of 1707 (Feldman 1997: 31).[1] Instead, the account of Roderick's home travels aims at a presentation of his dislocated and alienated self (*cf.* Beasley 1998: 6-18), constructed in opposition to the world he is forced to confront; his confrontation with the southern part of Britain is, in fact, a confrontation with a foreign country. Having left his native Scotland, Roderick is permanently homeless. The initial excitement at the possibility of discovering the world gives way to feelings of desolation and displacement.

The protagonist's national identity, established and justified already in the Preface, is confirmed shortly after he sets out for England. When he stays overnight in Newcastle, he meets a barber there – his old friend Strap, as it appears later on – who addresses him with the words: "Sir, I presume you are a Scotchman" (*RR*, 41). Roderick's origin is also exposed when he is confronted with the representatives of the southern parts of Britain. When at an inn, Roderick and Strap, who accompanies him, have their Scottishness commented upon by Betty, the chambermaid (*RR*, 44), whereas when already in London, neither Roderick nor Strap are understood by a passing carman, who as a result damns them "for a lousy Scotch guard" (*RR*, 68). Their linguistic otherness is addressed for the second time shortly after, when they are insulted in a London alehouse and involved in a fight (*RR*, 68). Finally, both Roderick and his companion are identified as Scotchmen on the same basis by a gambler, who imposes on them praising their nation and eventually lures them into playing cards, as a result of which they lose all the money they have at their disposal (*RR*, 74-75).

The London of Roderick's account is thus by no means the glorious capital of Defoe's relation – "the great center of England", as he writes (Defoe 1991: 133). Instead, it is a place in which the atmosphere of hostility, defining the chronotope of Roderick's road, is amplified. Summing up the first two days of their stay in the city, Strap bewails:

> God send us well out of this place, we have not been in London eight and forty hours, and I believe we have met with eight and forty thousand misfortunes.—We have been jeered, reproached, buffeted, pissed upon, and at last stript of our money: and I suppose by and by we shall be stript of our skins. (*RR*, 76)

---

[1] This objective, as Lutz argues (2001), lies behind *The Expedition of Humphry Clinker*, where Scotland is no longer represented as an enclave but as part of Great Britain.

The presentation of urban spaces lacks topographical descriptions, whereas the inns visited by the protagonist, the streets gone down, and the lodgings taken are usually not called by any names. Nowicki rightly observes that this indeterminacy "stresses the labyrinthine nature of the metropolis and exposes the loneliness and helplessness of the protagonists stranded in unfamiliar surroundings" (Nowicki 1986: 113). Indeed, London, as accounted for by Roderick, does not seem to be a happily reached destination of a tedious journey, but a place in which the travellers cannot find their way, are misunderstood, imposed upon and cheated. The only friendly space within this large *locus horridus* is the one that is related to their homeland:

> we were pretty much fatigued with our walk, and not knowing how to proceed, I went into a small snuff-shop hard by, encouraged by the sign of the highlander, where I found, to my inexpressible satisfaction, the shop-keeper was my country-man. (*RR*, 69)

This meeting with their fellow countryman suspends the London hostility for a while. The shopkeeper instructs the travellers as to the way they should follow and recommends a lodging worth taking. His snuff-shop functions as a peaceful enclave where the two wayfarers can take momentary shelter. This could not be said of their encounter with another fellow countryman, Strap's friend,

> who had come from Scotland three or four years before, kept a school in town, where he taught the Latin, French and Italian languages; but what he chiefly professed was the pronunciation of the English tongue, after a method more speedy and uncommon than any practised heretofore [...]. (*RR*, 72)

The friend has betrayed his Scotishness by speaking a non-Scotch dialect, and Roderick feels obliged to criticise the apostate fiercely. Not only does he present a derogatory caricature of the language teacher, referring to his stooped figure and his frightful face "pitted with the small-pox", but also ironically observes that the English he speaks is as unintelligible as if it were Arabic or Irish (*RR*, 72). From the perspective of Roderick, the one who is not true to his national identity deserves scorn.

The protagonist's alienation on the grounds of his national identity also comes to the fore when he finds himself on board the man-of-war Thunder on the expedition to Cartagena. As Roderick reports, when he was examined by Captain Oakhum, "[t]he first question put to [him], was touching the place of

[his] nativity, which [he] declared to be the north of Scotland" (*RR*, 152). After the examination, Roderick becomes imprisoned on suspicion of having "entered into a conspiracy [...] against the life of Captain Oakhum" (*RR*, 153). Even though no explicit association is made between Roderick's nationality and his alleged crime, the juxtaposition of the accusation and his Scottishness being exposed is quite telling.

The manner of Roderick's return from the expedition likewise brings to mind the idea of an alienated self. Having reached the coast of England, the protagonist becomes engaged in a fight with his old enemy, the midshipman Crampley, as a result of which he is abandoned senseless on the ground. When he regains consciousness, he reflects on his situation, which is thus related in the protagonist's narrative:

> I cursed the hour of my birth, the parents that gave me being, the sea that did not swallow me up, the poignard of the enemy, which could not find the way to my heart, the villainy of those who had left me in that miserable condition; and in the extasy of despair, resolved to lie still where I was and perish. (*RR*, 194)

The complaint is very much in line with the one I have already quoted, articulated by Strap after the first day in London. Just as was the case in his previous journeys, the protagonist's alienation after he returns from his voyages is either amplified or alleviated by the figures he encounters. Shortly after he becomes conscious, Roderick directs his steps towards a barn where he is accosted by the country people who, given his bloody appearance, take him for "the devil or a dead mon" (*RR*, 195). In spite of the comic dimension of the scene, what is conveyed between the lines is Roderick's rejection by the English. His second entrance into the southern part of Britain again highlights the protagonist's alterity. Similarly to what happened in London, he finds shelter, a peaceful enclave, in the periphery – at the house of an old woman who "bears the character" of a witch, living a "recluse way of life", her "conversation being different from that of the inhabitants of the village" (*RR*, 198). It is by no means a coincidence that the protagonist finds a kindred spirit in a solitary woman – her alienation highlights Roderick's. When he is at most tormented by the hostile world, he finds asylum in the peripheral – at "a small snuff-shop" run by a Scot or at a desolate witch's hut.

Roderick's encounter with the alleged witch constitutes a turning point in his life story. The old woman takes the role of a fortune-teller and, judging by the diverse vicissitudes Roderick has suffered, predicts "a happy presage of [his] future life" (*RR*, 197). She provides him with occupation, recommending him as a footman to a lady, but at the same time counsels him to "conceal [his] story" (*RR*, 199). In other words, she advises him to put a mask covering the identity of an alienated and homeless North Briton, buffeted by fate and tormented by the hostile world. Roderick willingly follows her advice and, on being presented to his new lady, finds it "proper to conceal [his real name] under that of John Brown" (*RR*, 200). From then on, Roderick's narrative is no longer limited to a series of misfortunes but, for the most part, depicts the protagonist willingly taking on any social role. Having "concealed his story" and adopted a new name, Roderick becomes a protean man capable of adapting to any circumstances.

2. Peregrine as a disowned exile

Peregrine's homelessness, already indicated by his name, is explicitly and literally established at the beginning of the novel. Soon after his birth, the protagonist's mother develops a very peculiar aversion to her son, which is to last throughout the narrative. His father, not being able to defy Mrs Pickle, maintains a similar distance from his son, as a result of which Peregrine, already in his early youth, becomes emotionally separated from his parents. What initially takes place at the emotional level becomes a factual situation shortly thereafter. First, on the grounds of insubordination, the six-year-old Peregrine is sent to a boarding school. On return, he is by no means welcomed with parental affection:

> In the afternoon he was conducted by the commodore to the house of his parents; and strange to tell, no sooner was he presented to his mother than her countenance changed, she eyed him with tokens of affliction and surprize, and bursting into tears, exclaimed her child was dead, and this was no other than an impostor whom they had brought to defraud her sorrow. (*PP*, 76)

Given his mother's unchanging aversion, Peregrine becomes "exiled from his father's house" and "left entirely to the disposal of the commodore" (*PP*, 76). From then on, it is his uncle's country seat – the garrison – that functions as his home, which he visits every now and then, and which he lawfully inherits in the end.

Peregrine's separation from his parents is an experience he shares with Roderick. The latter is not openly rejected but also abandoned by his parents – permanently by his mother, who dies shortly after Roderick is born, and temporarily by his father, who disappears mourning his beloved's death. Both Peregrine's rejection and Roderick's abandonment are in line with two characteristics of "the Smolletian world" in general; namely, "the dislocation of the family group" (Boucé 1976: 297) and "the unnatural family motif" (Nowicki 1986: 47). In a sense, the two novels in question are orphan narratives, which in the eighteenth century would frequently take the form of travel books (see Nixon 2011: 225-256). As Nixon argues, literary orphans are characterised by "multiplicity" and "conceptual fluidity", which, in turn, can be easily translated into "physical mobility" (Nixon 2011: 227). In fact, the idea of an orphan's fluidity and mobility is quite literally addressed in two of the interpolated tales in *Peregrine Pickle* – the memoirs of a prisoner (*PP*, 577-607) and the story of count D'Alvarez (*PP*, 607-609). They are both orphan narratives proper and depict turbulent lives of travelling parentless youths, who take on various roles struggling with the hostile world. This idea seems to form the basis for both Roderick's and Peregrine's adventures; however, the road offers different possibilities for them. For the former, it is the only way to a respected career; for the latter, in turn, a substitute for the stability he has never experienced.

In fact, Peregrine's life is depicted as a continuous search for substitutes and compensations. First, being disowned by his parents, he finds shelter in the Garrison, which quite literally functions as a substitute for his real home. Then, when his romantic love affair with Emilia is hindered by his uncle, he is sent to the Continent and finds compensation through numerous amours. On his return, when his attempt to resume his relationship with Emilia ends in a failure, he "vow[s] within himself, that he would seek consolation [...] in the possession of the first willing wench he should meet upon the road" (*PP*, 499) and transforms "*a nymph of the road*" into a lady (*PP*, 500). In psychological terms, his licentiousness is a direct consequence of his motherless childhood. As Beasley puts it, being unfamiliar with "the nurturing love of a mother", Peregrine "is forced to grow up without any gentling restraints upon [...] his adolescent libido" (Beasley 1998: 91). His unfamiliarity with "any model of the woman as a feeling person" limits his perception of the fair sex, and thus in seeking female substitutes, he is limited only to the physical and shows complete indifference towards their selfhood (Beasley 1998: 92). His search for a compensatory father figure is not as dramatic, given his reciprocated attachment to Hawser Trunnion, his godfather. However, when the latter passes away, Peregrine finds himself in need of a guardian and eventually seeks patronage in the world of politics. His longing for a father figure is correlated with his quest for social stability; he seeks patrons who would safeguard his economic situation and help him maintain his position in the high life. In other words, he wishes them to do what his natural father failed to do.

To conclude, the motifs of dislocation, alienation, homelessness and exile are all correlated with the protagonists' potential for change. The construction of the journey metaphor in Smollett's novels is therefore different from the one in the works by Fielding. The road Roderick and Peregrine go down does not lead to any discovery of their true selves but provides a background against which their selves are shaped. Being deprived of their homes, the ultimate point of reference, they find themselves on the road which appears to be a space of endless possibilities. It is there that they best exercise their adaptability (especially Roderick) and changeability (Peregrine).

Chapter Five

Roderick's and Peregrine's Protean Identities

In contemporary thought, the notion of protean identity has been most extensively dealt with by Robert Jay Lifton, a leading American psychohistorian.[1] In a 1967 article, Lifton introduced the character of a "Protean Man", whom he understood as a typically postmodern figure undergoing a continuous "self-process" in response to social and ideological turmoil (Lifton 1970: 319). Lifton's idea of proteanism is an elaboration on Erik Erikson's theory of adolescent identity crisis, which, if not successfully resolved, leads to identity diffusion and role confusion (Erikson 1959). It is also parallel to the theory of modern identity put forward by Peter Berger, Brigitte Berger and Hansfried Kellner in their *The Homeless Mind: Modernization and Consciousness* (1973). According to the authors, the modern individual struggles with a "loss of integrative meanings" and "pluralization of life-worlds" (1973: 142, 62), and in effect, his or her identity can be characterised as "peculiarly open" (1973: 73). In a similar vein, referring to both Lifton and Berger et al., Drew Westen considers modern selfhood to be defined by "fluidity and transitory character" (1985: 342). In his most comprehensive book-length study of proteanism, Lifton writes:

> We are becoming fluid and many-sided. Without quite realizing it, we have been evolving a sense of self appropriate to the restlessness and flux of our time. This mode of being differs radically from that of the past, and enables us to engage in continuous exploration and personal experiment. (Lifton 1993: 1)

---

[1] Generally, psychohistory can be defined as a form of an "interdisciplinary dialogue between psychology and history" (Tileagă and Byford 2014: 1), studying, among other issues, socio-historical determinants of the self. For a recent survey of psychohistory, see Tileagă and Byford 2014; for an overview of Lifton's thought, see Pomper 1985.

As such, proteanism with regard to personal identity is by nature anti-substantial – it assumes that human beings are not predetermined by any unchanging and stable qualities but are subject to constant metamorphoses. The term itself derives from Proteus, the Greek sea god capable of assuming many forms. According to Pierre Grimal,

> He had the ability to change himself into whatever form he desired. He used this power particularly when he wanted to elude those asking him questions: he possessed the gift of prophecy, but refused to provide information to those mortals who sought it from him. (Grimal 1990: 377-378)

In other words, Proteus changed forms whenever he found it appropriate and as a way of adapting to circumstances. Proteanism, therefore, implies intentional transformations with some defined objectives rather than accidental changes.

The category of the protean self is also present in the recent criticism of eighteenth-century culture and society, being one of numerous contemporary critical concepts which have entered eighteenth-century studies due to various affinities between the period and post-modern times. The eighteenth century, considered as the founding period of modernity broadly understood, has been treated by contemporary critics as a basis for modern fragmentation and instability and as such becomes an appropriate background for fluctuations and metamorphoses of the self. Barbara Stafford, for example, writes about "protean flexibility" of the period, manifesting itself in the metamorphoses of such seemingly "rigid categories" as "identity, gender, and social or racial stereotypes" (Stafford 1996: 55). The affinities between our time and the eighteenth century can be easily discerned from the following sketch:

> The protean self emerges from confusion, from the widespread feeling that we are losing our psychological moorings. We feel ourselves buffeted about the unmanageable historical forces and social uncertainties. Leaders appear suddenly, recede equally rapidly, and are difficult for us to believe in when they are around. We change ideas and partners frequently, and do the same with jobs and places of residence. Enduring moral convictions, clear principles of action and behaviour: we believe they must exist, but where? Whether dealing with world problems or child rearing, our behaviour tends to be ad hoc, more or less decided upon as we go along. We are beset by a contradiction: schooled in the virtues of constancy and stability – whether as individuals, groups, or nations – our world and our lives seem inconstant and utterly unpredictable. We ready come to view ourselves as unsteady, neurotic, or worse. (Lifton 1993: 1)

With very few, if any, exceptions, the sketch could just as well serve as a rendition of the eighteenth-century world in general and of Smollett's universe in particular. In *Roderick Random* and *Peregrine Pickle* the eponymous protagonists are for the most part of the novels emotionally homeless, as I have already discussed, and thus quite literally deprived of their "psychological moorings". Their personal histories are intertwined with the Grand Narrative, which reveals itself in such events as the Cartagena expedition (1740-41) and the battle of Dettingen (1743) in *Roderick Random*, or Peregrine's contacts with the court in Paris, Versailles, the Hague as well as his episode in politics. Their lives are made up of constant changes of roles, occupations and social standings, all of which take place in a social structure far from being stable and hierarchically organised. They both have difficulty identifying a universally recognised moral system, not to mention determining their own. Their lives are lives of confusion, inconstancy and unpredictability.

Kenneth Simpson in his *The Protean Scot* (1988), a study of eighteenth-century Scottish literature, calls the eighteenth-century Scot one of the prototypes of the contemporary protean man (Simpson 1988: 1). The critic argues that "multiplicity of voice, fragmentation of personality, and the projection of self-images" reappear in eighteenth-century Scottish literature "with a frequency and an intensity that are quite remarkable" (Simpson 1988: 2). Consequently, in his study of Smollett he applies the notion of proteanism both to the author himself and his fictional characters, despite the fact that not all of his protagonists were Scots. The aspect of Smollett's poetics that best correlates with proteanism is multiplicity of voices (Simpson 1988: 16); a quality that also comes to the fore in the studies by Richetti, who discusses it in the light of Bakhtinian dialogism (Richetti 1999: 162-195), and Blackwell (2011). What both Simpson and Blackwell suggest is that multiplicity of voices in Smollett's fiction corresponds with multiple identity – multiple in terms of consciousness, very much in line with Hume's and Bakhtin's understandings of personal identity. This, however, raises doubts, as Smollett's protagonists do not reveal any considerable psychological depth which would make it justifiable for the critic to refer to such ideas as fragmented or multiple consciousness. Instead, what should be analysed is what Wahrman calls identity "determined outwardly by a matrix of social relations" (Wahrman 2004: 196). In an attempt to clarify its meaning Wahrman refers to a letter quoted by Edmund Law in his 1769 *A defence of Mr. Locke's opinion concerning personal identity*. We read in it that "[t]he word person" should be understood as:

standing for a certain guise, character, quality, i.e. being in fact a mixed mode, or relation, and not a substance [...] it amounts to no more that saying, a man puts on a mask – continues to wear it for some time – puts off one mask and takes another. (quoted in Wahrman 2004: 196-197)

The model of personal identity emerging from the passage above is that of a continual masquerade or a series of roles adopted. Naturally, as the author of the quotation himself observed, selfhood thus understood does not rely on substance but is constantly being created by consequent acts of putting on masks. According to Grimes's typology, discussed in the Introduction, the mode of masking in question is masking as concretion, which implies that it constitutes rather than conceals identity. Consequently, in my reading of Smollett's two novels I will understand proteanism as a quality enabling the two protagonists to easily adapt, through changing roles and putting on masks, to various circumstances within the "matrix of social relations". This quality is what situates both characters in the picaresque tradition.

1. The protean protagonists and the picaresque tradition

I commented upon the correlation between proteanism and the picaresque already in the Introduction. The basic assumption is that protean characters are one of the aspects that constitute the picaresque novel as a genre and directly correspond to the fragmented and chaotic representation of the world. However, even though both *Roderick Random* and *Peregrine Pickle* feature protean characters set against the background of a destabilised and hostile world, the application of the term picaresque to the study of Smollett's novels has never gained unanimous approval.[2] One of the reasons for the ambiguity has been what Nowicki calls "the intrusion of the romance on the structure of the picaresque" (Nowicki 1986: 44), which manifests itself in references to characters' nobility and curiously romantic happy endings.[3] My perspective will assume the validity of the term picaresque to the study of Smollett's novels for one simple reason – the picaresque novel itself is a

---

[2] Numerous texts have been written on the problem, among which the two by Boucé (1972) and Rousseau (1971) best reveal the nature of the polemical debate, or, in Boucé's words, the "picaresque battle – or rather anti-picaresque battle" (Boucé 1972: 74).

[3] In fact, recent criticism has recognised that the picaresque is always tinged with "a pervasive longing for romance wish fulfilment" (Brownlee 1994: 28).

mutable construct[4] and it would be reckless to exclude Smollett's novels from the tradition on the grounds that not all its generic requirements are met, especially given the vagueness of the very idea of "generic requirements".

In fact, the dialogic constitution of characters, who fluctuate between the picaresque and the romantic poles, can only amplify the impression of their patchwork identities. Unlike Fielding's Tom Jones and Joseph Andrews, whose essential nobility is visible in their benevolence and knightly behaviour, Roderick and Peregrine are throughout the entire narratives capable of doings which stand in direct opposition to their alleged nobility. It surfaces especially in the final parts of the novels leading to romance-like endings, and thus nobility cannot be seen as some personal essence the protagonists discover through their adventures but rather as yet another form they assume when circumstances – in both cases inheritance of a large fortune – make it possible.

In Smollett's novels, the ideas of proteanism and the picaresque are probably best exposed in the character of Crabtree, with whom Peregrine contracts a very peculiar relationship. Crabtree's condensed life story could in fact function as a short picaresque narrative.[5] He presents himself as an outcast from the very beginning of his life, the nomadic nature of which was predefined by "a large share of choler" inherited from his father (*PP*, 328). His life was a constant journey, during which surviving was tantamount to adopting various roles – from a young gentleman through a weaver to a constant impostor. At the same time, it was a life of constant metamorphoses of his body:

> I was once maimed by a carman, with whom I quarrelled, because he ridiculed my leek on St. David's day; my skull was fractured by a butcher's cleaver, on the like occasion. I have been run thro' the body five times, and lost the tip of my left ear by a pistol bullet. (*PP*, 328)

This disintegration of the physical correlates with his social instability but at the same time points to his resilience and indomitability – no matter what happened to him, he proceeded, even though his travels lacked a clearly determined destination. When circumstances demanded it, he also proved him-

---

[4] Interestingly, the idea of proteanism is also invoked with reference to the form of the picaresque novel itself (Mancing 1979).
[5] As Nowicki observes, what Smollett achieved in the figure of Crabtree was "a portrait of the picaro after he has ceased to be one" (Nowicki 1986: 66).

self capable of intentional changes to his appearance, which included "walk[ing] barefoot to Rome, in the habit of a pilgrim", disguising himself "by a change of dress, and a large patch on one eye" or pretending to be deaf (*PP*, 330). As a typical picaro, there was no role that he would not play, being able to "turn his hand to anything, assume the social disguise of every profession and vocation" (Miller 1967: 70). In a sense, Crabtree's life story constitutes an eighteenth-century translation of the myth of Proteus, relating it to a struggle for surviving in the hostile world.

As I have pointed out before, Roderick's and Peregrine's picaresque proteanism is a direct response to their experience of the world "in a flux" (Wicks 1974: 247). Deprived of a stable family structure, a fundamental identity-shaping factor, they come to realise that what they will become depends solely on themselves and on the twists and turns of fortune they will go through. They are made to understand that the sordid world they enter does not offer any logical patterns that can be followed but is rather governed by chance and coincidence. As such, it is inhabited by opportunists, hypocrites, posers and impostors, whose masquerading rules become dominant modes of behaviour. Therefore, their protean potential constitutes what Wicks calls "the picaro's survival kit" (Wicks 1974: 247), as it enables them to resist whatever misfortune they go through.[6]

The archetypal structure underpinning the picaro's adventures is that of a series of symbolic deaths and rebirths or, in other words, alternate periods of winter and spring. Comedy thus understood is by nature carnivalesque; as Bakhtin explains, a medley of births and deaths is one of the basic dualistic carnival images: "Birth is fraught with death, and death with new birth" (Bakhtin 1984a: 125). The intensity with which Roderick and Peregrine experience the vicissitudes of life differs in the two novels, depending on their ability to maintain the status of a gentleman (whenever their position is weakened, they are more susceptible to subsequent misfortunes). Consequently, Roderick is subject to more dynamic fluctuations, being practically deprived of his status the moment he sets out for London, whereas Peregrine, who preserves his position for the most part of the narrative, does not experi-

---

[6] The idea of the "survival kit" is also exposed in Smollett's interpolated tales. Miss Williams in her life story thus defines her resilience and adaptability: "—If one scheme of life should not succeed, I could have recourse to another, and so to a third, veering about to a thousand different shifts, according to the emergencies of my fate [...]" (*RR*, 125).

ence the bottom until cheated out of his fortune in the final phase of his adventures.

In *Roderick Random*, what lies behind the protagonist's travels is a quest for social stability. Roderick's ultimate aim is to appear in society in the quality of a gentleman, to which he considers himself "intitled by birth and education" (*RR*, 208). Bearing this aim in mind, the protagonist travels to London, where he expects to gradually ascend the social ladder. The first roles he takes up – that of a surgeon's and an apothecary's apprentice and a journeyman apothecary – are part of the scheme leading to the intended social ascent (Rory begins to "look upon [him]self as a gentleman in reality" [*RR*, 103]). The sordidness of London and its people, however, soon makes itself known to Rory again, and he finds himself "reduced to a starving condition" and ponders over his "beggarly fate" (*RR*, 127). Soon, he is battered unconscious by a Press gang and finds himself on board the Thunder, where he starts a new life, again struggling to improve his social status. In this he proves successful, being raised to the rank of a surgeon's mate – a position which, modest as it may seem, fills Roderick with pride: "—I found my spirit revive with my good fortune; and now I was an officer, resolved to maintain the dignity of my station, against all opposition or affronts" (*RR*, 139). His good fortune, however, once more proves to be unstable, when in effect of some fraudulent doings of his enemies in the crew, he is falsely accused of being a spy and imprisoned. The protagonist's rebirth is made possible after some time, when thanks to his friend Thompson's generosity, he is "provided with money, and all necessaries for the comfort of life" and, as a result, feels entitled to "look upon [him]self as a gentleman of some consequence" (*RR*, 178). Naturally, fortune's fickleness once more makes itself known to Roderick, as after a misunderstanding and the duel with Crampley, he is left alone on the shore in a "miserable condition" (*RR*, 194). This symbolic death becomes almost literal, when the two country people he encounters believe him to be a zombie (*RR*, 195). Roderick is reborn again, when on Mrs Sagely's recommendation he becomes a servant to Narcissa's eccentric aunt. Even though the role does not meet his high expectations, his learning and gentlemanly behaviour procure for him the title of "Gentleman John" (his proper name being concealed under that of John Brown) (*RR*, 207). High reputation among the servants, however, is not enough for Roderick, who "[a]t certain intervals" disdains himself for his "tame resignation to [his] sordid fate" (*RR*, 208). As a protean picaro proper, he "revolve[s] an hundred schemes for assuming the character of a gentleman" (*RR*, 208) and finally leaves his post after coming into conflict with Sir Timothy. Having ended his servitude, Roderick travels to the Continent, where he is subject to similarly dynamic fluctuations (these I will address later on), at the resolution of which he achieves his goal and assumes the character of a gentleman. It is then that he is finally able to reap the rewards of his efforts and live a life of indulgence. This life, however, just as the one he has lived so far, lacks stability. He performs various roles within the higher stratum of society, ranging from "a pretty fellow" (*RR*, 231), a coffee-house intellectual (*RR*, 233), through a "true French gallant" (*RR*, 249) and a fortune hunter, to a gamester (*RR*, 275) and an imprisoned debtor (*RR*, 317). On the other hand, whenever he comes into contact with Narcissa, the romance convention surfaces, and Roderick displays his sentimental disposition, which is manifested through the visible impact of the doings of his passion on his body and the use of pompous and highly emotional language. His presence in the high life comes to an end when he finds himself in the Marshalsea, imprisoned for debt. His gradual fall and growing melancholy, however, are interrupted by uncle Bowling, who makes it possible for him to be reborn once more and resume his career at sea. What follows is Roderick's continuous rise, which finds its culmination in a typically romance-like discovery of his father and, consequently, in Roderick's becoming a gentleman proper. As Nowicki puts it, "the romance world of harmony and order" triumphs over "the picaresque world of violence and disorder" (Nowicki 1986: 83-84).

As I have already pointed out, the sequence of alternate deaths and rebirths in *Peregrine Pickle* is not so widely developed as in Smollett's first novel. For the most part of the narrative, Peregrine maintains his social position, even though, just like Roderick, he is a constant exile being disowned by unnaturally cold-hearted parents. It does not mean, however, that his continuous life in the quality of a gentleman lacks the protean element. He does exercise his protean skills in different ways throughout the whole narrative, and what makes him a truly protean figure is the ease with which he adopts and changes his roles within the stratum of society he occupies. Depending on circumstances and his prevailing disposition, he makes himself known as a trickster, a gallant, a sentimental lover, a libertine, a politician, a wit or a man of letters. As a rule, it is the first character that Peregrine most frequently assumes. His talents in this matter surface from the beginning of his life when he reveals a tendency to "take indecent freedoms" with his uncle's tobacco, favourite beverage, as well as his nose and gouty toe (*PP*, 67). His predilection for jests is a quality which itself requires some protean potential, as it often makes Peregrine transform his body, put on masks and false identities. This dimension of Perry's trickery is also exposed at the very beginning:

> one day, when the commodore had chastised him by a gentle tap with his cane, he fell flat on the floor as if he had been deprived of all sense and motion, to the terror and amazement of the striker; and after having filled the whole house with confusion and dismay, opened his eyes and laughed heartily at the success of his own imposition. (*PP*, 67-68)

As a commentary on these jokes, the narrator reflects: "It would be an endless and perhaps no very agreeable task, to enumerate all the unlucky pranks he played upon his uncle and others, before he attained the fourth year of his age" (*PP*, 68); naturally, the same could be said about his adolescence and early adulthood. Peregrine's trickery can also be understood as a response to the sense of homelessness he continuously feels. In terms of Jungian psychology, the trickster as an archetype embodies what is unsocialised, unaccepted and marginalised (Jung 2003: 159-179), and as such correlates with Peregrine's exile and rejection.

The other three characters the protagonist assumes – a gallant, a sentimental lover and a libertine – come to the fore along with Perry's numerous affairs with the fair sex. In fact, his contacts with women prove how changeable his disposition can be, which is best visible in the history of his relationship with Emilia Gauntlet. When he first meets her, he displays his talent for gallantry, entertaining her with dances and *tête-à-tête* conversations; then, after momentary hesitation following the discovery of her poor financial standing, he dispenses with proprieties, quits his studies and lets Emilia take "entire possession of his heart" (*PP*, 103); on the other hand, the experience of the grand tour transforms him into a rapacious womaniser, so when he meets her on his return, he looks upon her "with the eyes of a libertine", and "his discourse into the focus of love [...] put[s] on a very different appearance from that which it ha[s] formerly worn" (*PP*, 311); conversely, when his ruthless stratagem to take advantage of her at the masquerade ends in failure, he again resorts to gallantry and sentimentality interchangeably to win back her heart; in the end, he reconciles with her assuming a sentimental air, perfectly corresponding with the romance-like conclusion of his adventures.

Finally, the roles of a politician, a wit and a man of letters come into focus along with Peregrine's attempts to secure his economic situation or to endure its deterioration. This period of financial instability, in fact, is the one that best illustrates the fickleness of fortune and thus subjects the protagonist to dynamic fluctuations. First, Peregrine ingratiates himself with a "noble patron", who takes him under his wing and advises that he should deposit a substantial part of his fortune and stand for Parliament (*PP*, 511-515). At this point, his protean skills prove to be very useful for running an effective campaign:

> He made balls for the ladies, visited the matrons of the corporation, adapted himself to their various humours with surprising facility, drank with those who loved a cherishing cup in private, made love to the amorous, prayed with the religious, gossiped with those who delighted in scandal, and with great sagacity contrived agreeable presents to them all. (*PP*, 516)

What follows, however, is the first of his symbolic deaths – Perry comes to realise that the state of his financial and political affairs is far from being promising: "He cursed his own folly and extravagance, by which he was reduced to such an uncomfortable situation" (*PP*, 519). His rebirth is made possible by an intentional descent on the social ladder: "he now found himself disabled from cultivating the society of [...] men of ample estates and liberal dispositions [...]; so that he was obliged to descend to another degree, and mingle with a set of old bachelors and younger brothers" (*PP*, 521). It is among them that he "constitute[s] himself a classic in wit", thanks to the fact that all the experiences he has gone through so far have provided him with "a thousand entertaining anecdotes" (*PP*, 522). This agreeable social position, however, cannot help him improve his finances, and thus, thinking over various schemes and being "determined to profit, in some shape or other", he decides on the career of a man of letters with a view to "establish his importance among the copy-purchasers in town" (*PP*, 532-533). This reversal of fortune, however, does not last long, and Peregrine hits bottom again, this time probably most severely, being imprisoned for debt. At this point, no role would give him a possibility to be reborn again, so what follows is a romance-like resolution making Peregrine a rightful inheritor of his parents' fortune and Emilia Gauntlet's tender and passionate husband.

To recapitulate, the aspect of the picaresque that is best realised in Smollett's two novels is the mutability of identity, reflecting itself in the ease with which the travellers adapt to changing circumstances. In *Roderick Random* this protean potential ensures the protagonist's resilience to the fickleness of fortune; whenever he falls, he is willing to adopt any role that would make it possible for him to be reborn. In *Peregrine Pickle*, in turn, Perry's proteanism is a quality which, on the one hand, allows him to enjoy various aspects of the high life, and on the other, to respond to his personal, social and economic fluctuations.

2. The protean grand tourists

Both *Roderick Random* and *Peregrine Pickle* at some point feature their protagonists on Continental tours. The discourse of identity inherent in the tours depends on the exercise of the travellers' protean potential – Roderick's and Peregrine's grand tours are both circumstances demanding personal transformations and perfect occasions to play with identity. What follows is a linear presentation of both Continental tours, which, I believe, will show that Smollett's fictionalisations of the grand tour aimed at highlighting its potential to become a series of roles adopted.

The application of the term grand tour to *Roderick Random* may raise doubts, as, in fact, the protagonist does not travel to France with the intention of familiarising himself with "the treasured artifacts and ennobling society of the Continent" (Buzard 2002: 38). Instead, Roderick's journey starts when he finds himself "in the hands of ruffians" on board "a smuggling cutter" heading to France (*RR*, 210). When they arrive on shore, Roderick has his pocket "emptied [...] of the contents" and is forced to exchange his hat and wig with one of the outlaws (*RR*, 210). Roderick's change is highlighted shortly after, when he is at first not recognised by his uncle Bowling, whom he discovers, similarly transformed (by means of an "alteration of dress, and disguise of a long beard" [*RR*, 211]), at a public house. Thus, he begins his adventures on the Continent with no possessions and with a changed appearance, which symbolically defines his social status – he is a nobody; a shapeless and dislocated being ready to take on new forms which would vindicate him in the social structure.

The protagonist's adventures in France are arranged in such a way as would bring to mind typical grand tour occupations and itineraries. The places Roderick visits and the characters he meets on his way would certainly find their place in accounts of Continental travels, and his attitude suggests some aspiration to the status of a grand tourist. His itinerary, even though it is never carefully planned but rather spontaneously constructed, includes such celebrated spots as Paris (though he does not reach it at first), Abbeville, Amiens and Noyons, which could all well appear in any grand tour programme. On his way, he encounters a Catholic priest and a Capuchin, who both stand for Continental Catholicism, the experience of which was an important theme in grand tour accounts (Haynes 2010: 197).[7] The presentation of the Capuchin is very much in line with typical eighteenth-century British observations on the popish religion:

> It was not long before I discovered my fellow-traveller to be a merry facetious fellow, who, notwithstanding his profession and appearance of mortification, loved good eating and drinking better than his rosary, and paid more adoration to a pretty girl than to the Virgin Mary, or St. Genevieve.——He was a thick brawny young man, with red eyebrows, a hook-nose, a face cover'd with freckles; and his name was Frere Balthazar. [...] he was none of the cleanliest animals in the world; and his constitution was naturally so strongly scented, that I always thought it convenient to keep to the windward of him in our march. [...] the fatigue of our journey was much alleviated by the good humour of my companion, who sang an infinite number of catches on the subjects of love and wine. (*RR*, 217)

The caricature of Frere Balthazar consists of typical anti-Catholic invectives, touching upon gluttony and promiscuity, on the one hand, and repulsive appearance, on the other. Moreover, Roderick does not fail to notice the Capuchin's masquerading nature – he discovers his lewdness and excess in drinking and eating despite the latter's "profession and appearance of mortification". Later on it also appears that the monk is a successful procurer (*RR*, 217-218) as well as a cunning thief (*RR*, 219).

Roderick's contact with Catholicism is not the only experience he has on the Continent which brings to mind the idea of grand touring. The protagonist reports having "sauntered about the town [Boulogne] to satisfy [his] curiosity" (*RR*, 214), and being shown "every thing that was remarkable in the [Catholic priest's] monastery" (*RR*, 216); he constructs detailed accounts of the lodgings he has taken and meals he has been offered, and is capable of formulating a highly critical observation on inn-keepers – "an inn-keeper is the same sordid animal all the world over" (*RR*, 219) – which corresponds to Smollett's derogatory commentaries in his proper grand tour narrative.[8] I would argue, then, that even though Roderick's early adventures in France are no part of any grand tour *sensu stricto*, the way he reports them indicates

---

[7] To read more on anti-Catholicism in grand tour accounts, see Black 1992: 238-244, Haynes 2010.

[8] In Smollett's *Travels through France and Italy*, inn-keepers frequently turn out to be the traveller's principal antagonists. The words the narrator resorts to when accounting for his encounters with landlords include "mortifying indifference", "ill manners", "extortion", "villainous house", "impertinent rascal", "ill-looking fellow", "miscreants", and others similarly offensive (Smollett 1979: 43, 110, 300-1).

some ambition to be seen as a travelling gentleman; a status he always feels "intitled by birth and education".

Apart from adopting these self-fashioning techniques, Roderick on his quasi-grand tour experiences the potential of the journey to become a series of roles adopted. His susceptibility to change, as I have mentioned, is already indicated at the beginning of his stay on the Continent – he is reduced to a nobody by the thieves and thus may become whoever he wishes. The first opportunity for Roderick to exercise his protean power arises when the Catholic priest, whose reliability is augmented by his Scottish origin, recommends that the protagonist should decide on a monastic life, as this is the only "way of life in which a person of [his] talents could not fail of making a great figure" (*RR*, 216). The recommendation is not accepted by Roderick, but the reasons he gives tell a lot about his disposition – he does not take any ideological issues into account, "the difference of religion" being "a thing of too small moment to come in competition with a man's fortune" (*RR*, 217), and rejects the offer simply on the grounds of his "aversion to an ecclesiastical life" (*RR*, 217) and his promise to Bowling to "persevere in the religion of [his] forefathers" (*RR*, 216). Nevertheless, Roderick's argument that the matter of religion should not be taken into consideration when it comes to "man's fortune", and thus his disregard for "the religion of forefathers", reveal his capability of going to any lengths when circumstances demand it. His disrespect for family heritage correlates with the atmosphere of homelessness and dislocation maintained throughout the narrative.

After his unsuccessful attempt to transform the traveller into a monk, the Catholic priest provides Roderick with letters of recommendation addressed to his acquaintances from Versailles – another typical grand tour location – who may employ him "in quality of *maitre d'hotel*", with prospects for "a better provision" (given Roderick's "qualifications" [*RR*, 217]), which is accepted by the protagonist "with great eagerness" (*RR*, 217). It is the second time the priest has commented upon Roderick's capabilities – first, calling him "a person of talents" likely to become "a great figure", and now, mentioning his "qualifications" which "entitle" him to a successful career. Even though neither of the priest's schemes is eventually realised – the first being rejected by Roderick himself, the second being hindered by the villainous Capuchin – the episode depicts Roderick as a protean figure ready to transform himself in response to the doings of fortune.

The first social role Roderick does adopt on his tour is that of a soldier, which happens when the traveller is again reduced to a nobody having been robbed by the Capuchin. The encounter with "a party of soldiers" (*RR*, 220) is thus an episode built around the motif of a symbolic death and rebirth. The former is elaborately reported by Roderick:

> I quitted Noyons, and betook myself to the fields, where I wandered about like one distracted, till my spirits were quite exhausted, and I was obliged to throw myself down at the root of a tree, to rest my wearied limbs.—Here my rage forsook me, I began to feel the importunate cravings of nature, and relapsed into silent sorrow, and melancholy reflection. I revolved all the crimes I had been guilty of, and found them so few and venial, that I could not comprehend the justice of that providence, which after having exposed me to so much wretchedness and danger, left me a prey to famine at last in a foreign country, where I had not one friend or acquaintance to close my eyes, and do the last offices of humanity to my miserable carcase. (*RR*, 220)

This short passage touches upon three dimensions of Roderick's symbolic death – he finds himself exhausted both mentally and physically, and reflects on his social alienation. In a sense, he laments the death of his mind, his body and social self – the three aspects of life he recognises. The encounter with a regiment of soldiers leads to his rebirth, constituted by the new role he adopts. As I have argued before, in contrast to a similar scene in *Tom Jones*, Roderick's enlistment does not stem from any character traits that would predispose him to become a soldier. He does so solely in response to the circumstances he has found himself in – "the more I considered my own condition, the more I was convinced of the necessity I was under to come to a speedy determination" (*RR*, 221-222).

Roderick's objective – that is, securing his social standing – becomes apparent once again, when after serving for some time in the army, he meets his old friend Strap "in the sphere of a gentleman", using a modified name of Monsieur d'Estrapes (*RR*, 226). By this time, Rory has grown tired of his military service, which he emphasises complaining about hunger and uncomfortable clothes. Both needs are satisfied by Strap, who invites his friend to dinner and provides him with "a very fine ruffled holland shirt, and cambrick neck-cloth" (*RR*, 227), the high quality of which foreshadows Roderick's forthcoming transformation into a gentleman. This happens in consequence of a masquerading scheme, in which Strap plays the role of Rory's brother in order to implore for his discharge. When the scheme is successfully realised, the two friends continue their Continental adventures, which now take the form of a grand tour proper. At this point, Strap observes:

—I have cloaths in my possession that a Duke need not be ashamed to wear.—I believe they will fit you as they are; if not, there are plenty of taylors in France.— Let us take a short trip to Paris, and provide ourselves in all other necessaries, then set out for England, where I intend to do myself the honour of attending you in quality of a valet. (*RR*, 229)

In accord with Strap's plan, Roderick is to appear in "the character of a gentleman", as there is "none so likely to succeed" in attempts to find "some lady of fortune", who could render them both financially independent (*RR*, 229). Roderick literally becomes a man of quality, which is established not only by the clothes he starts to wear but also by his social status – Strap puts on the mask of his valet. From then on, Roderick's grand tour becomes more dynamic and is practically free of any misfortunes:

> Thus equipped, I put on the gentleman of figure, and attended by my honest friend, who was contented with the station of my valet, visited the Louvre, examined the gallery of Luxemburgh, and appeared at Versailles, where I had the honour of seeing his Most Christian Majesty eat a considerable quantity of olives.— During the month I spent at Paris, I went several times to court, the Italian comedy, opera and play-house, danced at a masquerade, and in short, saw every thing remarkable in and about that capital.—Then we set out for England by the way of Flanders, passed through Brussels, Ghent, and Bruges, and took shipping at Ostend, from whence in fourteen hours we arrived at Deal, hired a post-chaise, and in twelve hours more got safe to London [...]. (*RR*, 230)

This short report includes not only typical grand tour destinations, such as Paris, Versailles, Brussels, Ghent and Bruges, but also forms of entertainment and occupations, which all constitute Roderick's identity as a grand touring gentleman. Confirming this status are mentions of Rory's contact with the aristocracy – the king in Versailles and the Parisian court. In the end, thus, Roderick manages to assume the role he has aspired for. Some time later, at a tavern in London, Mr Banter calls him "a mighty pretty sort of a gentleman— —a man of fortune" who "has made the grand tour—and seen the best company in Europe" (*RR*, 240). As is clear from this observation, and from Roderick's travels in the character of a man of fashion, being a gentleman is perceived a socialising device which enables the protagonist to keep company with the representatives of the highest stratum of society, who, in turn, strengthen the protagonist's sense of belonging to elite social circles.

What in *Roderick Random* constitutes a successful resolution, forms the basis for the tour embarked on by Peregrine Pickle. The gentlemanly status of the undertaking is already established at its outset – Perry receives "an annui-ty of eight hundred pounds" and is to be accompanied by Mr Jolter, "[a] Swiss valet de chambre, who ha[s] already made the tour of Europe", and "a Parisian lacquey" (*PP*, 153). However, what is seen by Roderick as an index of his status, does not impress Perry that much – the fashionable and educa-tional potential of the Continental tour is not what Peregrine wishes to be limited to. He treats the tour as an opportunity to abandon himself to a life of pleasure and practical jokes, and it is also in this life that he exercises his protean powers.

The first of the forms the protagonist assumes is that of "a young English lord", which, in accord with Jolter's plan, helps him pass the gate of Calais without any obstruction (*PP*, 177). Then, he proceeds to make first "*attempt in gallantry*" (*PP*, 178-188), which euphemistically denotes his struggle to satisfy his lust with Mrs Hornbeck. When the travellers arrive in Paris, Pere-grine sends a letter to Gauntlet, "with a very tender billet inclosed for his dear Emilia, to whom he repeated all his former vows of constancy and love" (*PP*, 189). The central idea of this short report is Peregrine's alleged constancy, which in fact has just been questioned by his advances to Mrs Hornbeck. The protagonist's disposition is thus already defined at the beginning of the tour – his departure for France, being the first step of the journey, both physically and psychologically, is for him tantamount to disengagement not only from his homeland but also from his social environment and self (Leed 1991:11). On the grand tour, Peregrine opens up for new experiences and new forms.

Having arrived in Paris, he "bespeak[s] several suits of cloaths suitable to the French mode" (*PP*, 189) and starts fashioning himself as a Parisian gen-tleman. Being ready to "appear a la Françoise, he hire[s] a genteel chariot by the month" (*PP*, 191) and performs typical grand tourist duties, such as visit-ing galleries, remarkable sights and institutions providing entertainment. What, however, interests him most is "profit[ing] by his talents among the fair sex" by means of "his utmost art and address" (*PP*, 192). Yet, this time the transformation is not entirely successful – he finds himself

> a mere novice in French gallantry, which is supported by an amazing volubility of tongue, an obsequious and incredible attention to trifles, a surprising faculty of laughing out of pure complaisance, and a nothingness of conversation, which he could never attain. (*PP*, 192)

Despite all the indicators of fluidity in terms of personal and social identity expressed throughout Smollett's two novels, one's national characteristics prevail over any attempts to transform or conceal them. The most vivid of these is the mother tongue and its conventions, which will always take the better of one's efforts to modify it. As is frequently indicated throughout both novels, Peregrine's Englishness as well as Roderick's Scottishness are the two constituents of their identity that are not subject to change.[9]

The next role Peregrine takes on is that of an intellectual, which, similarly to those previously discussed, is socially-oriented. The protagonist defines himself by means of the social circle he enters – "a noted academy" – where he "contract[s] an acquaintance with a few sensible people [...] contribut[ing] not a little to the improvement of his knowledge and taste" (*PP*, 193). Peregrine's interests in intellectual debates are for some time interrupted by some further "*amorous recreations*" with a certain "Dulcinea" (*PP*, 193-196) and then again with Mrs Hornbeck (*PP*, 199-200), but they come to the fore once more when roused by "*the odd characters*" of the Swiss Doctor and Mr Pallet (*PP*, 203). It is with them that Peregrine enters into quasi-scholarly debates, the culmination of which is the carnivalesque "*entertainment in the manner of the ancients*" (*PP*, 210-217). As their acquaintance continues, more or less serious debates occur, the most notable of which being "*a conversation upon the* English *stage*" (*PP*, 242-246), but the feast organised by Pallet marks a turn towards the ridiculous on Peregrine's tour. From then on, the traveller resorts to his skills as a prankster more often.

The first opportunity to demonstrate these skills is the masked ball that Perry attends accompanied by Pallet in the aftermath of the banquet, which I will study in greater detail later on. Then, when both characters are imprisoned, Peregrine conceals the news of their approaching release and informs Pallet, having "modelled his physiognomy" into "the woeful appearance", that he is doomed to be locked in the Bastille for life (*PP*, 226). As if that were not enough, Perry "*persecutes him with his mischievous talent, upon the road to* Flanders" (*PP*, 231), when "recollecting the story of Scipio and the mulcteer in Gil Blas", he proceeds to "perpetrate a joke upon the stomach of Pallet", which he accomplishes resorting once more to his talent for mislead-

---

[9] Though he never literally becomes a French gallant, what he learns during his stay in Paris is not entirely lost on him. He proves it when he sees Emilia for the first time after his return from the grand tour: "he practised his Parisian improvements on the art of conversation, and uttered a thousand prettinesses in the way of compliment, with such incredible rotation of tongue, that his rivals were struck dumb with astonishment" (*PP*, 311).

ing facial expressions – he "affect[s] to gaze with peculiar eagerness at the painter" and "assum[es] a mysterious air" (*PP*, 233).

Peregrine's libertine disposition takes precedence in the subsequent part of the journey, being stimulated by his coach travel in the company of "a very handsome young lady" (*PP*, 248). Just because it happens that she is accompanied by a Capuchin, Perry finds it proper to make a donation for his order, and then, our "hypocritical projector" gives the following demonstration of his religious zeal "with transport half natural and half affected":

> O father! [...] if I could be favoured but for one half hour with the private instructions of that inspired devotee, my mind presages, that I should be a stray'd sheep brought back into the fold, and that I should find easy entrance at the gates of heaven! There is something supernatural in her aspect; I gaze upon her with the most pious fervor, and my whole soul is agitated with tumults of hope and despair! (*PP*, 250)

Even though the whole "rhapsody" testifies to Peregrine's hypocrisy and lewdness covered by the mask of religion, the metaphor he resorts to – that of "a stray'd sheep" – is, I believe, not accidental. I take it as evidence of some ongoing sense of homelessness Peregrine feels, which, however, is suppressed by other considerations at the moment. The affair ends in a disappointment, but Peregrine soon finds consolation in another encounter with Mrs Hornbeck. It again demands that he should use his protean skills:

> This lady no sooner beheld her gallant, than her cheeks reddened with a double glow; and she exclaimed, 'Dear brother, I am overjoy'd to see you! Pray come into our coach.' He took the hint immediately, and complying with her request, embraced this new sister with great affection. (*PP*, 274).

Unluckily for him, their artful plan is eventually hindered by the jealous husband, who, having been informed about his wife's encounter with "the pretended brother" (*PP*, 277), considers it necessary to intervene.

Towards the end of his tour, Peregrine once more derives pleasure from his role as a prankster – this time acting as a "mischievous fomentor" inciting both Pallet and the doctor to a ridiculous duel (*PP*, 292-297). Then, when already in Holland, the protagonist re-appears in the highest stratum of society. First, having arrived in the Hague, he "dresse[s] himself in a rich suit of the Parisian cut" and visits the court of the Dutch Princess "without any introduction" (*PP*, 301). He continues his stay making "a tour to all the remarkable places" there (*PP*, 301) and proceeds to Amsterdam, where he "visit[s] every thing worth seeing" (*PP*, 302) but also becomes involved in a brawl over "a sprightly French girl" (*PP*, 303). Finally, he appears in "the antient city of Leyden", where, having enjoyed a learned conversation with some students, he makes sure that he visits all the spots "recommended to their view" (*PP*, 303-304).

When he returns to England, he proudly believes in "his own improvement since he left his native soil" (*PP*, 304). However, as the narrator argues, this improvement should rather be called "degeneracy in the sentiments". Peregrine has become aware of "his own qualifications, vain of his fortune, and elated on the wings of imaginary expectation". What is more, "his charming Emily" appears to be far from "the ultimate aim of his gallantry", which, as he assumes, should "triumph over the most illustrious females of the land" (*PP*, 304-305). Thus, just as the grand tour enables Roderick to climb the social ladder, it helps Peregrine to recognise his potential. In the aftermath of the tour, Peregrine is not only "initiated in the beau monde" of London (*PP*, 306) but also achieves excellence both in practical jokes (manifested especially in his masquerading collaboration with Crabtree) and in libertinage (as reflected by the masquerade at Haymarket).

3. The protean bodies

Throughout both novels, Roderick's and Peregrine's transformations are as a rule correlated with metamorphoses of their bodies. This should not come as a surprise in an age revealing not only a "preoccupation with the physical" but also "readiness to make the body a subject" (Douglas 1995: xiii-xiv). The eighteenth-century novel, recognising this preoccupation, provided space to explore the potential of the physical, and thus, as Douglas rightly observes, whenever characters or their adventures were described, "physicality and physical events" always came to the fore (Douglas 1995: xvi). These characteristics both of the epoch and of the genre were accurately reflected in Smollett's fiction. The author, on the one hand involved in medical activities and, on the other, preoccupied with caricature in the arts, frequently let the physical dominate his narratives. This dominance manifests itself in various forms, from scatological humour through medically precise observations on defects and wounds to physical symptoms of passions and feelings. What, however, I will concentrate on here is the body in motion and its metamorphoses, the basic assumption being that it "remains at the very core of the representational enterprise of travel writing" (Białas 2010: 10). The body that will come into my focus is both the picaresque body, with its complete plasticity, and the grand touring body, adapting to the circumstances of the institution.

In Smollett's two novels, the protagonists' bodies undergo both natural and artificial changes. For the "outwardly or socially turned" self of the eighteenth century "putting on or taking off of clothes constituted the gist of a successful change of identity" (Wahrman 2004: 177-179). It is impossible, therefore, to separate the physical aspect of the body from the artificial one, especially as the boundary between artifice and nature is frequently indistinct in the eighteenth-century context.[10] On the one hand, some popular sartorial accessories of the time, such as wigs or masks, were thought of as imitations of nature; on the other, as is revealed in fiction, expressions, grimaces, emotions, etc. were literally "worn" and thus artificially evoked. For these reasons, my analysis of the transformations of the body in Smollett's two novels will cover both natural and artificial aspects, without drawing any boundaries between the two.

In *Roderick Random* the protagonist's social fluctuations are accompanied by his observations on his bodily status. In other words, the sequence of symbolic deaths and rebirths is, in a sense, imprinted on Roderick's appearance. At times, just as was the case with Fielding's Tom and Joseph, his body is taken as an index of his noble descent. When *"entertained by Mr. Crab"*, Roderick protests about being called a ragamuffin on the grounds that he has "a whole coat on [his] back" (*RR*, 38); then, when already in London, in order to appear as a gentleman, he does his best to improve his looks, even though he is not entirely successful:

> —I had dressed myself to the greatest advantage; that is, put on a clean ruffled shirt, and my best thread stockings, my hair (which was of the deepest red) hung down upon my shoulders, as lank and streight as a pound of candles; and the skirts of my coat reached to the middle of my leg; my waistcoat and breeches were of the same piece, and cut in the same taste; and my hat very much resembled a barber's bason, in the shallowness of the crown and narrowness of the brims. (*RR*, 65-68)

---

[10] The boundary between nature and artifice in terms of appearance was itself an important eighteenth-century motif, most notably elaborated on in Jonathan Swift's satirical "A Beautiful Young Nymph Going to Bed" (1734), in which the bodily status of the prostitute Corinna is constituted by artificial accessories imitating natural body parts.

This "whimsical appearance", as Roderick himself observes (*RR*, 65), does not receive approbation in the world of London. When the protagonist visits Strap's friend, the latter provides Rory with some practical advice: "I vaw to Gad, 'tis a masquerade here.—No christian will admit such a figure into his hawse" (*RR*, 72). In effect, Roderick agrees to be taken to "a perriwig ware-house, in the neighbourhood" in order to be deprived of "these carroty locks" (*RR*, 73). When Roderick is about to take on his first role in London, that of Mr Lavement's apprentice, he again thinks it fit to improve his appearance – he first visits a tailor, where he receives "a suit of clothes" and "a new hat" (*RR*, 95), and then dresses himself "to the greatest advantage" making "no contemptible figure" (*RR*, 96). At another time, Roderick starts a new life on board the Lizard, having been presented with "half a dozen fine shirts, and as many linen waistcoats and caps, with twelve pair of new thread-stockings", which all make it possible for him to "look upon [him]self as a gentleman of some consequence" and entertain himself at Port Royal making "a swagger-ing figure" (*RR*, 178). Then, when after some time he finds himself in France in the quality of a soldier, Strap relieves him of the military duties and makes it possible for him to take on the role of a grand touring gentleman. The pro-tagonist proudly illustrates "this sudden transition of fate" (*RR*, 230) with a detailed description of clothes and accessories:

> —My wardrobe consisted of five fashionable coats full-mounted, two of which were plain, one of cut velvet, one trimmed with gold, and another with silver-lace; two frocks, one of white drab with large plate buttons, the other of blue, with gold binding; one waistcoat of gold brocard; one of blue sattin, embroidered with sil-ver; one of green silk, trimmed with broad figured gold lace; one of black silk, with fringes; one of white sattin, one of black cloth, and one of scarlet; six pair of cloth breeches; one pair of crimson, and another of black velvet; twelve pair of white silk stockings, as many of black silk, and the same number of fine cotton; one hat, laced with gold *point d'Espagne*, another with silver-lace scolloped, a third with gold binding, and a fourth plain; three dozen of fine ruffled shirts, as many neckcloths; one dozen of cambrick handkerchiefs, and the like number of silk. (*RR*, 230)

The passage makes it clear that Roderick literally exploits the potential of lavish clothes to improve his social status. This enumerative account, concre-tising his consumerist mentality, proves his awareness that he can "establish" his identity through "consumption and display" (Hundert 1997: 76). Thus equipped, he concludes his Continental tour as a gentleman and enjoys himself in the London high life.

At times, when Roderick, and also Peregrine, fashion themselves as men of quality, their protean bodies are correlated with their immediate surroundings. In terms of Erving Goffman's sociology, their *fronts* are not only constituted by *appearance* and *manner* but also by *setting*, which involves all "background items which supply the scenery and stage props for the spate of human action" (Goffman 1956: 13). In other words, their performances are most meaningfully delivered when supported by suitable items and set against appropriate backgrounds. In order to become more successful, they carefully arrange their *settings*. They choose such appropriate venues as theatres, music halls, popular parks, assembly halls or famous sights when abroad. They surround themselves with valets, who arrange comfortable lodgings, with objects of value, such as "a genteel chariot" (*PP*, 191) or a whole set of jewellery, precious weapons and fashionable accessories (*RR*, 230). The following sketch of Roderick's attempts to appear as a proper *beau* in a theatre best illustrates this performative aspect of their quest for identity:

> —I rose and sat down, covered and uncovered my head twenty times between the acts; pulled out my watch, clapped it to my ear, wound it up, set it, gave it the hearing again;—displayed my snuff-box, affected to take snuff, that I might have an opportunity of shewing my brilliant, and wiped my nose with perfumed handkerchief;—then dangled my cane, and adjusted my sword-knot, and acted many more fooleries of the same kind, in hopes of obtaining the character of a pretty fellow [...]. (*RR*, 231)

In fact, Roderick's display of his foppish body is a kind of metatheatre – a performance within a performance. He exhibits himself while a play is being performed. The detailed account of his gestures, in a way foreshadowing the extensive body language in Sterne's fiction, can be taken as a very peculiar form of stage directions.

Roderick's life of luxury, however, ends when his financial reserves are exhausted. He decides to resort to "the gaming-table as a certain resource for a gentleman in want", which is again accompanied by a subtle change of his appearance:

> —Although my cloaths were almost as good as new, I grew ashamed of wearing them, because I thought every body, by this time, had got an inventory of my

wardrobe.—For which reason, I disposed of a good part of my apparel [...], and bought two new suits with the money. (*RR*, 279)

Finally, when his uncle Bowling pays off his debts and releases him from Marshalsea, Roderick has his beard trimmed, "perform[s] the ceremony of ablution", puts on his "gayest apparel" and in effect not only surprises his uncle at his "sudden transformation" (*RR*, 338) but also makes his friend Banter "confounded at the magnificence of [his] dress" (*RR*, 341). Roderick's vindication by his family member, in a way, foreshadows his ensuing reunion with his father, which is tantamount to being officially recognised as a gentleman. It is then that Strap, seeing "the magnificence of [Roderick's] apparel", loses his speech "in amazement" (*RR*, 353).

Even when Roderick finds himself in no position to appear as a gentleman, the metamorphoses of his body are still correlated with subsequent transformations of his social identity. When on board the Thunder, Roderick has his hair cut off and receives a new wig (*RR*, 137), and having been appointed surgeon's mate, he receives "a chest and some cloaths [...] to support the rank" (*RR*, 139). Having become a servant on Mrs Sagely's recommendation, in turn, he is provided with "a very good suit of livery", which belonged to his predecessor in the position (*RR*, 201), whereas joining the army means selling the livery suit and purchasing linen, as well as being "accommodated with cloaths, arms and accoutrements" (*RR*, 222).

On the other hand, poor sartorial status is tantamount to being reduced to poverty. When Roderick sets out for London, he defines his "whole fortune" as "consisting of one suit of cloaths, half a dozen of ruffled shirts, as many plain; two pair worsted and a like number of thread stockings", along with some indicators of his status as a surgeon's apprentice (*RR*, 40). Some time later, at the outset of his Continental tour, he is assaulted by smugglers and deprived of his hat and wig (*RR*, 210), whereas when he attempts to improve his financial situation in London, he is "advised [...] to take off two or three suits of rich cloaths, and convert them into cash" (*RR*, 316).

What is more, when Roderick finds himself at the bottom of the social ladder, his low status is either reflected by the physical or gives rise to appropriate bodily symptoms. Having spent the first misfortunate day in London, Rory throws himself "into the bed in an agony of despair" and cannot "refrain from weeping" (*RR*, 76). Then, when again "reduced to a starving condition", he encounters a Press gang, and the ensuing impressment is imprinted on his body:

I received a large wound on the head, and another on my left cheek, I was dis-
armed, taken prisoner, and carried on board a pressing tender; where, after being
pinioned like a malefactor, I was thrust down into the hold, among a parcel of
miserable wretches [...]. (*RR*, 127)[11]

Roderick's physical degradation following his impressment is brought into
focus again when the protagonist encounters his old friend Thompson. As
Roderick himself observes, he is not easy to recognise, "disfigured with
blood and dirt, and altered by [...] misery", and thus he asks Thompson if the
adversities he has gone through "disguised" him to such an extent as to make
his recognition impossible. Having posed this question, Roderick has his
body scrutinised – "he observed me with great earnestness for some time" –
but it does not lead to any identification – "he could not recollect one feature
of my countenance" (*RR*, 130). Having ended his service in the navy, Roderick hits bottom again. He finds himself *treacherously knocked down,
wounded and robbed*" on shore (*RR*, 191) and puts on "a seaman's old jack-
et" thrown away by his robber (*RR*, 194). Thus disfigured, he enters a barn,
where he is believed to be "either the devil or a dead mon" (*RR*, 195). Shortly
after, having arrived in Boulogne and being robbed again, he is not recognised by Lieutenant Bowling (*RR*, 211), whereas when reduced to ultimate
poverty by the villainous Capuchin, he is "so much transported with grief,
anger, and disdain, that a torrent of blood gushe[s] from [his] nostrils", and
when he lies down to "rest [his] wearied limbs", he starts lamenting his "miserable carcase" (*RR*, 220). Then, after he joins the regiment of soldiers, what
initially seems to be his redemption quickly turns out to be a curse:

—It is impossible to describe the hunger and thirst I sustained, and the fatigue I
underwent in a march of so many hundred miles; during which, I was so much
chafed with the heat and motion of my limbs, that in a very short time the inside
of my thighs and legs were deprived of skin, and I proceeded in the utmost tor-
ture. (*RR*, 222)

---

[11] In both cases, Roderick's is not the only body reflecting his status – when he starts
weeping, he does so being accompanied by Strap, and they are "mingle[ing] [their]
tears together" (*RR*, 76); when taken by force by the Press gang, in turn, Roderick
finds himself "among a parcel of miserable wretches". Thus, the bodies that surround
him help define the status of his own body, which in turn corresponds to his social
position – as Douglas observes, "social change does alter the ways in which bodies
surround one another" (Douglas 1995: 48).

Finally, when he finds himself imprisoned for debt, he reports being "neither washed, shifted nor shaved" and having his face "meagre with abstinence", "obscured with dirt, and overshadowed with hair". As such he makes a "squalid and even frightful" figure and is again not recognised by his uncle Bowling (*RR*, 337-338).

The body of Peregrine does not undergo such dynamic metamorphoses, just as the protagonist himself is not subject to such extreme social fluctuations. Nevertheless, his proteanism does reflect itself through his appearance. He transforms it both when adopting different roles and when arranging schemes, stratagems and pranks. The first notable instance of an intentional use of his body takes place when the protagonist is fourteen and starts to "adopt the pride and sentiments of a man" (*PP*, 98). It is then that we learn of his interest in "gymnastic exercises" and "parties of gallantry", in which he has become "particularly adapted for succeeding" (*PP*, 98). For Perry, being a gallant means becoming "remarkably rich and fashionable in his cloaths" and taking "every opportunity to display himself" (*PP*, 99; see Hundert 1997: 76). His abilities are at their height when he prepares for his forthcoming meeting with Emilia:

> He arose with the lark, adjusted his hair into an agreeable negligence of curl, and dressing himself in a genteel grey frock trimmed with silver binding, waited with the utmost impatience for the hour of ten, which no sooner struck, than he hied him to the place of appointment [...]. (*PP*, 101)

In contrast, when Peregrine learns about Miss Gauntlet's poor financial standing, the conflict "between his interest and love" produces "a perplexity which had an evident effect upon his behaviour; he became pensive, solitary and peevish, avoided all publick diversions, and grew so remarkably negligent in his dress, that he was scarce distinguishable by his own acquaintance" (*PP*, 102). Thus, just as in *Roderick Random*, Smollett signals the protagonist's bodily transformation by his friends' inability to recognise him. After some time, however, when after a misunderstanding he is cured of his sentimental disposition, his body returns to its former shape: "his countenance gradually resumed its former serenity; and [...] he appeared again at public diversions with an air of gaiety and unconcern" (*PP*, 109). His foppish appearance is also constituted by his outstanding looks: "He was already taller than a middle-sized man, his shape ascertained, his sinews well knit, his mien greatly improved, and his whole figure [...] elegant and graceful" (*PP*, 110).

The grand tour is another opportunity for the protagonist to transform his appearance. For the most part, he attempts to maintain his status by clothes, and thus we read about Perry ordering "several suits of cloaths suitable to the French mode" (*PP*, 189) or "dress[ing] himself in a rich suit of the Parisian cut" (*PP*, 301). As I have already shown, Peregrine's Continental tour is also a time of satisfying his libertine wishes. To this end, he treats his Frenchified body as an exhibit which is to be "presented [...] at all the *Spectacles* for many weeks", in order to "attract the notice of some distinguished inamorata" (*PP*, 191). When, however, he finds it difficult to follow the rules of French gallantry, he dexterously transforms himself into a sentimental lover and addresses his target "not in the superficial manner of a French gallant, but with all the ardor of an enthusiast" (*PP*, 250). Then, having returned to England and entered the London *beau monde*, Peregrine travels to Bath, where he immediately safeguards his position by means of exhibiting his facade: "The splendor of his appearance excited the inquiries of envy, which [...] was cursed with the information of his being a young gentleman of a good family, and heir to an immense fortune" (*PP*, 318).

Peregrine is also capable of momentary transformations, which constitute parts of his stratagems and practical jokes. One of these, a prank arranged during his stay at the University of Oxford, is by nature dependant on the metamorphosis of the body. During a typical "midnight consistor[y]", Peregrine puts himself in the position of a master of revels and makes his fellow students "join in the most extravagant proposal that could be made":

> They had already broke their glasses in consequence of his suggestion, drank healths out of their shoes, caps, and the bottoms of the candle-sticks that stood before them, sometimes standing with one foot on a chair, and the knee bent on the edge of the table; and when they could no longer stand in that posture, setting their bare posteriors on the cold floor, they huzza'd, hollowed, danced, and sung, and in short were elevated to such a pitch of intoxication, that when Peregrine proposed that they should burn their perriwigs, the hint was immediately approved, and they executed the frolic as one man; their shoes and caps underwent the same fate by the same instigation, and in this trim he led them forth into the street, where they resolved to compel every body they should find to subscribe to their political creed, and pronounce the Shiboleth of their party. (*PP*, 115)

As is frequently the case with Peregrine's pranks, the construction of the body is based on the carnivalesque grotesque. In the passage above, the bodies of Peregrine and his companions are subject to disintegration and dismemberment, which situates them within the "system of grotesque images" (Bakhtin 1984b: 25) interlarding the whole narrative.[12]

When Peregrine is close to hitting bottom, having realised that his vast fortune is almost gone, this "uncomfortable situation" manifests itself through his appearance – he is "abandoned by his gayety and good humour", and "his countenance gradually contract[s] itself into a representation of severity and care" (*PP*, 519). At this point Smollett again resorts to the technique of highlighting the protagonist's transformation by means of its potential to evoke consternation in his friends. When Peregrine meets Mrs Gauntlet, she notices that "his former sprightly air was metamorphosed into [...] austerity, or rather dejection of feature", and thus, finding it difficult to "believe her own eyes", she exclaims: "Is it possible [...] that the gay Mr. Pickle should be so much altered in such a short space of time!" (*PP*, 519). The following phase of instability with regard to his social position, during which he tries to secure it through ingratiating himself with politicians, is duly reflected through his body. When he believes to have succeeded, "[h]is countenance [is] again lifted up, his good humour retrieved, and his mien reexalted" (*PP*, 530), whereas when he learns about his eventual failure, he saunters through a park "so discontented" that he is not able to determine whether he walks "upon his head or heels" (*PP*, 531).

Peregrine's ensuing struggle for his social position is similarly recorded by his body. First, in an attempt to remedy "the deficiencies of his yearly income", he enters "*a college of authors*" (*PP*, 532). He is initiated into the new role through a quasi-ritualistic ceremony, at the culmination of which "his temples [are] bound with a wreath of laurel" (*PP*, 534). However, even though he accepts this outward sign of his transformation, the physical responds negatively:

> This sudden change from his former way of life agreed so ill with his disposition, that, for the first time, he was troubled with flatulencies and indigestion, which produced anxiety and dejection of spirits, and the nature of his situation began in some measure to discompose his brain; (*PP*, 551)

---

[12] The body drinking "healths" out of shoes or other accessories designed to perform different functions has a curious correspondence with the body of slapstick comedies of the silent cinema. Using pieces of clothing for other purposes than those for which they were originally designed was one of the basic techniques adopted by Charlie Chaplin.

Then, when the protagonist hits bottom being imprisoned for debt in the Fleet, his symbolic death corresponds with the degradation of his body: "his health suffered by his sedentary life and austere application; his eye-sight failed, his appetite forsook him, his spirits decayed" (*PP*, 618). Finally, when fortune smiles on him after all, he surprises Godfrey by "a favourable alteration in his externals"; namely, having "purified himself from the dregs of his distress", he appears "in a decent suit, with clean linnen", his face being "disencumbered of the hair that overshadowed it" (*PP*, 624).

Apart from using the body in the ways I have so far discussed, the protagonists of both novels display a command of their faces. They are capable of intentionally modifying their countenances, depending on the circumstances they find themselves in. And thus, throughout their adventures they prove themselves to be masters of their faces, being able to deliberately "assume" such expressions as "a sullen look" (*RR*, 276), "a most seducing tenderness of look" (*PP*, 119), "a stern, or rather frantic countenance" (*PP*, 498), "an air of serenity" (*PP*, 132) or "an air of fraternal concern" (*PP*, 274); their hypocritical disposition allows them to "affect to smile" (*PP*, 135) and to display "feigned amazement" (*RR*, 44), "affected surprize" (*RR*, 44), "the appearance of disappointment and chagrin" (*RR*, 272) as well as "the appearance of extraordinary fondness" (*PP*, 195); their limitless plasticity, in turn, makes it possible for them to "preserve [...] gravity of countenance" (*PP*, 226) as well as "model" their "physiognomy" (*PP*, 226) or "looks [...] into the characters of humility and love" (*RR*, 288). At one point in *Roderick Random*, the protagonist is accused of "possess[ing] all the mimickry and mischievous qualities of an ape" (*RR*, 245); it seems that this invective could just as well be addressed to either of the two protean characters.

In conclusion, the narrative patterns adopted by Smollett – that is, picaresque adventures and the grand tour – are both built around the motif of protean identity. Roderick and Peregrine are constantly negotiating their identities, and their journeys, instead of being oriented towards some discovery of their true selves, are depicted as series of roles adopted. What highlights the impression of proteanism is the theme of the metamorphosing body. Roderick's and Peregrine's transformations and social fluctuations reflect themselves in the appearance of the characters, which is constituted both by the physical and by the sartorial. The mutability of their bodies, given Smollett's predilection for the carnivalesque, brings to mind what Bakhtin defines as the grotesque body, undergoing "unfinished metamorphosis, of death and birth, growth and becoming" (Bakhtin 1984b: 24). As such, Smollett's protean travellers stand in opposition to "the classic images of the finished, completed man" (Bakhtin 1984b: 25), which, in turn, rely on the substantialist approach to identity.

Chapter Six

The Masquerading Protagonists

What contributes to the atmosphere of confusion and destabilisation, created on the one hand by the protagonists' homelessness and displacement, and on the other by their protean selves, are the diversified masquerades they take part in. Naturally, these are not limited to literal masked balls but also take the forms of stratagems and practical jokes, which are based on the motif of identity play. What I will also treat here as a form of metaphorical and passive masquerade are scenes in which the characters' identities are mistaken, confused or not recognised, which however does not result from any of their schemes. All these help to constitute what I have defined as masquerade poetics, or the transposition of the masquerade into the language of literature, in which the idea of identity play comes to the fore.

1. Masked balls
In both *Roderick Random* and *Peregrine Pickle* there are mentions of masked assemblies in which the protagonists take part. The basic difference between the masquerades in the two novels is that in *Roderick Random* there are only references to the activity, whereas *Peregrine Pickle* offers two full-length masquerade scenes, taking up whole chapters. Smollett's masquerades lack the subversive dimension of the one in *Tom Jones* and instead of showing some hitherto-unknown personal features of the attendants, illustrate the currently prevailing dispositions.

Roderick reports having attended masked balls while in Paris and London, when he finds himself at the top of the social ladder passing as a gentleman and a man of fashion:

—During the month I spent at Paris, I went several times to court, the Italian comedy, opera, and play-house, danced at a masquerade, and in short saw every thing remarkable in and about that capital. (*RR*, 230)

I soon became acquainted with a good many people of fashion, and spent my time in the modish diversions of the town, such as plays, operas, masquerades, drums, assemblies, and puppet-shews; (*RR*, 258)

In both excerpts, masquerades are listed along with other popular urban diversions suitable for men of fashion, and they help to strengthen the impression of social identity Roderick wishes to display. The listed forms of entertainment correspond with those enjoyed by Thomas Rakewell in Hogarth's *A Rake's Progress*, who similarly to Roderick fashions himself as a man of quality after inheriting his father's wealth.[1] Both in Smollett's novel and in Hogarth's cycle, and in fact in any other didactic writing of the time, high life entertainment is tantamount to vanity; however, Roderick's absorption into the Paris and London *beau monde* is not as disastrous for him as it is for Rakewell, who ends up in Bedlam. Roderick's episodes as a Parisian and London gentleman are no part of any systematic moral discourse but elements of the dialogic texture of this generically diversified novel.

In Smollett's second novel the report of the first masked assembly attended by the protagonist takes up the whole Chapter XLIX, where we learn that Peregrine, "being rendered frolicsome by the wine he ha[s] drank, propose[s] that he and Pallet should go to a masquerade [...] to be given that night" (*PP*, 219). Their Parisian landlady – for it all happens in Paris during Perry's Continental tour – advises Pallet to "appear in a woman's dress" (*PP*, 219), so that both the protagonist and his companion would be able to stay together for the whole night without raising any controversy. Pallet's appearance in a woman's dress is itself an interesting aspect of the scene, telling a lot about the turmoil over gender identity at the time, partially caused and partially reflected by masked balls.[2] What is, however, more important for the study of Peregrine's development as a hero is the comic potential of the event, imme-

---

[1] For a detailed study of correspondences between Smollett's novels and Hogarth's progresses, see Moore 1948: 162-195.

[2] Cross-dressing was in fact a phenomenon inextricably related to the masquerade. As a factor contributing to sexual chaos, it was frequently attacked by anti-masquerade writers. To read more on cross-dressing at eighteenth-century masked balls, see Castle: 1986: 46-49, 63-64. For a comprehensive analysis of gender identities in the eighteenth century, see Wahrman 2004: 3-82.

diately recognised by the protagonist, who "forsee[s] abundance of diversion in the execution of this project" (*PP*, 219). Thus, the masked assembly joined by Perry, just as is the case with masquerades attended by Roderick, serves as an illustration of the protagonist's disposition. Peregrine, who on the grand tour exploits his potential as a prankster, derives from the masquerade what it has to offer in terms of practical jokes:

> After they had taken a view of all the remarkable masques, and the painter had been treated with a of glass of liqueur, his mischievous companion gave him the slip, and vanishing in an instant, returned with another mask and a domino over his habit, that he might enjoy Pallet's perplexity, and be at hand to protect him from insult.
>
> The poor painter having lost his guide, was almost distracted with anxiety, and stalked about the room, in quest of him, with such huge strides and oddity of gesture, that he was followed by a whole multitude, who gazed at him as a preternatural phænomenon. (*PP*, 219)

As will be the case with other pranks arranged by Peregrine, the one he organises at the masquerade is the source of carnivalesque laughter, targeted at the grotesque body of cross-dressed Pallet, taking "huge strides", displaying "oddity of gesture" and thus making "a preternatural phænomenon". The aura of carnival becomes amplified in the continuation of the scene, when a masked nobleman "beg[ins] to be very free with the supposed lady, and attempt[s] to plunge his hand into her bosom", which is followed by yet another sexual attempt "in a manner still more indelicate". Pallet's response perfectly fits this carnivalesque poetics, as it takes the form of "a box on the ear", bringing the two involved to the verge of a fight. This, however, is prevented by Peregrine who, being aware of everything happening, decides to interpose (*PP*, 220). The first masquerade scene thus features Perry in the role of a master of revels, who both provides entertainment and brings it to an end when he finds it appropriate. The amusement offered by the protagonist contains the hallmarks of the carnivalesque as defined by Bakhtin (1984b), such as gender reversal, identity play, as well as sexual content and the grotesque image of the body.

The second masquerade attended by Peregrine likewise functions as an illustration of his prevailing disposition. This time, however, the protagonist does not appear as a frivolous prankster but as a determined and villainous libertine. The potential of the masked assembly that he wishes to exploit is its promiscuous atmosphere – the ball is supposed to serve as an introduction to

his seduction of Emilia. The masquerade proper is preceded by Perry's stratagem which aims at dissuading Emilia's friend from accompanying them at
the ball. The stratagem, typically of Peregrine, is itself a masquerading
scheme, in which the author puts on a false identity to misinform others:

> he conveyed a letter to her [Emilia's friend] mother, intimating, that her daughter,
> on pretence of going to the masquerade, intended to bestow herself in marriage to
> a certain person, and that in a few days she would be informed of the circum-
> stances of the whole intrigue, provided she would keep this information secret,
> and contrive some excuse for detaining the young lady at home, without giving
> her cause to believe she was apprized of her intention. This billet, subscribed *Your
> well-wisher and unknown humble servant*, had the desired effect upon the careful
> matron, who, on the ball-day, feigned herself so extremely ill, that miss could not,
> with any decency, quit her mamma's apartment; and therefore sent her apology to
> Emilia in the afternoon, immediately after the arrival of Peregrine, who pretended
> to be very much afflicted with the disappointment, while his heart throbbed with a
> transport of joy. (*PP*, 349)

This short report of Perry's stratagem exudes an aura of deception and dissimulation, which most appropriately introduces the masked ball. It is not
only about Peregrine's fraudulent letter[3] and pretended sadness at the resolution of the plot but also about the friend being endowed with false identity by
the protagonist and her mother "feign[ing] herself so extremely ill".

As is foreshadowed by the preceding stratagem, the masked ball centres
around Perry's treacherous disposition, which manifests itself in his vicious
and cold-blooded, but at the same time systematic and carefully planned,
attempt at seducing his companion. The power relationship between the protagonist and Emilia is indicated by their costumes – that of Pantaloon and
Columbine respectively. In a standard plot of eighteenth-century harlequin-
ades, Pantaloon was Columbine's devious and greedy father who attempted
to separate her from her beloved Harlequin.[4] Peregrine by donning this particular dress situates himself in a dominant position, which he maintains

---

[3] Deceptive letters as part of masquerading schemes are by no means an innovative
theme in the eighteenth-century novel. The novels of the time abound in forgeries and
misinforming letters, which function as plot catalysts leading to narrative twists and
complications. The technique was also adopted by Fielding (Tom's fraudulent proposal to Lady Bellaston), which I commented upon in Chapter Three.
[4] Costumes referring to *commedia dell'arte* or harlequinade – a genre derived from
the former – were typical character costumes at eighteenth-century masquerades
(Castle 1986: 70).

throughout the masked ball. His scheme to seduce Emilia is by no means refined and consists of making his companion drunk at the ball and taking advantage of her afterwards in a previously arranged bagnio. The way he proceeds with the realisation of his plan is at times surprisingly ruthless:

> our adventurer concluded, that his partner's blood was sufficiently warmed for the prosecution of his design. On this supposition, which was built upon her declaring, that she was thirsty and fatigued, he persuaded her to take a little refreshment and repose; and for that purpose, handed her down stairs into the eating-room, where having seated her on the floor, he presented her with a glass of wine and water; and as she complained of being faint, enriched the draught with some drops of a certain elixir, which he recommended as a most excellent restorative, though it was no other than a stimulating tincture, which he had treacherously provided for the occasion. (*PP*, 349)

The Peregrine before our eyes is no longer a childish practical joker of the previous masquerade scene, and of the earlier part of the narrative in general, but rather a villainous libertine, who would stop at nothing to achieve his goal.

When his design proves unsuccessful – "Emilia had too much penetration to be imposed upon" (*PP*, 350) – he does not resign but transforms his facade. First, he pretends to be concerned with her safety, being worried about "a multitude of robbers and cut-throats" in the streets, and "urge[s] her, with a thousand remonstrances, to consult her own ease and safety" (*PP*, 350). Then, he plays the role of a desperate lover:

> He then fell upon his knees before her, and the tears gushing from his eyes, swore that his passion was wound up to such a pitch of impatience, that he could no longer live upon the unsubstantial food of expectation; and that, if she would not vouchsafe to crown his happiness, he would forthwith sacrifice himself to her disdain. (*PP*, 351)

When this disguise also turns out ineffective, the protagonist modifies his discourse and resorts to all the flatteries of gallantry he learnt during his stay on the Continent. He pompously addresses Emilia as "Divine creature" and "My dear angel" and tempts her with the prospect of becoming "mistress of [his] whole estate" (*PP*, 351), which however makes little impression on the prudent heroine. She remains unyielding to his advances and rejects him definitively, showing great power of observation in discerning his "little arts [...] practised to ensnare [her] heart", his "most perfidious dissimulation", "the mask of the most delicate respect" as well as "other impious stratagems" (*PP*, 351-352). In a word, she unmasks Peregrine and identifies him as "a treacherous villain" (*PP*, 352).

To recapitulate, as I have argued, Smollett's masquerade scenes do not display such a rich interpretative potential as the one in *Tom Jones* or, better yet, those in *Amelia*. In Fielding's novels, masquerades threaten the allegorical consistency of characterisation, as the participants reveal traits so far unknown and consequently unexpected. Both Roderick and Peregrine, on the other hand, are true to their currently prevailing identities when taking part in masked assemblies. Roderick attends them, just like other urban diversions, to reinforce his status as a man of fashion, whereas Peregrine, in accordance with the adopted roles of a prankster and a libertine, attempts to exploit their comic and promiscuous potential.

2. Masquerading pranks and stratagems

Apart from the masquerade scenes proper, the two novels offer numerous quasi-masquerades in the form of practical jokes and stratagems, which are both well-grounded in the picaresque tradition. The former category, under the Spanish name of *burla*, was one of those that constituted the picaresque as a genre. Its literal meaning – "it deceives" – only proves that deception forms the basis for picaresque pranks and as such is central to Smollett's understanding of the tradition (Gibson 2007: 573). Pranks and stratagems that the two protagonists arrange result from their performances in the roles of tricksters and men of stratagem. These roles, correlated with their homelessness and dislocation, are also indispensably dependent on the masquerade and dissimulation. What accurately defines Roderick's and especially Peregrine's function in Smollett's world are Bakhtin's observations on the roles of the rogue, the clown and the fool in the novel:

> They are life's maskers; their being coincides with their role, and outside this role they simply do not exist.
>
> Essential to these three figures is a distinctive feature that is as well a privilege – the right to be "other" in this world, the right not to make common cause with any single one of the existing categories that life makes available; none of these categories quite suits them, they see the underside and the falseness of every situation. Therefore, they can exploit any position they choose, but only as a mask. (Bakhtin 1981: 159)

As Bakhtin continues, the picaresque novel, and eighteenth-century fiction in general, feature protagonists who, thanks to their distanced position, expose and unmask conventions governing social structures (Bakhtin 1981: 164-165). The motif of unmasking is clearly one of the basic ones behind Roderick's and Peregrine's pranks and stratagems, which can be best illustrated by probably the most celebrated stratagem of Perry's invention – Crabtree's fraudulent clairvoyance – in effect of which "the whole variety of character undisguised, passed" (*PP*, 474). What, however, I will focus on here is not the satirical dimension of the pranks and stratagems arranged by the two protagonists but rather the masquerading element they involve; in other words, all the masks and disguises put on either by the protagonists or by other characters involved in the process of carrying them out.

In *Roderick Random*, where the intensity with which pranks and stratagems interlard the narrative is rather lower than in Smollett's second novel, there are three basic structures governing their arrangement: surviving, taking revenge and fooling a friend. There is a variety of ways in which Roderick exercises his masquerading potential through carrying them out. In Chapter VIII, when Rory and Strap find themselves in the same room with a pedlar who is being sought by an armed thief, they let him run away and design "a proper method of behaviour, to render [them] unsuspected in the morning", which, in a word, comes down to pretending ignorance through producing "affected surprize", "feigned amazement" or "seeming concern" (*RR*, 44). In Chapter XLIV, when surviving is tantamount to quitting the army, Roderick assumes the role of Straps's long-lost brother and makes the other ask for his discharge. The most elaborate stratagems are those which are inspired by Roderick's determination to take revenge on his enemies. In Chapter XX the protagonist's design to pay Captain O'Donnell back for his assault comprises two masquerading techniques. First, he forges a letter in which, putting on the mask of a lady whom the captain holds in affection, he proposes a meeting. Then, having provided both himself and his companion Strap with disguises, they interrupt him on his way to his inamorata and chastise him severely (*RR*, 102). Taking revenge on Melinda, in turn, is probably even more complex. In order to fill her with envy, Roderick organises a ball in the character of a French marquis, accompanied by Miss Gripewell playing the role of a rich heiress. To expose his antagonist to further ridicule, he sets Banter's barber on her, who, having been equipped with "a tawdry suit of cloaths", acts the part of "a very pretty fellow, just returned from his travels" (*RR*, 261). As the narrator reports it, the metamorphosed barber took her out, and acted his part with such ridiculous extravagance, that the mirth of the whole company was excited at his expence, and his partner so much ashamed, that before the country dances began, she retired in great confusion, under pretence of being taken suddenly ill [...]. (*RR*, 261)

Just as surviving and taking revenge lie at the core of Roderick's stratagems, fooling his friends forms the basis for his pranks. The principle behind these pranks is triggering off extreme reactions in their friends, which can be easily turned into ridicule. It can be best exemplified by two scenes in which Rory mocks Morgan and Strap respectively. When he is taken by a fever on board the Thunder, he fools Morgan into believing that he is dead "by fixing [his] eyes, and dropping [his] under-jaw", and by assuming a "distortion of [his] face", convinces the other that he "must have had a strong struggle" (*RR*, 167). As if that were not enough, when Morgan proceeds to "perform the last duty of a friend, in closing [his] eyes and [his] mouth", Roderick "suddenly snap[s] at his fingers", making the other look "pale as ashes, and [...] like the picture of horror" – an appearance Roderick cannot help laughing at (*RR*, 168). Strap, in turn, falls victim to Roderick's mockery when the latter realises the uneasiness with which his friend has been expecting to learn about the protagonist's achievements at a gaming table. Having "guessed the situation of his thoughts", Roderick prolongs the suspense, and through "assuming a sullen look" and "a peremptory tone", arouses feelings of hopelessness in his friend (*RR*, 276-277). When Roderick finally reveals the true state of affairs, the abrupt reversal of fortune gives way to Strap's ridiculous behaviour: "he danced about the room, in an extasy [...] So that [Roderick] was afraid the sudden change of fortune had disordered his intellects, and that he was run mad with joy" (*RR*, 277).

The concentration of practical jokes and stratagems in *Peregrine Pickle* is even higher. Consequently, there is naturally a greater diversity in terms of structures underpinning them, so that at times it is even hard to discern any governing structures or principles at all. As Grant argues, even if Perry was originally conceived as a medium of satire, he lacks moral principles which could impart the satire with meaning, and thus his life is, in fact, reduced to "a practical joke [...], endlessly and tediously repeated" (Grant 1977: 48). What can then shed more light on Peregrine's games is Bakhtinian carnivalesque – Peregrine in the role of the fool chastising society comes up with "highly developed forms of games", including "carnival, disguise, and the masquerade" (Skinner 1996: 23), and exudes an aura of the carnivalesque over all the presented events.

It would be too tedious a task to discuss all the pranks and stratagems in detail, and consequently I will focus here only on the masquerading techniques Peregrine repetitiously adopts. The one he exercises when still an infant is feigning death, which, as I have pointed out, is also one of those Roderick has at his disposal. Peregrine resorts to it when fooling uncle Trunnion (*PP*, 67) as well as when arranging a stratagem which is to expose Emilia's true feelings for him (*PP*, 497-498). He also proves capable of forgery when still a child; again entertaining himself at the expense of his uncle drafting letters signed with the name of the latter (*PP*, 80, 85). Another form of childish masquerade for which Peregrine has a special liking is putting on ghastly figures. For example, he is able to frighten uncle Trunnion with an apparition made from "a leathern vizor", "the jaws of a shark" and "a couple of broad glasses instead of eyes" (*PP*, 81). He also displays predilection for the macabre some time later, when he offers to cover the bruises on his tutor Jolter's face with "a slight coat of flesh-colour", which provides "a staring addiction to the natural ghastliness of his features", making the latter bear "a very apt resemblance to some of those ferocious countenances that hang over the doors of certain taverns and alehouses, under the denomination of the Saracen's head" (*PP*, 116). A further technique is the intentional use and transformation of his voice and countenance, which I have already discussed along with other uses of the body. Finally, external circumstances and surroundings are at times also part of Perry's masquerades. He frequently arranges his pranks and stratagems under cover of darkness, which provides him with a natural mask concealing his identity, not only for his ghastly pranks but also, for example, for a fake duel (*PP*, 161), nocturnal meetings with the fair sex (e.g. *PP*, 186, 276) or attempts to chastise his adversaries (e.g. *PP*, 146-147). In his schemes he is also mindful of his immediate surroundings, hiding himself "under a large table" (*PP*, 253) or "behind a hedge" (*PP*, 356), which brings to mind conventional seventeenth- and eighteenth-century theatrical motifs.

An indispensable element of Peregrine's masquerading pranks and stratagems is the participation of his comrades. When Perry forges a letter of recommendation in the name of his uncle, Hatchway is to "personate the man in whose favour it was feigned to be writ" (*PP*, 84). On another occasion, when he arranges a fake duel between his father and uncle (satiating the latter's pride), Godfrey Gauntlet is asked to "personate old Pickle's friend", the role of the antagonist being played by Peregrine himself. They both proceed to the field "being muffled in a greatcoat, which, with the dimness of the light, effectually shield[s] them from the knowledge of the one-eyed commander" (*PP*, 161). The most celebrated instance of Peregrine's friends' participation in his masquerading endeavours is the fraudulent clairvoyance of the misanthrope Crabtree (*PP*, 459-474), which, however, deserves a detailed commentary.

What makes the episode special is the complexity with which different patterns of the masquerade cooperate. The constitutive pattern is the following: Peregrine persuades Crabtree to wear the mask of a counselling clairvoyant and makes his valet personate the fortune-teller's assistant under the name of Hadgi Rourk; the enterprise is to be housed in a previously hired apartment, which itself is subject to transformation "being furnished with the apparatus of a magician, such as globes, telescopes, a magic lanthorn, a skeleton, a dried monkey, together with the skins of an alligator, otter and snake" (*PP*, 460). This basic masquerade, however, is interrelated with other complementary patterns. The whole venture may succeed through Crabtree's feigned deafness, thanks to which the misanthrope has accumulated vast knowledge of society's rumours and secrets. In other words, Crabtree's constant masquerade guarantees a successful execution of the new masquerading stratagem. Furthermore, Peregrine himself plays a double game – he "affect[s] to talk of the pretensions of this sage with ridicule and contempt" (*PP*, 460) in order to ingratiate himself with possible clients and thus obtain valuable information (a similar double game is played by his valet). As if that were not enough, Crabtree's clients are masquerading characters themselves. The fraud is visited by a lady dressed in her maid's clothes, who at the same time is personating her mistress, by a lady disguised as "the wife of a substantial tradesman", by a lady wearing a mask or by a Levite disguised as a country squire (*PP*, 460, 463, 471). In sum, Perry's stratagem is constituted by dual masquerades on the part of Crabtree, himself and his valet, and provides space for masked performances on the part of society.

To recapitulate, Roderick's and Peregrine's pranks and stratagems are among the most transparent ways in which the two protagonists expose their masquerading potential. There is a variety of reasons behind their execution and a variety of ways in which they are carried out, but what they all have in common is a potential which makes the doers, those cooperating and those affected put on masks, wear disguises, conceal or transform identity. If life in Smollett's universe seems at times reduced to a practical joke, to elaborate on Grant's metaphor, it is this potential that most appropriately defines it.

3. Confusions of identity

The manifestations of "the ephemerality of both social and physical identity" I have discussed so far are also related to the abundance of scenes in which identities are mistaken, confused or not recognised (Blackwell 2011: 426). Naturally, this refers not only to Roderick and Peregrine – other characters are also frequently endowed with false identities or not identified, which all contributes to the atmosphere of instability regarding the self. However, on the same basis as before, my scope will be the two eponymous protagonists. I have already dealt with their mutable and changeable identities, and now it is the way they are perceived by others that merits attention.

An accurate introduction to this discussion can be found in Banter's commentary on Roderick's obscure image in the London high life:

> One suspects you to be a Jesuit in disguise; another thinks you are an agent from the pretender; a third believes you to be an upstart gamester, because no body knows any thing of your family or fortune; a fourth is of opinion, that you are an Irish fortune-hunter. (*RR*, 250)

This controversy over Roderick's identity not only reveals a lot about the social context – in the masquerading metropolis, to use the idea from the epigraph, imposture and disguise are taken for granted – but also about Roderick's proteanism. In fact, all these attributed identities are in some way related to the protagonist – at one point, he is invited to assume the role of a monk, some time later becomes a soldier, and finally, when already in the quality of a gentleman, he resorts both to gaming and fortune hunting. Of the four attributed identities related by Banter, it is the last one – "an Irish fortune-hunter" – that irritates Roderick the most: "This last hypothesis touched me so nearly, that, to conceal my confusion, I was fain to interrupt his detail, and damn the world for an envious meddling community" (*RR*, 250-251). Naturally, it is not fortune-hunting that touches Roderick but his alleged Irishness. National identity, thus, again comes to the fore as a category that is not negotiable, as the only limitation to Roderick's exercise of his protean and masquerading potential.

As Roderick reports, his whole life was marked by false readings of his character. As a young boy, he served as a scapegoat who had to accept various unjust accusations:

> I was often inhumanly scourged for crimes I did not commit, because, having the character of a vagabond in the village, every piece of mischief whose author lay

unknown, was charged upon me. I have been found guilty of robbing orchards I never entered, of killing cats I never hurted, of stealing gingerbread I never touched, and of abusing old women I never saw. (*RR*, 21)

These false allegations contribute to Roderick's image as "a consoling personification of randomness" – whenever something is difficult to be explained, it is attributed to the protagonist's doings (Blackwell 2011: 426). Later on in his life, Roderick is mistaken for the criminal Patrick Gaghagan (*RR*, 91), a corrupt rake (*RR*, 166), a devil or a zombie (*RR*, 195), a spy (*RR*, 210), "an Irish fortune-hunter, without either birth or estate" (*RR*, 307) or a "pretended son" of his father (*RR*, 362). Additionally, as I have previously demonstrated, the continuing modifications of his appearance make him a difficult object of recognition and identification – even his close friends, such as Strap, uncle Bowling or Morgan, fail to recognise him after some time of separation. All these troublesome identifications, false identities attributed to Roderick as well as the variety of roles he does take on make the reader wonder, as Blackwell argues, how it can all be "knit together into a single person" (Blackwell 2011: 427).

In *Peregrine Pickle*, scenes in which the protagonist's identity is mistaken do not create the impression of randomness, as is the case in the first novel, but are surprisingly related to the roles the protagonist does assume. Peregrine's passive masquerade is thus interrelated with his active masquerade. The first three misunderstandings regard his relationship with Emilia. The first results from Pipe's delivery of a forged letter (the original one being destroyed) to Peregrine's beloved one, in which the protagonist's original tender feelings are substituted with ridiculously pathetic remarks, taken by Emilia as a proof of her lover's levity (*PP*, 108). Then, when trying to become reconciled with her, he attempts to ingratiate himself with her cousin Sophy's father, who, however, "look[s] upon him as one of those forward fortune-hunters who go about the country seeking whom they may devour" (*PP*, 122). Finally, when his departure for the Continent has already been decided, Emilia is "invaded by a suspicion, that this scheme of travelling was the effect of her lover's inconstancy" (*PP*, 136). All these imputations, though groundless at the moment when they are formulated, foreshadow Peregrine's transformation on his grand tour and in its aftermath. Even though he never becomes a fortune hunter proper – his economic situation for the most part of his adventures is satisfactory – he does treat women as objects over which he can triumph to satisfy his "appetite and ambition" (*PP*, 305).

A similar correspondence governs other misunderstandings regarding Peregrine's identity. When he is taken for a robber (*PP*, 358), the mistake is well-grounded, given the whole ambuscade he has arranged and his roguish appearance – he bursts into the chamber where he wrongly supposes to find Emilia and her alleged suitor "with a pistol ready cock'd in his hand" (*PP*, 359). Then, in the final part of the narrative, when Peregrine falls out of Minister Steady's favour, the latter spreads rumours about Peregrine's alleged mental problems and "his disorder" turns out to be "the general topic of conversation" (*PP*, 559). Even though the rumour has no basis in reality, the narrator admits that "Peregrine's fiery disposition [...] would have actually justified any remarks of this kind" (*PP*, 559). What is more, his friend Crabtree himself, recalling Perry's "impatience and impetuosity", is on the verge of "becoming a proselyte to Sir Steady's opinion" (*PP*, 559). Finally, when the protagonist finds himself imprisoned in the Fleet, his misfortune again becomes a common topic "discoursed upon at several tea and card-tables" (*PP*, 576). As Crabtree reports, the way society has it is

> that Peregrine was a bite from the beginning, who had found credit on account of his effrontery and appearance, and imposed himself upon the town as a young gentleman of fortune. They rejoiced, therefore, at his calamity, which they considered as a just punishment for his fraud and presumption, and began to review certain particulars of his conduct, that plainly demonstrated him to be a rank adventurer, long before he had arrived at this end of his career. (*PP*, 576)

The reader is well aware that the true reasons behind Perry's imprisonment are different but at the same time cannot help but get the impression that there is a grain of truth in these allegations. Effrontery, appearance, imposture, fraud and presumption are all by no means alien to Peregrine and his conduct, and the reader is much more likely to share society's critical stance rather than sympathise with the imprisoned protagonist.

In sum, it should appear quite apparent that Roderick's and Peregrine's presence in the masquerade of the world clearly differs from that of Joseph and Tom. Fielding's protagonists do their best to distance themselves from the world of hypocrisy and affectation, even if it is at times impossible. Roderick and Peregrine, on the other hand, are true "men of stratagem", who do not hesitate to exploit their masquerading potential. This difference is most interestingly exposed through the motif of passive masquerade. Whenever Fielding's characters are endowed with some false identities, their role is always to highlight their true selves and expose their essential qualities. In

Smollett's novels, on the other hand, misunderstandings and confusions over the protagonists' identities are as a rule somehow related to their active masquerades and thus tell a lot about their protean selves.

Roderick Random and *Peregrine Pickle* feature protagonists who, being deprived of the basic psychological moorings – homes and stable family backgrounds – find themselves on the road, which provides them with opportunities to exercise their protean potential. Their proteanism is a response to their experience of the world in flux – they come to realise that in a world of instability their survival depends, on the one hand, on adaptability to changing circumstances, but on the other, on accepting and adopting the dominant patterns of behaviour; that is, role playing and the masquerade. Their journeys are thus constituted by numerous roles they adopt and masked performances they put on. This understanding of the chronotope of the road situates both novels within the picaresque tradition – one of the constitutive elements of which is a protean and masquerading picaro – and corresponds with the literary representation of the institution of the grand tour; an enterprise which was by nature correlated with the discourse of the self. Roderick and Peregrine as both picaros and grand tourists are also subject to physical transformations, which illustrate their subsequent metamorphoses. The two novels offer diverse variations on the masquerade topos. Apart from literal masquerade scenes, which function as vivid illustrations of the protagonists' prevailing dispositions, the novels abound in quasi-masquerades in the form of pranks and stratagems built around the motifs of affectation, fraud, disguise and impersonation. Roderick and Peregrine, just like Fielding's protagonists, are also subject to passive masquerades, when they are endowed with false identities by those who perceive them. Contrary to Joseph and Tom, however, the identities attributed to them are frequently closely related to those identities they do assume throughout their adventures, which can be taken as evidence of a rather different role they play in the masquerading world.

PART THREE

A SENTIMENTAL JOURNEY THROUGH FRANCE AND ITALY :
MASQUERADE AND SENTIMENTALISM

> —every thing in this world seems in Masquer-
> ade, but thee dear Woman—and therefore I am
> sick of all the world but thee—
>
> Laurence Sterne, *Continuation of the
> Bramine's Journal*

Chapter Seven

Tradition and Novelty in Yorick's *Journey*

The novels of Fielding and Smollett offered diametrically-opposed approaches to the categories of masquerade, travel and self, as well as the related idea of the *ancien régime* of identity. My aim in what follows will be to demonstrate that Laurence Sterne's *A Sentimental Journey through France and Italy* (1768) can be seen as a dialogic work juxtaposing the contradictory attitudes of Fielding and Smollett. I will argue that Sterne's work is a polyphonic texture which includes diverse stances on the categories in question. Therefore, I will study the masquerade as both the allegory of affectation and one's potential to change identity, travel as a teleological structure of self discovery as well as a series of random experiences and impressions, whereas the discourse of the self as grounded in both substantialist and anti-substantialist traditions.

This patchwork constitution of Sterne's work is a quality that accurately defines the disposition of the author himself. A certain anonymous writer of his time accounted for it in the following way: "one of the odd qualities of this very odd person, to join contradictions" (quoted in Ross 2001: 6).[1] Joining contradictions was thus a quality that already in Sterne's time was thought to define the author's character. His contemporaries were perplexed by the possibility of a single author publishing such dissimilar works as the bawdy *Life and Opinions of Tristram Shandy, Gentleman* (the first instalment appeared in 1759) and the latitudinarian *Sermons of Mr. Yorick* (the first two volumes were published in 1760). One can only wonder with what reaction the latter would have met if Sterne had not drawn back from putting in print the originally intended title for the work: *The Dramatic Sermons of Mr. Yo-*

---

[1] In fact, Sterne himself argued that personal identity is a complex and versatile category: "Man surely is a compound of riddles and contradictions" (*Sermons*, 188).

rick, by Tristram Shandy, Gentleman – "a yoking together of the Word of God, the playhouse, a jester, and a facetious fictional hero", as Ross puts it (Ross 2009: 12). The intended title clearly demonstrates that Sterne was very much aware of his established reputation as a man of contradictory faces. By no means, however, did he attempt to change it but rather reinforced it through his ambiguous social performances. Depending on his mood and circumstances, he would either "Shandy it" – that is, play the role of Tristram Shandy – or present himself as the good-natured and sentimental Mr Yorick. Sterne's patchwork identity is thus the immediate background for his *A Sentimental Journey*, which I understand as a work reconciling the author's two masks.

This complexity of Sterne's poetics can be most clearly exposed when read from the perspective of the Bakhtinian aesthetics of dialogue and polyphony. I will treat the former as the methodological framework for the study of the *Journey*'s double-voiced poetics, constituted by interweaving discourses of the masquerade and sentimentalism. The latter, in turn, will serve as an approach to the complexities of Yorick as a literary character. The application of the notion of polyphony, understood as "a plurality of independent and unmerged voices and consciousnesses, a genuine polyphony of fully valid voices" (Bakhtin 1984a: 6), is, I believe, justified, even though it was Fyodor Dostoevsky that was credited by the Soviet scholar with the title of the inventor of the polyphonic novel.[2] Originally, Bakhtin's argument was supposed to relate to a situation in which the narrator refrains from holding the dominant position within the narrative and makes the voices of other characters equally valid. In effect, the narrative becomes a space on which "the discourses of space and other interpenetrate each other" (Dentith 1995: 40). In the following study of Sterne's text, however, I will understand polyphony as a quality defining the narrator himself, who appears to be a versatile construction within which many equally legitimate voices operate. Yet, apart from the polyphonic construction of Yorick and the double-voiced poetics, which I will discuss later on, what also makes Sterne's text a rewarding object of a Bakhtinian reading is its generic status.

In his study of literary genre, Bakhtin argues:

A literary genre, by its very nature, reflects the most stable, "eternal" tendencies in literature's development. Always preserved in a genre are undying elements of

---

[2] In fact, Bakhtin himself noticed that Sterne's novels can be treated as prototypes of the polyphonic novel (Bakhtin 1984a: 227).

the archaic. True, these archaic elements are preserved in it only thanks to their constant renewal, which is to say, their contemporization. A genre is always the same and yet not the same, always old and new simultaneously. Genre is reborn and renewed at every new stage in the development of literature and in every individual work of a given genre. This constitutes the life of the genre. Therefore even the archaic elements preserved in a genre are not dead but eternally alive; that is, archaic elements are capable of renewing themselves. (Bakhtin 1984a: 106)

In other words, the genre's life is a series of constant renewals resulting from the evolutions of some undying elements; consequently, what always lies behind is the interplay of tradition and novelty. Seen in this light, Sterne's *A Sentimental Journey* is a text contributing to the renewal of travel narrative.

1. Sterne on travelling and travel writing

Sterne's attitude towards travel, especially the grand tour, is systematically articulated in one of his most celebrated sermons – "The Prodigal Son", published in the third volume of *Sermons of Mr. Yorick* (1766). Having vividly discussed the psychological intricacies of both the son and the father, the author changes focus, and being aware of the fact that the allegorical meaning of the parable has been "so ably set forth, in so many good sermons upon the prodigal son" (*Sermons*, 191), he decides to concentrate on the idea of travel as such. First, he draws the reader's attention to the natural disposition of man inclining him to travels:

> The love of variety, or curiosity of seeing new things, which is the same, or at least a sister passion to it,——seems wove into the frame of every son and daughter of Adam; we usually speak of it as one of nature's levities, tho' planted within us for the solid purposes of carrying forwards the mind to fresh inquiry and knowledge [...]. (*Sermons*, 192)

At this point, Sterne's argument about man's inherent curiosity, which stands behind the desire for visiting foreign countries, resembles other eighteenth-century texts analysing the importance and popularity of the institution of travel.[3] The quoted excerpt from Sterne's sermon seems, in fact, a paraphrase of Lord Kames's observations on the phenomenon articulated in his *Elements of Criticism* (1762):

---

[3] For an interesting survey of the eighteenth-century understandings of the category of curiosity, see Chard 1999: 26-30.

Men tear themselves from their native country in search of things rare and new; and curiosity converts into a pleasure, the fatigues, and even perils of travelling. [...] Curiosity is implanted in human nature, for a purpose extremely beneficial, that of acquiring knowledge. (quoted in Chard 1999: 27)

In this way, Sterne situates himself among notable figures of the British Enlightenment, arguing for the educational value of travel.

Having defined man's natural disposition towards mobility, Sterne proceeds to enumerate the advantages of travelling (if we "order it rightly"):

———to learn the languages, the laws and customs, and understand the government and interest of other nations,———to acquire an urbanity and confidence of behaviour, and fit the mind more easily for conversation and discourse;———to take us out of the company of our aunts and grandmothers, and from the track of nursery mistakes; and by shewing us new objects, or old ones in new lights, to reform our judgements——— (*Sermons*, 192)

So far, nothing extraordinary has been mentioned. Visiting other countries contributes to the traveller's educational development, awareness of foreign political systems and aspirations, as well as polishing his or her manners, conduct and aesthetic judgements. Furthermore, it separates the traveller from his or her immediate surroundings and directly exposes to diverse experiences. Having enumerated these advantages, however, Sterne concentrates on others, which are not to be found in any standard eighteenth-century approach to travelling:

———by tasting perpetually the varieties of nature, to know what *is good*———by observing the address and arts of men, to conceive what *is sincere*,———and by seeing the difference of so many various humours and manners,———to look into ourselves and form our own. (*Sermons*, 192)

In this way, Sterne points to those benefits of travel which seem to have been forgotten in the highly conventionalised tradition of travelling abroad. The sermonist highlights such essentialist categories as goodness, sincerity and selfhood, arguing that the traveller's exposure to the variety of the world will contribute to a proper understanding of them. Thus, Sterne argues that what forms the basis for the idea of travel is the ancient precept "know then thyself", in both individual and general terms – travel is to be a quest for one's self as well as the process of understanding human nature in general. This potential of the road is a quality that in Sterne's opinion is to renew the institution of travel and as such will play a crucial role in the author's conceptual-isation of sentimental travelling. What is also indicated in the quoted passage is the traveller's search for sincerity concealed by "the address and arts of men". In a sense then, Sterne's reflection over the idea of travel implies an anti-masquerade approach – the traveller's task is to reveal nature by taking off the masks of artificial addresses and arts.

The author's awareness of the need to reform the institution of travel cor-responds with his uneasiness about the prevailing conventions of travel writ-ing. Before he took up the role of the reformer, however, he proved to be a successful satirist. In a letter to Robert Foley, Sterne thus advertises the up-coming volumes of his *Tristram Shandy*: "You will read as odd a Tour thro' france, as ever was projected or executed by traveller or travell Writer, since the world began. / —tis a laughing good temperd Satyr against Travelling (as puppies travel)" (*Letters*, 391-392; Nov. 11, 1764). What he has in mind is, of course, the grand tour narrative in the seventh volume of *Tristram Shandy* (1765). The narrative, being a surprisingly literal flight from Death, reveals the author's profound understanding of the conventions governing contempo-rary travel writing. Tristram appears to be a highly self-conscious travel writ-er, mocking the typical motifs, ways of presentation and narrative patterns of the eighteenth-century grand tour account. He also frequently refers to the horizon of expectations about the genre and deliberately does not meet them for the most part. One of the most celebrated passages defining the peculiari-ty of Tristram's account is to be found in Chapter IV:

> "Now before I quit Calais," a travel-writer would say, "it would not be amiss to give some account of it."—Now I think it very much amiss—that a man cannot go quietly through a town, and let it alone, when it does not meddle with him, but that he must be turning about and drawing his pen at every kennel he crosses over, merely o'my conscience, for the sake of drawing it; (*TS*, 580)

This short passage accurately characterises the nature of Tristram's self-reflexivity; it is about mocking what in the eighteenth-century understanding constitutes the grand tour account as a genre – the observations on the places visited. Nevertheless, because consistency is not Shandy's strong point, the following Chapter V contains a detailed description of the town of Calais, very much in line with Charles Batten's definition of the genre as an "imper-sonal relating of facts" (Batten 1978: 41).

Elsewhere, the narrator satirically refers to another generic feature of grand tour accounts – the observations on the people encountered:

—No;—I cannot stop a moment to give you the character of the people—their genius—their manners—their customs—their laws—their religion—their government—their manufactures—their commerce—their finances, with all the resources and hidden springs which sustain them: qualified as I may be, by spending three days and two nights amongst them, and during all that time, making these things the entire subject of my enquiries and reflections— (*TS*, 604)

One can only wonder what is to be within Tristram's scope of interest if it is neither the places visited nor the people encountered. What comes to the fore is the dynamically moving Tristram, who finds it appropriate to interrupt the narrative only when deciding to digress and acquaint the reader with his rather non-standard or hobby-horsical observations and reflections. For example, the account of his visit in Paris does not include any conventional descriptions of the popular sights but a rather surprising enumeration of the streets the city contains (*TS*, 602).

Throughout the whole volume the travelling narrator makes it clear that his account is by no means a standard one. Tristram's satire, however, is not limited to mockery but offers substitutes for the ridiculed conventions, which will appear again in *A Sentimental Journey*. The first of these is certainly the motif of encounter, especially with the fair sex. For example, the traveller observes that even though the town of Montreuil "looks most pitifully", "[t]here is one thing however in it at present very handsome; and that is the inn-keeper's daughter" (*TS*, 588). What follows is a detailed description of her looks and character, which Tristram provides at the cost of meeting the reader's expectations by presenting "the length, breadth, and perpendicular height of the parish church, or a drawing of the fascade of the abbey of Saint Austreberte" (*TS*, 589). Soon after, the traveller reaches Amiens – a standard stopover in any grand tour itinerary – about which, however, he has "nothing to inform you [i.e. the reader]" but the fact "that Janatone [the inn-keeper's daughter] went there to school" (*TS*, 596).

A further peculiarity of Tristram's narrative is the interplay of dynamic motion and stasis. As a rule, Shandy's tour is a hyperbolically dynamic one, being, as I have mentioned, a literal flight from Death. In fact, as Tristram himself declares, its hasty nature corresponds with its literary representation – its fragmentation, infiniteness and abruptness result from the fact that the narrator "*wrote-galloping*" (*TS*, 580). Among various narrative techniques representing Tristram's haste are enumerations, parallelisms of subsequent structures and run-on-lines:

And so making all possible speed, from

Ailly au clochers, I got to Hixcourt,
from Hixcourt, I got to Pequignay, and
from Pequignay, I got to AMIENS [...] (*TS*, 596)

Such passages of acceleration, in which discourse time is much shorter than story time, are interlarded with moments of stasis, in which the narrator digresses or becomes preoccupied with seemingly insignificant issues, such as the already-mentioned enumeration of Parisian streets or the absurdist story of the abbess of Andouillets and a novice (Chapter XXI). Admittedly, the interplay of acceleration and stasis is typical of travel narratives, in which the narrator is expected to account not only for the road gone down but also for his or her observations and reflections. Tristram's peculiarity as a travel writer, however, lies in his proneness to interrupt the narrative when it is not expected at all or in a manner that is not expected – for example, he meets the reader's expectations and provides some commentary on Paris, but the content of the commentary appears to be entirely irrelevant. The object of satire in this case is quite clear – Sterne ridicules the standard itinerary of the Continental tour, the canon of sights and places to be commented upon, and the derivative and conventionalised ways of writing about them. He suggests that other considerations may become equally valid objects of the traveller's attention and that the manner of representing them in literature may differ from the received standard.

Finally, there are elements of sentimentalism in Tristram's account, which are thought of as yet another substitute for the missing representations of the commonplace objects. One notable example of this is the interpolated tale of two sentimental lovers from Lyons – Amandus and Amanda – whose tomb for Tristram is "as valuable as that of Mecca, and so little short, except in wealth, of the Santa Casa itself" (*TS*, 629). Tristram openly pronounces the superiority of the sentimental story related to the place over any work of art it might contain: "There is a soft æra in every gentle mortal's life, where such a story affords more *pabulum* to the brain, than all the *Frusts*, and *Crusts*, and *Rusts* of antiquity, which travellers can cook up for it" (*TS*, 628). At the same time, the narrator, as a "gentle mortal", admits to being under strong influence of both the story and the tomb testifying to the lover's feeling: "such a kind of empire had it establish'd over me, that I could seldom think or speak of Lyons—and sometimes not so much as see even a *Lyons-waistcoat*, but this remnant of antiquity would present itself to my fancy" (*TS*, 629). The narrator's credulity and seriousness at this point are at least dubious, but the ambiguity of sentimentalism is a quality inherent in the mood, and I will discuss it as such later on.

To recapitulate, the sermon on the Prodigal Son and the grand tour narrative in *Tristram Shandy* testify to Sterne's dialogue with the tradition of both the grand tour as an institution and its literary representations. The sermon includes not only typical observations on the benefits of travel but also provides rather non-standard remarks on the importance of discovering one's self and human nature in general, which follow from the sermonist's preoccupation with the classical precept "know then thyself". Volume VII of *Tristram Shandy*, in turn, reveals the author's uneasiness about the prevailing conventions of grand tour accounts. In a satirical vein, the narrating traveller not only mocks typical features of the genre, and thus the reader's expectations, but also foreshadows the ways in which the grand tour account as a form will be renewed by *A Sentimental Journey*.

2. *A Sentimental Journey* and the tradition of grand tour accounts

What clearly situates Sterne's *Journey* within the tradition of grand tour accounts is not necessarily the Continent as the object of representation (especially given the non-standard way in which the places visited are accounted for) but the educational purpose, which is explicitly stated after Yorick's first encounter with the Franciscan Father Lorenzo in Calais: "I have only just set upon my travels; and shall learn better manners as I get along" (*ASJ*, 11). Elsewhere, the traveller declares "a mortal aversion for returning back no wiser than [he] set out" and proclaims his journey to be "one of the greatest efforts [he] ha[s] ever made for knowledge" (*ASJ*, 91). The idea of improvement thus lies behind the travels of Yorick, who is supposed to become a better man thanks to all the experiences he will have gone through along his way. What is not clear at this point, however, is the traveller's understanding of the idea of improvement. As becomes apparent in the course of his narrative, the lesson he expects to take on his tour corresponds to the nature of travelling he advocates. In the "Preface" (which, however, is not included at the beginning of the narrative), the narrator puts forward a curious classification of travellers:

> the whole circle of travellers may be reduced to the following *Heads*.
>
> Idle Travellers,
> Inquisitive Travellers,

> Lying Travellers,
> Proud Travellers,
> Vain Travellers
> Splenetic Travellers.

> Then follow the Travellers of Necessity.
> The delinquent and felonious Traveller,
> The unfortunate and innocent Traveller,
> The simple Traveller,
> And last of all (if you please) The

> Sentimental Traveller (meaning thereby myself) who have travell'd, and of which I am now sitting down to give an account— (*ASJ*, 15)

The classification, however satirical, proves Sterne's acquaintance with travel writing and the institution of travel in general.[4] Being aware of various forms it took, he feels the need to distinguish a new category which would most accurately render the nature of his journey. As the unique Sentimental Traveller, he informs the reader about the "*Novelty of* [his] *Vehicle*" (*ASJ*, 15), believing that "both [his] travels and observations will be altogether of a different cast from any of [his] fore-runners" (*ASJ*, 15). A similar conviction about the *Journey*'s innovativeness is expressed in one of his letters addressed to his daughter: "I have laid a plan for something new, quite out of the beaten track" (*Letters*, 536; Feb. 23, 1767).

A major novelty concerns the shift from linearity to circularity, which makes the narrative "an unprecedented travelogue of subjective spiritual exploration" (Curley 1990: 203). In terms of Tzvetan Todorov's taxonomy, Yorick's sentimental journey is a spiritual journey of the interior (as opposed to material journeys of the exterior) (Todorov 1995: 62). Thus, Sterne's renewal of the genre, as foreshadowed in Volume VII of *Tristram Shandy*, concerns the basic generic constituent of travel narrative – movement through space. What in Tristram's narrative took the form of a dynamic interplay of stasis and motion is pushed to the extreme in *A Sentimental Journey* – there is hardly any mobility on the part of Yorick, and what constitutes his narrative are digressions, observations and reflections, as well as tableaux-like representations, none of which conveys the impression of motion. The linearity of

---

[4] As Curley points out, Sterne's library holdings included sixty-seven works of geographic literature, of which at least eight were grand tour guidebooks (Curley 1990: 204).

travel is also undermined by the fragmented narration – the narrative both begins and ends with an interrupted conversation and not, as would be typical of travel narratives, with departure and arrival. The reader soon realises that no spatial destinations will govern the narrative but rather the sentimental traveller's whims and fancies. His narrative, then, becomes a series of loosely related episodes held together solely by the figure of the traveller (Bystydzieńska 1993: 102).

As was the case with Tristram's satirical grand tour, it is not only the manner of presentation but also the object of presentation that is far from the conventional one. In Versailles, conversing with Count de B****, Yorick thus explains his interest in French women:

> —But I could wish [...] to spy the *nakedness* of their hearts, and through the different disguises of customs, climates, and religion, find out what is good in them to fashion my own by—and therefore I am come.
>
> It is for this reason, Monsieur le Compte, continued I, that I have not seen the Palais royal—nor the Luxembourg—nor the Façade of the Louvre—nor have attempted to swell the catalogues we have of pictures, statues, and churches—I conceive every fair being as a temple, and would rather enter in, and see the original drawings and loose sketches hung up in it, than the transfiguration of Raphael itself. (*ASJ*, 111).

At this point, it becomes clear what the traveller has in mind when writing about "learning better manners", "returning wiser" and "making an effort for knowledge". In his "quiet journey of the heart in pursuit of NATURE" (*ASJ*, 111), as he himself defines it, Yorick wishes to depart from the tradition of travelling which has hitherto been subject to the artifice of both the arts and human behaviours, and aims at discovering what is true and natural in others and thus also in himself. What lies at the core of his journey is the "know then thyself" principle, which implies both a search for the universality of human nature and a struggle for self-definition (Bystydzieńska 1993: 103).

Consequently, what is to serve as a substitute for typical objects of representation are encounters with others, which, apart from being themselves elements of the sentimental discourse, help to construct the image of Yorick as a sentimental traveller. It is through contacts with others that the narrator can best display his charity, passions and tender feelings; his encounters thus function as a "touchstone of his emotionality" (Bystydzieńska 1993: 103, my translation). Paradoxically, then, in renewing the genre of the grand tour account, Sterne undermines its basic generic constituent – the representation of the countries and people visited. The sentimental traveller comes to the fore instead and resorts to representation solely for the purposes of self-presentation.

The quoted passage is also telling of Yorick's approach towards the masquerade. His quest for nature implies seeing through "different disguises of customs, climates, and religion" in order to identify the essence of human nature. The masquerade, thus, obscures what is natural, and a true encounter with the other is only possible when the different masks one puts on are taken off. And this is what Yorick, the traveller unmasked, aims at. This objective corresponds with Sterne's prevailing mood in the final stage of his life, which can be discerned from his correspondence and *Continuation of the Bramine's Journal* (1767). In his letters for the year 1767, he believes his feelings to be "too nice for the world [he] live[s] in" (*Letters*, 582; To John Dillon, May 22, 1767); praises God "for [his] sensibility" and assures that his "feelings are from the heart" (*Letters*, 621-622; To Sir W., Sept. 27, 1767);[5] and also admits to having "long been a sentimental being" (*Letters*, 633; To the Earl of——, Nov. 28, 1767). The epigraph to this part, taken from the latter work, points to Sterne's binary distinction between the world "in Masquerade" and his beloved person (*BJ*, 190). In general terms, I would argue that what Sterne sets in opposition is a sentimental union with another person and the masquerading world. Yorick's journey "in pursuit of NATURE" can be thus seen as the one on which the traveller escapes from the world of masquerade and devotes himself to the quest for unobscured essence.

In conclusion, Bakhtin's idea of a genre's renewal through the potential of some undying elements very accurately renders Sterne's attempt at modernising the grand tour account, which he successfully accomplishes in *A Sentimental Journey*. At the core of his reform lies the ancient precept of "know then thyself", which is an archetypal pattern of travel. Sterne's uneasiness about the form of grand tour accounts results from his dismissal of highly conventionalised itineraries and objects of attention. He destabilises the model of a grand tour itinerary (most notably by never reaching Italy) and

---

[5] I distinguish sentimentalism from sensibility in the way proposed by Janet Todd (1986) and Ann Jessie Van Sant (1993). Namely, I understand the former as "a moral reflection [...] or a thought, often an elevated one, influenced by emotion", whereas the latter as "emotional and physical susceptibility [...] revealing itself in a variety of spontaneous activities such as crying, swooning and kneeling" (Tood 1986: 7). In other words, I associate the former with the mind and the latter with the body (Van Sant 1993: 4). In fact, both words were frequently used interchangeably in Sterne's time.

draws attention to other considerations at the cost of typically observed and represented sights, manners and customs. The stopovers throughout his journey are not marked by spatial destinations but by sentimental encounters with others, thanks to which the traveller is supposed to derive knowledge of himself and human nature in general. This shift of attention is also reflected through the fragmented, elliptic and for the most part static narrative. The beginning and the ending, which both take the form of interrupted conversations, suggest a turn from linearity to circularity, even though the changing place names preserve a semblance of the former. Yorick's journey is predominantly a quest for the self, and subsequent departures and arrivals are mere pretexts rather than the fabric of the narrative.

Chapter Eight

The Poetics of Mask and Sentiment

I have argued that one of the basic aspects of Sterne's modernisation of the grand tour account is the vindication of sentimentalism as a disposition making the advocated pursuit of nature possible. Yorick's pursuit of nature is thus proclaimed along with the abandonment of the masquerade as artificial patterns of behaviour obscuring nature. Consequently, I will point out, sentimentalism and the masquerade are contradictory within such a framework of thought. This opposition is clearly visible in the epigraph to this part, in which Sterne's "dear Woman" is juxtaposed with the world "in Masquerade". Eliza is, in fact, a sentimental object for which the diarist can only sigh, being aware of the impossibility of their union.[1] Therefore, she functions as an ideal against which his sentimentalism is defined. Distinguishing Eliza from the masquerading world, Sterne constructs a binary opposition between sentimentalism and the world "in Masquerade".

In the case of Sterne, however, seemingly clear dichotomies and lines of argument should not be taken for granted. Sentimentalism as a disposition and a pattern of behaviour reveals ambiguities, and they definitely merit attention if the author in question is Laurence Sterne – "the great master of ambiguity", as Nietzsche labelled him (1986: 238). In what follows I will trace the dialogic nature of Sterne's sentimentalism, arguing that the poetics of *A Sentimental Journey* is constituted by an interplay of seemingly contradictory elements.

---

[1] Eliza Draper was the wife of Daniel Draper, a director of the East India Company, and had to leave London and return to Bombay shortly after her sentimental relationship with Sterne began.

1. The mask of sentiment?

In his *Confessions*, Jean-Jacques Rousseau thus expresses his dissatisfaction with the high life:

> Why should it be that, having encountered so many good people in my youth, I should find so few in later life; are they a dying breed? Clearly not, although the order of men among whom I am obliged to seek them today is not the same as that where I once found them. Among the ordinary people, where grand passions speak only at intervals, the sentiments of nature are more often heard. In more elevated ranks the latter are completely stifled, while, from behind a mask of sentiment, all that speaks is self-interest and vanity. (Rousseau 2000: 144)

Rousseau, typically of him, juxtaposes nature with civilisation, but what is of greater importance for my argument is the fact that already one of the pioneers and most enthusiastic advocates of sentimentalism recognises its potential to become merely a mask and thus something that it by definition rejects. Contemporary criticism has also addressed this ambivalence – affectation, posturing, theatricality or performance are frequently invoked in recent studies of the phenomenon, even though they openly undermine the advocated cult of nature and authenticity.[2]

In an attempt to reconcile these paradoxes, Paul E. Parnell coins the term "Sentimental Mask", suggesting a close connection between the seemingly incompatible ideas of masquerade and sentimentalism. According to the critic, "sentimental thinking" is, in fact, a dialogic disposition "balanced delicately between hypocrisy and sincerity, simplicity and duplicity, self-consciousness and spontaneity" (Parnell 1963: 530). What, however, raises doubts, at least with regard to Sterne, is Parnell's conviction about the stability of the sentimentalist's self: "the sentimentalist sees himself as sincerely, simply, and spontaneously virtuous, but only achieves this belief at the cost of a constant demonstration to himself that his mask of virtue and his face are one" (Parnell 1963: 530). This unity of the self would be hard to defend in the case of Yorick, who himself undermines it declaring that "THERE is not a more perplexing affair in life to [him], than to set about telling any one who [he is]" (*ASJ*, 112), and that "there is nothing unmixt in this world" (*ASJ*, 116). The quest for the unity of the self does not apply to Sterne's *Journey* – it is contradictions rather than unity that are in question here.

---

[2] See, for example, Bell 2000: 47, Wikander 2002: 79-89, Spacks 2003: 55-86, Manning 2004: 96, Goring 2005: 142-147.

The relationship between these contradictions has given way to various critical interpretations. What already in Sterne's time was considered dubious was the sincerity of the advocated sentimentalism (Howes 1974: 3). Zofia Sinko, accounting for the controversy, points to several both textual and extra-textual reasons. The former include the *Journey*'s excessive soppiness, half-heartedness, volatile mood and sexual ambiguities, whereas the latter are related to Sterne as the author of the bawdy *Tristram Shandy* and disloyal spouse and father (Sinko 1973: LV). These ambiguities were critically addressed already in the first half of the twentieth century in the studies of Putney (1940) and Dilworth (1948). Ever since their works were published, critics have pondered the authenticity of Sterne's sentimentalism, and the *Journey* has been perceived as either "the Bible of sentimentalism" or "mock emotionalism" (Sinko 1973: LIV, my translation). More recent studies focusing on these aspects of the *Journey* include the essays by Chadwick (1978-79) and Markley (1987), who argue for the performativity of Yorick's sentimentalism. In the twenty-first century there has been a tendency for reconciling the seemingly contradictory interpretations of Sterne's work. Pfister, for example, approaches Yorick's sentimentalism in a way that may be regarded as openly questioning classical logic: "Both his spoken and written sentiments and the sentimental vibrations of his body, the sensitive glances, the tender blushes and benevolent and sympathetic tears, are sincerely felt and a staged performance at one and the same time" (Pfister 2001: 89). Keymer, in turn, defines the *Journey* as "an exploratory, delicately balanced work that could be read as celebrating the refinement of sensibility or as mocking its shortcomings and excesses" (Keymer 2009: 89).[3] The critic concludes that bearing these qualities in mind, one should only approach the text considering both these interpretative possibilities, "for on close inspection the novel fails, or refuses, to sustain any clear distinction between sentimental sincerity and Shandean satire" (Keymer 2009: 89-90). Drawing on Pfister and Keymer, I will argue that sentimentalism and the masquerade are similarly reconciled in the *Journey*. As I have pointed out, the masquerade in Sterne's text stands for patterns of behaviour obscuring nature; thus, there is a close relationship between the masquerade and artifice, as both are notions juxtaposed with nature and authenticity. In what follows I will demonstrate that the discourses of nature and artifice, as well as the masquerade and sentimen-

---

[3] Being partially a mockery of the excesses of sensibility, *A Sentimental Journey* opened the tradition of sentimental parody, which culminated in Jane Austen's *Northanger Abbey* and *Sense and Sensibility*.

talism, are all equally valid in constituting the dialogic texture of *A Sentimental Journey*.

2. Sentimental encounters or masquerading schemes?
– The art of conversation

Conversation as a socio-cultural institution is a phenomenon usually associated with the long eighteenth century. It came into being much earlier with sixteenth-century normative court literature and was extensively addressed, for example, in Stefano Guazzo's *La Civil Conversazione* (1574), one of the earliest treatises on the practice. The treatise focuses on aspects which appeared to be crucial in the seventeenth and eighteenth centuries, when conversation was considered indispensable in refined society. Guazzo is concerned with such issues as the relationships between appearances and one's true character, between the individual and the community, between the private and the public spheres, and the courtly and political societies (Courtine and Haroche 2007: 111). Guazzo's treatise gave way to numerous conduct books on the art of conversation, which treated it as an essential component of one's social competence. In the seventeenth and eighteenth centuries its practice was, in fact, what lay behind the ideas of the salon (France) and the coffeehouse (England). In France, along with the publications of subsequent conduct books, conversation evolved into a highly conventionalised form, subject to various normative rules of etiquette. As such, in the seventeenth century it had already become subject to criticism, focusing for the most part on its artificiality and inauthenticity. One of the basic critical remarks about conversations was concerned with their being founded on appearances which hide true selves. Consequently, it was argued, conversations gave way to a situation in which the participants, exhibiting an artificially constructed public self, lost a sense of who they really were; they became "runaways from their true selves" (Courtine and Haroche 2007: 122-123, my translation). The concept of civility, which determined the form of the French conversation (Tadié 2003: 28), was so closely related to appearances and affectation that its criticism frequently revolved around the idea of masking and the topos of the masquerade of the world (Courtine and Haroche 2007: 149).

In the eighteenth century, conversation continued to be frequently addressed by numerous treatises and conduct books but also became an issue which aroused the interest of periodicals. It was then that conversation as a socio-cultural practice ceased to be limited only to aristocratic circles and evolved into a commonly shared experience.[4] In England, due to the emerging sense of Englishness and the need to differentiate what was considered English from what was considered French, men of letters were faced with the necessity of distinguishing the English conversation from the French conversation. What formed the basis for the differentiation was one of the prevailing stereotypes of the French – their alleged artificiality and lack of authenticity. It was argued, not groundlessly in fact, that the French practice was a highly conventionalised, insincere and contrived form and as such made a true communication of thoughts and feelings impossible (Tadié 2003: 30). The English conversation, in turn, was to be founded on what Mr Spectator called "the Old English Plainness and Sincerity" (*Spectator*, June 28, 1711, quoted in Tadié 2003: 30), and thus affected behaviours and the display of a facade concealing the true self in order to satisfy the company were superseded by "a quest for sincerity, for true and natural eloquence" (Tadié 2003: 31). The English conversation as a practice allowing the experience of sincerity at the cost of civility opened up "the whole space of sensibility" (Tadié 2003: 32). It became what constituted a sentimental encounter, in which the self and the other were to be joined in a natural union.

Sterne's place in "the age of conversation", to use Craveri's terms (Craveri 2006), was a very significant one given his status as a literary celebrity and his presence in the celebrated social circles not only in Yorkshire and London but also in Paris. Ever since he published the first two volumes of his *Tristram Shandy*, he was very much welcome in the elitist gatherings convened by his friend John Hall-Stevenson and in Baron d'Holbach's and Madame du Deffand's salons in Paris. As Briggs argues, "celebrity involves public performance" (Briggs 2006: 81), and thus the polished conversations Sterne attended were part of his scheme to sustain his popular status. His correspondence proves Sterne's awareness of the role of conversation and public performance. In a letter addressed to David Garrick, whom Sterne considered his close friend, the author explicitly accounts for his success in Parisian salons:

> I have been introduced to one half of their best Goddesses, and in a month more shall be admitted to the shrines of the other half—but I neither worship—or fall (much) upon my knees before them; but on the contrary, have converted many unto Shandeism—for be it known I Shandy it away fifty times more than I was ever

---

[4] The same could be said of masked balls, which, being originally enjoyed by the aristocracy exclusively, evolved into democratic forms of entertainment.

wont, talk more nonsense than ever you heard me talk in your days—and to all sorts of people. (*Letters*, 242; Mar. 19, 1762)

The passage above clearly indicates not only Sterne's success in Paris but also his ambiguous attitude towards the practice of conversation. In the light of the quoted excerpt, it is by no means founded on "Plainness and Sincerity", advocated by Mr Spectator, but rather on talking "nonsense [...] to all sorts of people". On the other hand, in the final years of his life, as his letters attest, he seems to be tired of "Shandying it" and expresses preference for private and authentic conversation, which best exemplified in his correspondence with Eliza Draper and with Ann and William James.

A similar ambivalence can be found in *A Sentimental Journey*. On the one hand, as a travel book the *Journey* is to a large extent based on Sterne's own experiences on his Continental tours, during which, as I have mentioned, he would "Shandy it away" more often than usual; on the other hand, as a "*Work of Redemption*", to use words attributed to Sterne (Battestin 1994: 191), the text was conceived to account for the author's true feelings and emotions. I would argue that the consequence is that the *Journey* represents the practice of conversation dialogically, exposing its potential for both a sentimental encounter and a masquerading scheme. A similar idea is put forward by Tadié, for whom Yorick "represents the transition between a form of conversation inspired by French theories which emphasises its social dimension, to a form determined by the English model which lays greater stress on sensibility" (Tadié 2003: 44). What, however, raises doubts in the critic's argument is the statement that Yorick's conversations are represented "through the lack of rhetorical artificiality" (Tadié 2003: 44). I will demonstrate in what follows that conversations in Sterne's text are constituted by seemingly exclusive discourses of the masquerade and sentimentalism, sincerity and fraud, as well as nature and artifice.

The first extensive conversation Yorick enjoys takes place at the Remise door in Calais. The protagonist converses with the lady he has previously seen "in conference" with the Franciscan monk. For the most part the scene seems to be an epitome of a sentimental conversation, and both Yorick and the lady appear to be naturally predisposed to it – the former with his self-proclaimed good nature, benevolence and the kind-hearted will to know the reasons behind the lady's sorrow and distress, and the latter with a face "—of a clear transparent brown, simply set off without rouge or powder—" (*ASJ*,

23), testifying to her naturalness.[5] Their union is endowed with a universal dimension, being perceived by Yorick as a consequence of the workings of Fortune:

> THIS certainly, fair lady! said I, raising her hand up a little lightly as I begun, must be one of Fortune's whimsical doings: to take two utter strangers by their hands— of different sexes, and perhaps from different corners of the globe, and in one moment place them together in such a cordial situation, as Friendship herself could scarce have atchieved for them, had she projected it for a month— (*ASJ*, 24)

Their conversation does not, however, rely on language. In Sinko's words, "a true communion of the hearts is founded on a communion of senses, especially of sight and touch" (Sinko 1973: XLV, my translation).[6] As "utter strangers" they depend on sensual contact, holding each other's hands, and consider silence to be even more meaningful than words: "The pulsations of the arteries along my fingers pressing across hers, told her what was passing within me: she looked down—a silence of some moments followed" (*ASJ*, 25). When they are joined by the Franciscan monk, silence is what sustains the conversation when they cannot come to an agreement through linguistic expressions: "—We remained silent, without any sensation of that foolish pain which takes place, when in such a circle you look for ten minutes in one another's faces without saying a word" (*ASJ*, 26-27). This period of speech-lessness leads to the ultimate reconciliation between Yorick and the monk, the foundation of which has been laid by the exchange of their snuff boxes. As Courtine and Haroche explain, silence is what makes an open and kind countenance ready to listen and enter into a true dialogue (Courtine and Haroche 2007: 141). Silence and natural body language are thus what form the basis for a sentimental conversation, being a reaction against the artificial and contrived conversation depending on an exchange of clichéd phrases.

Seeming to be an epitome of a sentimental conversation, the scene is not free, however, from elements of artificiality and the masquerade. The former are hinted at when Yorick considers himself to be in possession of refined

---

[5] Her face is clearly represented as deprived of what Smollett in his *Travels* called "[t]his hideous mask of painting" (Smollett 1979: 54). By highlighting the naturalness of the lady, Yorick clearly distinguishes himself from "the learned Smelfungus", who expresses indignation over the artificiality of the French.

[6] Van Sant considers sight and touch to be "the 'philosophical senses'", given their special epistemological function acknowledged by empiricist philosophers of the time (van Sant 1993: 84).

verbal skills. He claims to be acquainted with the "same *bon ton* of conversation [...] as in the days of Esdras" (*ASJ*, 23), proves able to "model" conversation (*ASJ*, 25) and expresses readiness to speak to the lady "with the best address [he] was master of" (*ASJ*, 29). The masquerade, in turn, can be discerned from the celebrated moment when Yorick and Father Lorenzo exchange their snuff boxes. The episode, regardless of its impact on the culture of sensibility (e.g. Lorenzo Order in Germany), raises doubts as far as its naturalness and sincerity are concerned. In fact, its status as a scene of mutual reconciliation or, better yet, as an index of Yorick's good nature and benevolence can easily be undermined if its immediate context is taken into account. Just before the monk joins the conversing couple, Yorick muses over the way the lady perceived his rejection of the monk's humble request for alms: "I set myself to consider how I should undo the ill impressions which the poor monk's story, in case he had told it her, must have planted in her breast against me" (*ASJ*, 25). The ensuing scene of reconciliation and snuffbox exchange, when read against the background of the quoted passage, can thus be seen as a form of public performance, which aims at presenting Yorick in the most favourable light.

In Goffman's terms, the protagonist displays his *front* (constituted both by *appearance* and *manner*) in a "dramatic realisation" which is infused "with signs which dramatically highlight and portray confirmatory facts that might otherwise remain unapparent or obscure" (Goffman 1956: 19). Yorick's performance in front of the lady, depending on the critical stance adopted, can be understood either in terms of *idealisation, misrepresentation* or even *mystification*, to use Goffman's categories. If the protagonist's sentimentalism is taken as a sincere disposition, the way he presents himself can be seen as a way of idealising his sentimental qualities. As Goffman explains, "idealisation" as a form of public performance "tend[s] to incorporate and exemplify the officially accredited values of the society" (Goffman 1956: 23). The reconciliation scene, seen in this light, aims at constructing the image of Yorick as an embodiment of benevolence; a quality which is to be admired both by the present lady and the reader.[7] On the other hand, if Yorick's sentiments are not taken for granted, his performance may be perceived as a "misrepresentation" – that is, a representation of "a false front" (Goffman 1956: 38) – or even as a "mystification", having "secret powers and mysteries behind [it]"

---

[7] The same might be said of Yorick's act of charity in Montriul, which is called by the protagonist himself "the first publick act of my charity in France" (*ASJ*, 47) – a phrase pointing to its performative nature.

(Goffman 1956: 46). Seen in this light, Yorick's reconciliation with the monk can be understood as a performance in the "mask of sentiment" with some hidden agenda. This hidden agenda is thus identified by Kraft: "Yorick can be read as a philosopher of sentiment, but he can also be read as a sensualist who tries to disguise, even from himself, the truth that his impulses are carnal, not sentimental at all" (Kraft 1996: 106). Drawing on Kraft's argument, it is possible to understand the scene merely as Yorick's masked performance, which aims at endearing himself to the lady. Seen in this light, Yorick can be considered "a libertine in masquerade habit", to use the invective formulated by an anonymous reviewer of Sterne's *Sermons* (*The Monthly Review* 1760: 424).

A similar duality may be discerned from other conversations Yorick takes part in. When in Paris, the protagonist expresses his disinterestedness in the place as such, with its "glittering clatter" (*ASJ*, 65), and comforts himself with the prospect of enjoying true conversations:

> —seek—seek some winding alley, with a tourniquet at the end of it, where chariot never rolled or flambeau shot its rays—there thou mayest solace thy soul in converse sweet with some kind *grisset* of a barber's wife, and get into such coteries!— (*ASJ*, 65)

As the sentimental traveller, Yorick is not satisfied with marvelling at cityscapes from a privileged position (through his hotel room's window) but wishes to immerse himself in the life of Paris through conversing with some local women in a remote spot. However, what initially seems to be a response to a heartfelt need then takes the form of a well thought-out scheme:

> I had given a cast with my eye into half a dozen shops as I came along in search of a face not likely to be disordered by such an interruption [an enquiry about the way to the Opera comique]; till at last, this hitting my fancy, I had walked in. (*ASJ*, 69)

One can have serious reservations concerning the sincerity of Yorick's sentimental disposition. He not only carefully selects the observed women, choosing the one who suits his whim, but also starts the conversation with an enquiry that has no *raison d'être* – he asks about the way to the Opera comique, having informed the reader that he "walk[s] forth without any determination where to go" (*ASJ*, 68). The grisette informs Yorick about the way, but the latter, instead of focusing on the message, is more attentive to the former's "cheerful" movements and looks, her "*tones and manners*" as well as "good natur'd patience" (*ASJ*, 69-70). Yorick informs the reader that she "repeated her instructions three times" (*ASJ*, 70), from which it can be inferred that the protagonist, with the intention of prolonging the conversation, makes the grisette understand that the repetitions are necessary. Typically of a sentimental conversation, it is not words that matter but sensual contact: "I remember, when I told her how much I was obliged to her, that I looked very full in her eyes,—and that I repeated my thanks as often as she had done her instructions" (*ASJ*, 70). Words, uttered repetitiously by both Yorick and the grisette, are meaningful only when taken as gestures; it is not their literal meaning that matters – Yorick does not really need the instructions and thus has no obligation to express gratitude for them – but the way they fulfil the deep eye contact; utterances matter as "*tones and manners*", so that the ear can complement the eye. This becomes apparent in the remaining part of the scene, when the reader learns that Yorick "ha[s] forgot every tittle of what she ha[s] said", which, he admits, is more that natural "when a man is thinking more of a woman than of her good advice" (*ASJ*, 70).

The nature of Yorick's conversation with the grisette is thus ambiguous. On the one hand, it begins as a scheme based on fraudulent and meaningless linguistic exchange; on the other hand, the verbal exchange becomes merely an excuse for a sensual union between the protagonist and the grisette, which is ultimately fulfilled when Yorick is feeling her pulse. The irrelevance of words and their incompatibility with true sensual experience is best rendered when the measurement of the pulse is interrupted by the entrance of the grisette's husband. The woman explains the situation in words which are completely at odds with the true nature of their sensual contact: "—Monsieur is so good, quoth she, as he pass'd us by, as to give himself the trouble of feeling my pulse—" (*ASJ*, 72). Throughout the whole scene words function as masks concealing true intentions and dispositions.[8]

Yorick explicitly admits to being well aware of the masquerading potential of conversation also when preparing himself for a meeting with Monsieur Le Duc de C*****, which, as the protagonist expects, should reduce the threat of him being imprisoned in the Bastille:

---

[8] This function of words is also addressed elsewhere, when Yorick endeavours to hide from La Fleur his concern about possible imprisonment in the Bastille through "talk[ing] to him with more than usual gaiety about Paris, and of the opera comique" (*ASJ*, 93).

> How many mean plans of dirty address, as I went along, did my servile heart form! I deserved the Bastile for every one of them.
> Then nothing would serve me, when I got within sight of Versailles, but putting words and sentences together, and conceiving attitudes and tones to wreath myself into Monsieur Le Duc de C*****'s good graces—This will do—said I—Just as well, retorted I again, as a coat carried up to him by an adventurous taylor, without taking his measure— (*ASJ*, 101)

I have already accounted for Yorick's ambiguous approach to language, but also serving as a masquerading technique in the excerpt above are "attitudes and tones", which hitherto have rather been associated with a sentimental union (the sartorial metaphor, I believe, is by no means accidental here). As if that were not enough, in an internal dialogue the protagonist expresses readiness to use his face as a mask:

> Go to the Duc de C***** with the Bastile in thy looks—my life for it, thou wilt be sent back to Paris in about half an hour, with an escort.
> I believe so, said I—Then I'll go to the Duke, by heaven! With all the gaiety and debonairness in the world.— (*ASJ*, 102)

Surprisingly enough, the protagonist declares that he would be able to convey deceptive emotions to his countenance. In effect, he undermines one of the fundamental assumptions of the culture of sensibility – the idea that faces, revealing emotions and dispositions, are indexes of the soul (see Benedict 1995). Yorick on many occasions proves that he shares this conviction and is a staunch physiognomist – he has a tendency to read faces and to inform the reader about the characters of the people he has encountered. Paradoxically then, through ascertaining his ability to present a masked countenance to others, he throws doubt on the sentimental politics of reading characters he himself advocates.

When the actual conversation about Yorick's possible imprisonment does take place, though the protagonist eventually decides to turn to Count de B**** instead of the Duc de C*****, he does not implement the masquerading schemes he intended:

> [The Count] seeing I look'd a little pale and sickly, insisted upon my taking an arm-chair: so I sat down; and to save him conjectures upon a visit so out of all rule, I told him simply of the incident in the bookseller's shop, and how that had impell'd me rather to go to him with the story of a little embarrassment I was under, than to any other man in France—And what is your embarrassment? let me

hear it, said the Count. So I told him the story just as I have told it the reader—
(*ASJ*, 109)

The "gaiety and debonairness" (*ASJ*, 102) in which Yorick intended to dress his countenance are in the actual conversation juxtaposed with his "pale and sickly" looks, testifying to the true state of his mind. The "mean plans of dirty address" and fraudulent "attitudes and tones" (*ASJ*, 101), in turn, give way to simplicity and truthfulness with which Yorick tells the Count about his concern – "I told him simply of the incident", "I told him the story just as I have told it the reader".

In fact, it is the conversation with the Count de B**** that explicitly defines Yorick's understanding of sentimental travel; it is then that he labels his travel "a quiet journey of the heart in pursuit of NATURE" (*ASJ*, 111). Furthermore, it is also then that he asserts his Englishness, the construction of which, typically of his time, sets the French as the opposite extreme and revolves around the notions of benevolence, naturalness and sincerity:

> should it ever be the case of the English, in the progress of their refinements, to arrive at the same polish which distinguishes the French, if we did not lose the *politesse de cœur*, which inclines men more to humane actions than courteous ones—we should at least lose that distinct variety and originality of character, which distinguishes them, not only from each other, but from all the world besides. [...]
> The English [...] preserve the first sharpnesses which the fine hand of nature has given them—they are so pleasant to feel— (*ASJ*, 119)

The oppositions included here between "*politesse de cœur*" and "polish", "humane actions" and "courteous ones", which refer to the English and the French respectively, help to define the "originality of character" of the former nation, which predisposes them to sentimentalism.

As if to remain consistent, Yorick constructs the representation of another conversation – that is, the one between himself and "the fair *fille de chambre*" (*ASJ*, 115) in the scene entitled "The Temptation" – in such a way as to bring to mind the idea of an authentically sentimental conversation exclusively. There are hardly any words uttered, and the conversation depends solely on an exchange of blushes and gestures as well as on sensual contact: "[the *fille de chambre*] gave me both her hands, closed together, into mine—it was impossible not to compress them in that situation –" (*ASJ*, 122). However, the true nature and the purpose of the conversation are rather obscure, and its conclusion is highly ambiguous, to say the least:[9]

> The foot of the bed was within a yard and a half of the place where we were standing—I had still hold of her hands—and how it happened I can give no account, but I neither ask'd her—nor drew her—nor did I think of the bed—but so it did happen, we both sat down. [...]
> A strap had given way in her walk, and the buckle of her shoe was just falling off—See, said the *fille de chambre*, holding up her foot—I could not for my soul but fasten the buckle in return, and putting in the strap—and lifting up the other foot with it, when I had done [...] it unavoidably threw the fair *fille de chambre* off her center—and then— (*ASJ*, 123)

Even though the representation of the conversation highlights its naturalness, its consequence and Yorick's imprecise account of it can undermine the sincerity of the protagonist's relation. He does not openly address the outcome of the scene, limiting its presentation to the vague "and then—", and insists that their gradual turn towards an ambiguously erotic posture is perfectly unintentional: "so did it happen", "it unavoidably threw the fair *fille de chambre* off her center". What clearly aims at highlighting the unintentionality of the scene is the syntactic form of the phrases – the agent is not stated explicitly, and the fact that they both end up in bed seems to result from some providential scheme rather than from Yorick's own doings. In effect, the reader cannot help but have the impression that Yorick puts on a sentimental mask when representing the conversation, which conceals his "carnal impulses", to invoke the argument of Elizabeth Kraft again.

Curiously enough, as if foreshadowing the reception of his conversation with the *fille de chambre*, in the following chapter entitled "The Conquest" Yorick defends his sentimentalism, and thus its representation, constructing an opposition between those who do express their true sentiments and those who hide them: "YES—and then—Ye whose clay-cold heads and luke-warm hearts can argue down or mask your passions—tell me, what trespass is it that man should have them?" (*ASJ*, 124). This opposition, resembling the one in the epigraph to this part, is used here rather paradoxically, for, in fact, Yorick himself masks his passions not stating openly what his true intentions and their consequences are.

---

[9] The word conversation itself could be a source of ambiguity in the eighteenth century, serving at times as a euphemism of sexual intercourse. *Cf.* Tom's "Conversation" with Lady Bellaston (*TJ*, 717).

Yorick's potential as a participant in purely contrived conversations becomes apparent in the chapter entitled "Paris" (*ASJ*, 145-148). It is there that he reports his popularity in Parisian salons: "Mons. Le Compte de B**** [...] [made] me known to a few people of rank; and they were to present me to others, and so on" (*ASJ*, 145). What follows is an enumerative account of his encounters with the representatives of the *beau monde*, who make Yorick converse about such diverse matters as English ladies, taxes or deist religion.[10] His presence among Parisian coteries, which might be taken as a fictional representation of Sterne's own popularity during his visits to Paris, leads, however, to his dissatisfaction with the high life:

> —the higher I got, the more I was forced upon my *beggarly system*—the better the *Coterie*—the more children of Art—I languish'd for those of Nature: and one night after a most vile prostitution of myself to half a dozen different people, I grew sick—went to bed—order'd La Fleur to get me horses in the morning to set out for Italy. (*ASJ*, 148)

In the archetypal terms invoked in the previous chapters, Yorick experiences here his symbolic death. His contacts with the *beau monde* have become "a most vile prostitution of [him]self" and, in consequence, he alienates himself from society. Being satiated with artifice, he yearns for nature and foreshadows his upcoming rebirth – just as "children of Art" have brought him down, "those of Nature" will be the agents of his revival.

The first of them is the insane Maria of Moulines, with whom the reader of Sterne was already familiarised in Volume IX of *Tristram Shandy*. In a sense, Yorick's encounter with Maria compensates for his exposure to Parisian artifice. It is set against a pastoral background, "in the hay-day of the vintage, when Nature is pouring her abundance into every one's lap" (*ASJ*, 149). Yorick's rebirth is thus to take place in a rural paradise, just as his symbolic death was a consequence of his urban experiences. Yorick comes across Maria "at a little opening in the road leading to a thicket" and finds her "sitting under a poplar", at the foot of which runs "a small brook" (*ASJ*, 150) – these features make the place a perfect example of a *locus amoenus* (Curtius 1990: 1995). It appears to be the most appropriate locale for a sentimental conversation, the climax of which is the union of tears:

---

[10] The vast spectrum of seemingly unrelated topics was, as Ryba explains, a peculiarity of conversations enjoyed in Parisian salons (Ryba 2011: 46).

[...] the tears trickled down her cheeks.

> I sat down close by her; and Maria let me wipe them away as they fell with my handkerchief.—I then steep'd it in my own—and then in hers—and then in mine—and then I wip'd hers again—and as I did it, I felt such undescribable emotions within me, as I am sure could not be accounted for from any combinations of matter and motion. (*ASJ*, 150-151)

In accord with the convention Yorick has followed so far, he emphasises the indescribability of a sentimental conversation, which is again constituted by sight ("I look'd in Maria's eyes" [*ASJ*, 150]), sensual contact and also physiological symptoms. Given her insanity, linguistic utterances cannot possibly lead to their mutual understanding. It is granted though by the closeness of their bodies, their warmth ("Nature melted within me" [*ASJ*, 153], "I'll dry [your handkerchief] in my bosom" [*ASJ*, 153]), physiological reactions and exchanges of looks. All this culminates in a pathetic self-recognition – "I am positive I have a soul" (*ASJ*, 151) – which marks Yorick's rebirth as a sentimental being. It is reasserted shortly after the couple separate in a lofty apostrophe to "Dear sensibility", the "great SENSORIUM of the world" (*ASJ*, 155). Yorick's rebirth becomes complete at the supper and dance at a peasant's house, inhabited by a numerous family of "children of Nature".

If Yorick's journey were truly about some evolution towards pure sentimentalism, "The Supper" and "The Grace", bearing openly religious, or quasi-religious titles, would certainly make a successful conclusion. Linearity, however, was never Sterne's strong point, which he visually demonstrated in the final chapter of Volume VI of *Tristram Shandy*. The scene at the peasant's house is followed by "The Case of Delicacy", in which Yorick is engaged in conversation with a Piedmontese lady and her maid. In contrast to his recent contacts with the "children of Nature", the present conversation depends solely on linguistic exchange and takes the form of "a two hours negociation" over the way they should spend the night in the same chamber (*ASJ*, 163). Its result is a ridiculous "treaty of peace", meticulously determining the behaviours of both sides and carefully represented, in a dialogised form, in Yorick's account. Contrary to sentimental conversations, whose naturalness made a successful linguistic representation impossible, the encounter with the Piedmontese lady can easily be rendered in words, as its only effect is a conventionalised treaty. Its validity, however, appears to be easy to undermine, as the simple exclamation "Oh my God!" (*ASJ*, 164) on the part of Yorick is tantamount to its dissolution and gives way to the ambiguous scene with the *fille de chambre* closing the whole narrative.

In any conversation Yorick enjoys, there is a special role ascribed to the interlocutors' bodies. The interweaving discourses of sentimentalism and the masquerade are thus constituted not only by the representations of the conversations themselves but also by the bodies of the participants. In fact, the physical is an inseparable dimension of Sternean conversations, irrespective of the critical stance adopted. If Yorick's sentiments are taken as sincere expressions of his state of mind, his bodily reactions, such as tears, pulsations or vibrations can only reinforce the impression. Conversely, whenever the protagonist's disposition raises doubts, readers focus their attention on conventionalised gestures and poses. The dialogue between sentimentalism and the masquerade is thus a dominant structure governing the poetics of the body in *A Sentimental Journey*.

3. A mask or a gateway to the soul? – The poetics of the body

One of the fundamental aspects of sentimental literature is the representation of somatic reactions to inner stimuli. In other words, it is necessary for true sentiments to be imprinted on the body, which, in turn, functions as an index of one's sentimentalism. As Goring puts it, sentimental novels elaborated on the notion of "sentimental somatic eloquence" and as such constituted "exhaustive dramatisations of contemporary thinking about the body's capacity to express character" (Goring 2005: 142-143).[11] Goring continues that sentimental heroes and heroines, whose bodies always transmit their true passions, are typically juxtaposed with "hypocrites and tricksters", whose bodies conceal their true disposition "beneath a deluding mask of sociability" (Goring 2005: 143). Sentimental figures are thus juxtaposed with masquerading ones on the grounds of the naturalness of their bodies. This juxtaposition, however, should not be taken for granted in the study of Sterne's *Journey*. As I have already demonstrated, naturalness and artifice, and also sentimentalism and the masquerade, are dispositions which can be ascribed to single characters or, better yet, single scenes. This duality is best visible in the pairing of Yorick and La Fleur.

Judging by appearances only – that is, by their clothes – one has the impression of them being set in radical opposition; the modest sentimental traveller finds his foil in a servant aspiring to become a Parisian *beau*. Yorick's humble clerical clothing is already addressed at the beginning of the narrative and functions as a definition of his modesty at the moment of departure: "—I

---

[11] For a comprehensive study of the eighteenth-century novel with reference to the tradition of physiognomy, see McMaster 2004.

went straight to my lodgings, put up half a dozen shirts and a black pair of silk breeches— 'the coat I have on, said I, looking at the sleeve, will do'—" (*ASJ*, 3). The quality of his dress does not change throughout the narrative, and nor does its quantity, which is openly stated when the protagonist meets La Fleur ("I delivered to him the key of my portmanteau with an inventory of my half a dozen shirts and silk pair of breeches" [*ASJ*, 44]) and in the "treaty of peace" in the final chapter of the *Journey* ("Monsieur is not worth a robe de chambre; he having nothing in his portmanteau but six shirts and a black silk pair of breeches" [*ASJ*, 163]). His simplicity in terms of clothes thus functions as an index of Yorick's identity (given the "literalness with which dress was taken to *make* identity" [Wahrman 2004: 177-178]), and the protagonist seems to be well aware of this potential. When he addresses his friend Eugenius while feeling the grisette's pulse, Yorick draws his friend's attention also to the way he is dressed:

> —Would to heaven! my dear Eugenius, thou hadst passed by, and beheld me sitting in my black coat, and in my lack-a-day-sical manner, counting the throbs of it, one by one, with as much true devotion as if I had been watching the critical ebb or flow of her fever— (*ASJ*, 71)

In the theatrical arrangement of the scene, he situates himself at the centre and draws attention to his appearance, before actually reporting his activity. The "black coat" and "lack-a-day-sical manner" are equally important in Yorick's presentation of himself as a sentimental clergyman.

La Fleur, in turn, makes himself known as a master of his appearance. In the chapter entitled "La Dimanche" the valet approaches Yorick "so gallantly array'd" that his master has difficulty recognising him (*ASJ*, 131). Sterne follows here the convention I discussed in the previous chapters – the sartorial metamorphosis and the consequent troublesome recognition. In accord with this convention, and similarly, for instance, to Roderick's transformation into a grand touring gentleman, Yorick provides a detailed account of the clothes making up the changed La Fleur:

> He had bought a bright, clean, good scarlet coat, and a pair of breeches of the same— [...]
> He had purchased, moreover, a handsome blue sattin waistcoat, fancifully enough embroidered—this was indeed something the worse for the service it had done, but 'twas clean scour'd [...]—and as the blue was not violent, it suited with the coat and breeches very well: he had squeez'd out of the money, moreover, a

new bag and a solitaire; and had insisted with the *fripier* upon a gold pair of gar-
ters to his breeches knees—He had purchased muslin ruffles, *bien brodées*, with
four livres of his own money—and a pair of white silk stockings for five more—
[...]

He enter'd the room thus set off, with his hair dress'd in the first style, and
with a handsome *bouquet* in his breast— (*ASJ*, 131-132)

Thus dressed, La Fleur situates himself in the numerous group of eighteenth-
century coxcombs and stands in opposition to the modestly clothed, clerical
Yorick. With his consumerist predilection for lavishness and his preoccupation with the material he acts as a foil for the demure Yorick, seemingly preoccupied with the immaterial. If Yorick, as he himself proposes, is to be
taken as "the Knight of the Woeful Countenance" (*ASJ*, 149), what makes La
Fleur a Sancho-like figure is his fondness for material goods.

This juxtaposition of Yorick and La Fleur on the grounds of their clothes
can be further supported by their language of countenance. Yorick, the sentimental traveller, represents his face as a gateway to his soul and meticulously accounts for the correspondence between his emotions, feelings and the
way they are imprinted on his countenance. He blushes when embarrassed;
"turn[s] pale with astonishment" (*ASJ*, 83); "look[s] a little pale and sickly"
when troubled (*ASJ*, 109); "stains [his] face with crimson" when ashamed
(*ASJ*, 117); and sheds tears when feeling "undescribable emotions within
[him]" (*ASJ*, 151). La Fleur, in turn, following the precepts of civility, is not
keen on revealing his true emotions on his countenance. As Yorick observes,

—I had a constant resource in his looks in all difficulties and distresses of my
own—I was going to have added, of his too; but La Fleur was out of the reach of
everything; for whether 'twas hunger or thirst, or cold or nakedness, or watchings,
or whatever stripes of ill luck La Fleur met with in our journeyings, there was no
index in his physiognomy to point them out by—he was eternally the same; (*ASJ*,
43)

Physiognomical readings of character, which enjoyed a revival in the culture
of feeling (Porter 1985: 393), fail when confronted with the civilised countenance of La Fleur, functioning as a mask concealing his inner self. Being
"eternally the same" means showing an unchanging facade which does not
correspond to the dynamics of one's person. A sentimental countenance, on
the other hand, is the one which perfectly renders the complexities of the self
and thus constitutes part of what Goring defines as "sentimental somatic

eloquence". What is more, La Fleur proves capable not only of displaying a civilised countenance masking what is happening inside him but also of modelling it for specific purposes. Surrounded by "half a dozen wenches", he "kisse[s] all their hands round and round again, and thrice he wipe[s] his eyes, and thrice he promise[s] he [will] bring them all pardons from Rome" (*ASJ*, 44).[12] Presenting an affectedly sensible countenance appears to be one of the techniques to which he resorts when endearing himself to the fair sex. Just like the beggar in "The Act of Charity", La Fleur succeeds in his contacts with women being able to put on what they expect to see.

These differences between Yorick and La Fleur can create the impression of some dichotomous paradigm standing behind the representation of their somatic constitution; a paradigm constituted by the binary oppositions of nature and artifice, as well as sentimentalism and the masquerade. In fact, just as is the case with the representations of the art of conversation, the dichotomy between the seemingly incompatible categories is by no means clear-cut. The bodies of both Yorick and La Fleur are spaces on which naturalness and artificiality, as well as sentimentalism and the masquerade are engaged in dialogue. If the body is to be read as a text, the texture of Yorick's and La Fleur's bodies is a highly dialogised form.

I have demonstrated that Yorick's clerical apparel, unchanging throughout, serves as an index of his sentimentalism, whereas La Fleur's foppishness as an index of his gallantry. In fact, however, both characters are capable of revealing dispositions which are rather contradictory to their seemingly well-established identities. When Yorick is about to leave his hotel room and set out for a wander in Paris for the first time, he "call[s] La Fleur to go seek [him] a barber directly—and come back and brush [his] coat" (*ASJ*, 66). Thus, he follows the convention I discussed in the previous chapters – just like the archetypal *beau* from Hogarth's *Rake Progress*, and a number of eighteenth-century protagonists (e.g. Joseph and Tom), Yorick must improve his appearance when entering the town. La Fleur, in turn, as Yorick himself admits, despite having "a small cast of the coxcomb [...] seem[s] at first sight to be more a coxcomb of nature than of art" and after some time – "no coxcomb at all" (*ASJ*, 43). What Yorick refers to, and what counterbalances La Fleur's foppishness, is "the genuine look and air of the fellow" (*ASJ*, 41), which is somehow surprising given what has been said so far about his face. Yorick's face, too, is not always consistent in its role as an index of his sen-

---

[12] *Cf.* "[Mrs Honour] thought fit to produce a Shower of Tears" (*TJ*, 813).

timental disposition. As I have already pointed out, Yorick also proves capable of hiding emotions (talking "with more than usual gaiety" rather than showing "a serious look upon the subject of [his] embarrassment" [*ASJ*, 93]) and expresses readiness to intentionally transform his countenance (by assuming "gaiety and debonairness" rather that revealing to the Duke "the Bastille in [his] looks" [*ASJ*, 102]).

The body of Yorick is also a space of continuous dialogue between physiological sensibility and posturing. On the one hand, in accordance with the convention of sentimental literature, Yorick frequently draws the reader's attention to the physiological reactions of his body, representing them as only natural responses to his sensibility – as Todd writes, "the body is a constant communicator" (Todd 1986: 99); on the other hand, he reveals a predilection for conventionalised gestures and poses.

As van Sant explains, Yorick's language of physiology is based on terms referring to "sensory processes" and "neural responsiveness", as well as on those which "feature the heart" (van Sant 1993: 9). The first category can be illustrated by such reactions as "a subtle sensation [Yorick] felt in the palm of [his] own" (*ASJ*, 25) or "an exquisite sensation [...] in wiping [the tears] away from off the cheeks of the first and fairest of women" (*ASJ*, 57). The reference to the doings of the nerves is present, for example, in such phrases as "so sweet and pleasurable a thing to the nerves" (*ASJ*, 26) or "he'll [the galloping postillion] go on tearing my nerves to pieces" (*ASJ*, 55). The heart, in turn, is addressed, for instance, when Yorick believes the grisette "look'd into [his] very heart and reins" and that he "could actually feel she did —" (*ASJ*, 75), or when he declares, on seeing the starling in a cage, that his "heart began to bleed" (*ASJ*, 97). The three aspects of his sensibility, however, are not always invoked separately and at times form what van Sant labels "the mixed physiological language" (van Sant 1993: 11-12). It is most vividly adopted in "The Temptation", when Yorick remarks on the exchange of blushes between himself and "the fair *fille de chambre*":

> There is a sort of a pleasing half-guilty blush, where the blood is more in fault than the man—'tis sent impetuous from the heart, and virtue flies after it—not to call it back, but to make the sensation of it more delicious to the nerves—'tis associated— (*ASJ*, 121-2)

The encounter activates Yorick's whole sensible being, and the associated reaction of the heart, the senses and the nerves is even reinforced, or made "more delicious", by the superseded moral concerns; it puts reason aside and gives way to a purely sensible pleasure.

The *Journey*, however, as Markeley aptly remarks, "suspends the reader [...] between passion and theatre" (Markley 1987: 221), and thus the sensible body of Yorick is counterbalanced by the theatrical body displayed in quasi-spectacles. In fact, theatricality itself is a significant theme in the *Journey*, and in sentimental literature in general – as McGuirk argues, "the world [in sentimental literature] was literally a stage – a backdrop for a series of histrionic gestures aimed at an audience of readers" (McGuirk 1980: 505). What helps create the proper background against which the theatrical body can be displayed are metaphors contributing to the aura of theatricality throughout the whole narrative. The life as stage topos, as constructed in the *Journey*, can be exemplified by such formulations as "[La Fleur] will be often upon the stage" (*ASJ*, 43); "[w]hat is grandeur in this painted scene of life!" (*ASJ*, 50); or "[t]he poor chevalier won my pity, and he finish'd the scene with winning my esteem too" (*ASJ*, 105). Furthermore, the very structuring of the novel, as Tadié explains, with brief chapter headings pointing, on the one hand, to the detail at the centre of attention and to the setting, on the other, suggests that reading the *Journey* is, in a sense, tantamount to watching a theatrical performance (Tadié 2003: 82). The critic rightly notices that empty spaces isolating each chapter visible on the manuscript of the *Journey* make the process of reading "not unlike the visual perception of a play" (Tadié 2003: 82). The idea of spectacle, however, is not limited to the communication between Yorick and the reader, which means that the performances of the former are not only intended to be observed and admired by the latter but find their audience also within the narrative itself. Being aware of the audience within the fictional realm, Yorick acts "like the actor of eighteenth-century theatre" (Bystydzieńska 1996: 41) and makes conscious uses of his body, which, in turn, are duly reported in his narrative. It is typical of him to account for his awareness of being looked at and the doings of his body at the same time. For example, being observed by two travellers he has already met, he "pull[s] out [his] monk's little horn-box to take a pinch of snuff" and "ma[kes] them a quiet bow" (*ASJ*, 28), whereas when being aware of "Maria observing", he t[akes] out [his] handkerchief" for "Nature melt[s] within [him]" (*ASJ*, 153). As Bystydzieńska observes, the precision with which Sterne accounts for the movements and gestures of his characters creates the impression of him "giving stage directions" (Bystydzieńska 1996: 43). The theatrical body also comes to the fore in the scene of feeling the pulse. It is then that Yorick suspends the progress of time and draws his friends Eugeni-us's attention to his motionless, posturing body "sitting in [his] black coat [...] in [his] lack-a-day-sical manner", having "applied two fore-fingers [...] to the [grisette's] artery" (*ASJ*, 71). The idea of spectacle inscribed in the scene, and thus its inherent pictorial appeal, made it a rewarding subject of visual representation,[13] and the theatricality of Yorick's body was at the centre of illustrators' attention. It is most vivid in Gilbert Stuart Newton's watercolour "Yorick and the Grisette", which hyperbolically depicts the protagonist's "lack-a-day-sical manner" by means of unnaturally crossed legs and the left arm propping up the body. Thus represented, Yorick performs parodic pos-turing and affectation rather than representing an epitome of sensibility. Yo-rick himself states that "Nature is shy, and hates to act before spectators" (*ASJ*, 131), and thus whenever he is aware of making a spectacle of himself, his body assumes poses and makes gestures which belong to the realm of artifice rather than nature.

To recapitulate, the analysis of the conversation scenes as well as the con-structions of the body in the *Journey* proves that the governing structure underpinning the narrative is what Bakhtin labels as "double-voiced dis-course" (Bakhtin 1984a: 185), referring to "the possibility and means for combining discourses belonging to various types within the limits of a single context" (Bakhtin 1984a: 186). In general terms, the dialogue shaping the poetics of the *Journey* is between the discourses of the *ancien régime* of identity, revolving around the notions of masquerade, theatricality, perfor-mance and artifice, and the language of sentimentalism, advocating authen-ticity, naturalness and truthfulness to one's self. In particular, however, the double-voiced principle refers to the idea of sentimentalism itself, whose ambiguity lies in the insoluble conflict between hypocrisy and sincerity, between being in jest and in earnest.

---

[13] For a discussion of Sterne's pictorial appeal, see Gerard 2006: 1-43.

Chapter Nine

Yorick as a Polyphonic Character

In his study of Dostoevsky's novels, Bakhtin introduced the idea of polyphony in an attempt to highlight their uniqueness in terms of a plurality of equally valid voices making up their versatile ideological constitution. I believe, however, that the category can also be applied to a single literary character to study his or her patchwork identity. This application, in fact, is also grounded in the Bakhtinian theory. The critic, in a 1961 essay rethinking the arguments put forward in "the Dostoevsky Book", writes: "A single consciousness is *contradictio in adjecto*. Consciousness is in essence multiple. *Pluralia tantum*" (Bakhtin 1984a: 288). The idea of the multiplicity of identity, of course, is not Bakhtin's invention. In fact, it is very much in line with David Hume's argument that "self or person is not any one impression, but that to which our several impressions and ideas are suppos'd to have a reference" (Hume 1975: 251), and that consequently, "The mind is a kind of theatre, where several perceptions successively make their appearance; pass, re-pass, glide away, and mingle in an infinite variety of postures and situations" (Hume 1975: 253).[1] I will argue in what follows that the construction of Yorick as a literary character can, on the one hand, be taken as an illustration of Hume's theory and, on the other, makes a rewarding subject of a Bakhtinian reading.

1. Yorick's intertextual and extratextual self

The figure of Yorick is perhaps the most complex literary creation in Sterne's *oeuvre*. His complexity depends, for the most part, on his existence in between different texts and also on his relationship to Sterne's life. In fact, his

---

[1] The affinities between Sterne's and Hume's approaches to the category of personal identity are also recognised by Dussinger (1974: 189).

identity as a literary character is an outcome of a dynamic dialogue between literary tradition, Sterne's life and his work.[2]

Chronologically speaking, his origins are to be found in Shakespeare's *Hamlet*, Act 5 Scene 1, in which the gravediggers dig up the skull of Yorick, "the king's jester". Taking over their find, Hamlet recalls the fool in the celebrated speech:

> Alas, poor Yorick. I knew him, Horatio. A fellow of infinite jest, of most excellent fancy. He hath borne me on his back a thousand times, and how abhorred my imagination is. My gorge rises at it. Here hung those lips that I have kissed I know not how oft. Where be your jibes now? Your gambols? Your songs? Your flashes of merriment that were wont to set the table on a roar? No one now to mock your own jeering? Quite chopfallen? (Shakespeare 2006: 335)

What the figure of Shakespeare's Yorick, and *Hamlet* in general, stood for in Sterne's understanding was, as Monkman writes, "its ever-tormentingly mysterious mixture of wit, humor, emotion, death, its jesting beside an open grave, its essential gaiety" (Monkman 1971: 113). These qualities define Sterne's Yorick throughout the author's work. In both *Tristram Shandy* and *A Sentimental Journey* the intertextual dependence on Shakespeare's deceased jester is explicitly established.

In Volume I of *Tristram Shandy* Mr Yorick, the local parson, is introduced and extensively characterised. Given Tristram's hobby-horsical obsession with origins, it is by no means surprising that a substantial part of the presentation refers to Parson Yorick's ancestry:

> [Yorick's] family was originally of *Danish* extraction, and had been transplanted into *England* as early as in the reign of *Horwendillus*, king of *Denmark*, in whose court it seems, an ancestor of this Mr. *Yorick*'s, and from whom he was lineally descended, held a considerable post to the day of his death. [...]
>
> It has often come into my head, that this post could be no other than that of the king's chief Jester;---and that *Hamlet*'s *Yorick*, in our *Shakespear*, many of whose plays, you know, are founded upon authenticated facts,--was certainly the very man. (*TS*, 25-26)

---

[2] In the following sketch, my examination of Yorick's intertextual constitution will be limited to his dependence on other figures bearing the name of Yorick. Therefore, it will not account for Yorick's quixotism, explicitly referred to in both *Tristram Shandy* and *A Sentimental Journey*. For a study of Sterne's Quixotes, including Yorick, see Niehus 1985: 41-60 and Paulson 1998: 150-158.

The Yorick of *Tristram Shandy* is thus not a direct transposition from Shakespeare's work but a descendant of the famous "king's chief Jester". Therefore, the pattern of intertextual communication is not only between Sterne's novel and Shakespeare's play but also between Yorick the ancestor and Yorick the descendant. Quite literally then, Sterne revives Shakespeare's work and makes it a prominent element of *Tristram Shandy*'s semantic structure.

Having accounted for Yorick's Danish origins, Tristram proceeds to present the reader with a character sketch of the parson:

> instead of that cold phlegm and exact regularity of sense and humours, you would have look'd for, in one so extracted;--he was, on the contrary, as mercurial and sublimated a composition,---as heteroclite a creature in all his declensions; ---- with as much life and whim, and *gaité de cœur* about him, as the kindliest climate could have engendered and put together. With all this sail, poor *Yorick* carried not one ounce of ballast; he was utterly unpractised in the world; and at the age of twenty-six, knew just about as well how to steer his course in it, as a romping, unsuspicious girl of thirteen [...] *Yorick* had an invincible dislike and opposition in his nature to gravity;----not to gravity as such;----for where gravity was wanted, he would be the most grave or serious of mortal men for days and weeks together;---but he was an enemy to the affectation of it, and declared open war against it, only as it appeared a cloak for ignorance, or for folly; and then, whenever it fell in his way, however sheltered and protected, he seldom gave it much quarter. (*TS*, 27-28)

The Yorick that emerges from Tristram's sketch is a good-natured and naive jester of a very complex and heterogeneous personality. Moreover, he is a man of feeling, having "the kindliest climate" about him. Importantly, he is also characterised as the enemy to false gravity, or, more appropriately, the affectation of gravity, treating it as a mask concealing ignorance and folly, and believing, as Tristram later informs us, that "[a] *mysterious carriage of the body* [...] *cover*[s] *the defects of the mind*" (*TS*, 28-29). Parson Yorick, as his Shakespearean predecessor, is also inextricably linked with death, dying shortly after being introduced (which, however, does not prevent Tristram from re-introducing him throughout the whole text).

In 1760, taking advantage of "the fashionable buzz generated by the novel" (Parnell 2009: 64), Sterne published the first two volumes of *The Sermons of Mr. Yorick*. Just like Tristram, Sterne himself did not find Yorick's death in *Tristram Shandy* to be a problem and resurrected him in the title of the collection. With the publication of *The Sermons*, Yorick's self became dependant not only on the intertextual network of correspondences, borrowings and allusions but also on the extratextual connection with Sterne's life. The author, by insisting on Yorick's authorship of *The Sermons*, began, in fact, "wearing a mask composed of intertextual fragments" (Rademacher 1996: 84). At the same time, by putting on the mask of Yorick, Sterne started to play a very peculiar game with his readers and critics – he deliberately related his collection to his fictional work, which was, in turn, criticised by many for its bawdiness and immorality. Consequently, he not only made his readers bear *Tristram Shandy* in mind when reading *The Sermons* but also ultimately dissolved the boundary between reality and literature, fact and fiction. What is especially important for the study of Yorick as a polyphonic character, though, is the fact that Sterne's decision to attribute *The Sermons* to the fictitious parson led his readers to identify the former with the latter and thus sanctioned autobiographical readings of his fiction. Consequently, one of the voices that make up the polyphonic Yorick is the voice of Sterne himself.

The Yorick of *The Sermons* is a latitudinarian divine believing in the essential goodness of human nature. At the same time, in accord with his characterisation in *Tristram Shandy*, he is an enemy to hypocrisy and affectation – personified in his sermons by such Biblical figures as the Pharisees or Shimei – and an advocate of simplicity and authenticity (Bystydzieńska 1993: 48, 50). He also ponders the brevity of human life, thus proving to be a rightful bearer of the name indispensably related to death, and analyses existential anxieties, epistemological problems and hidden motives of human actions, making himself known as an astute observer of the complexities of human nature (Bystydzieńska 1993: 51).

The early 1760s are also the time when Sterne started putting on his public performances, fashioning himself as his literary creations. As I have mentioned previously, he would alternately wear the masks of Shandy and Mr Yorick, depending on his mood and his audience. Consequently, the masks of his literary characters also come into use in his non-fiction writings. Apart from *The Sermons*, Sterne attributed to Yorick a substantial part of his correspondence. At first, Sterne does not sign his letters with the name of Yorick but refers to himself using the name of the parson. For example, in a letter to Mrs F. he complains that "insipidity there is in French characters has disgusted your friend Yorick" (*Letters*, 352; Feb. 1, 1764), whereas in a letter to an anonymous addressee he expresses his satisfaction with the recently concluded Continental tour, writing that "Never man [...] has had a more agreeable tour than your Yorick" (*Letters*, 502; July 23, 1766). Both of these mentions refer to Yorick in the third person and invoke the name in the context of

Sterne's Continental tour as if foreshadowing the (auto) fictional *Sentimental Journey*. The intensity with which the name of Yorick appears in Sterne's correspondence increases in 1767 when the author begins exchanging letters with Eliza Draper. In accord with the convention Sterne himself established, he refers to himself in the third person, using the name of Yorick. To give but a few examples:

> grateful and good girl! Yorick smiles contentedly over all thou dost, (*Letters*, 541; Mar., 1767)

> To whom shou'd Eliza apply in her distress, but to the friend that loves her; why then, my dear, do you apologize for employing me?
> Yorick wou'd be offended, and with reason, if you ever sent commissions to another [...]. (*Letters*, 547; Mar., 1767)

> may no doubt or misgivings disturb the serenity of thy mind, or awaken a painful thought about thy children, for they are Yorick's, and Yorick is thy friend for ever— (*Letters*, 569; Mar. 30, 1767)

The second of these excerpts is especially interesting in terms of its narrative stance. The author first refers to himself in the third person, then switches into the first, only to return to the third by invoking the name of Yorick; it seems as if there were three distinct voices speaking in the letter. Yet, apart from invoking the name of Yorick within the texts, Sterne also uses the name when signing the majority of his letters addressed to Eliza.

The correspondence of the final stage of his life reveals a similar intensity with which the name of Yorick appears; this time exclusively within the texts of the letters. The contexts for his appearances are Sterne's poor health and relationship with Mrs Draper. For example, when commenting on his treatment with mercury in a letter addressed to the Earl of Shelburne, he bewails: "Was it not as ridiculous an embarrassment as ever Yorick's spirit was involved in?" (*Letters*, 580; May 21, 1767), whereas when answering Earl of——'s "enquiry about Yorick", he complains that writing *A Sentimental Journey* "has worn out both his spirits and body" (*Letters*, 633; Nov. 28, 1767); he also refers to his affair with Eliza, writing "I heartily wish her well, and if Yorick was with her, he would tell her so" (*Letters*, 604; To Ann and William James, Aug. 2, 1767), which includes a similar dual narrative voice as one of the excerpts quoted before. There are thus three basic contexts for Yorick's

appearances in Sterne's correspondence – the Continental tour, the sentimental affair with Eliza Draper and poor health eventually leading to death.

The themes of travel, sentimentalism and death are also central for the final two texts featuring the parson – *Continuation of the Bramine's Journal*
(1767)[3] and, of course, *A Sentimental Journey*. The *Journal*, as Kraft notices,
"may have served as an exercise in sentimental expression that fuelled
Sterne's writing of *A Sentimental Journey*" (Kraft 1996: 122) and as such
features a narrator who fashions himself as an embodiment of sentimentalism. His disposition is inextricably related to poor physical and mental condition. In accord with the convention of referring to Yorick in the third person,
he writes, for example, about "poor Sick-headed, sick hearted Yorick!" (*BJ*,
173) or that "—thy [i.e. Eliza's] Yorick is going to waste himself on a rest-
less bed, where he will turn from side to side a thousand times—" (*BJ*, 175).
The Yorick of *The Journal* is also aware of the performative aspect of his
sentimentalism, expressing certitude that his journal will eventually be hand-
ed in to his Eliza: "—If I can write a Letter—I will—but this Journal must be
put into Eliza's hands by Yorick only—God grant you to read it soon.—"
(*BJ*, 203); "—I want to hear what You have to say to Y[r]. Yorick upon this
Text" (*BJ*, 212). Through such statements, he clearly demonstrates that sentimentalism is by no means limited to private contemplation but can only be
fulfilled when entering the public sphere and when becoming a spectacle.

Finally, Yorick appears in Sterne's last work – *A Sentimental Journey* –
taking the role of both the protagonist and the narrator. I will study the intricacies of his self later on, so now I will focus on his inter- and extratextual
constitution, as constructed in the *Journey*. When it comes to fictional inter-
texts, Yorick is quite explicit in maintaining relationships with them. His
Shakespearean provenance comes to the fore in the chapter entitled "The
Passport. Versailles", when Count de B**** asks the protagonist about his
name:

> I have often wish'd I could do it [tell the name] in a single word—and have an
> end of it. It was the only time and occasion in my life, I could accomplish this to
> any purpose—for Shakespear lying upon the table, and recollecting I was in his

---

[3] Sterne makes it clear at the beginning of the text that he will refer to himself as
Yorick: "This Journal wrote under the fictitious Names of Yorick & Draper—and
sometimes of the Bramin & Bramine—but tis a Diary of the miserable feelings of a
person separated from a Lady for whose Society he languish'd—" (*BJ*, 169)

books, I took up Hamlet, and turning immediately to the grave-diggers scene in the fifth act, I lay'd my finger upon YORICK, and advancing the book to the Count, with my finger all the way over the name—*Me, Voici!* said I. (*ASJ*, 112)

On the one hand, Yorick openly admits that his identity is a fictional entity, existing solely in literature; on the other, he plays with the audience, being aware that the reader of *Tristram Shandy* well remembers his lineage. In the *Journey* he suddenly becomes the actual king's jester rather than merely his descendant. This, however, is by no means tantamount to renouncing his affinities with the Yorick from the world of the previous novel. On the contrary, he makes explicit references to it every now and then in the narrative. For example, he calls Captain Tobias Shandy "the dearest of [his] flock and friends" (*ASJ*, 76) and alludes to Volume IX of *Tristram Shandy*, in which "[his] friend, Mr. Shandy, met with [Maria] near Mouliens" (*ASJ*, 149). As he admits,

> The story he [Tristram] had told of that disorder'd maid affect'd me not a little in the reading; but when I got within the neighbourhood where she lived, it returned so strong into my mind, that I could not resist an impulse which prompted me to go half a league out of the road to the village where her parents dwelt to enquire after her. (*ASJ*, 149)

Thus, in the Maria episode Yorick follows a typical grand tour account convention of imitating and re-enacting what a famous traveller accounted for in his report.

The characterisation of Yorick in the *Journey* is also dependent on the extratextual context. On the one hand, bearing in mind the earlier uses of the mask of Yorick in Sterne's personal writings, the reader must take into account the possibilities of autobiographical readings of the *Journey*, especially given the fact that what immediately preceded its publication was Sterne's Continental tour. On the other hand, Yorick explicitly refers to the realities of Sterne's life by addressing and recollecting his friend Eugenius (in reality John Hall-Stevenson) or his beloved Eliza, as well as by drawing the reader's attention to his clerical dress – the black coat. What is more, even though Yorick's accounts of the spaces he goes through and the people he encounters are rather cursory and impressionistic, some of them must have been based on Sterne's own experiences during his visits to France. For example, as New and Day explain, Mr Dessein, whom Yorick meets in Calais and who provides the protagonist with lodgings, was in 1762 the owner of Lyon d'Argent in Calais, where Sterne stayed on his way to Paris that year. The inn burned and Dessein built the new Hôtel d'Angleterre in 1764, where Sterne stayed in 1765 (New and Day 2002: 243).[4]

In sum, then, the Yorick of the *Journey* cannot be studied in isolation from other texts by Sterne. His nature is largely intertextual, or palimpsestic, as Genette would have it (Genette 1997). The French critic refers to the idea of a palimpsest, which is defined by OED as "a parchment, etc., which has been written upon twice, the original writing having been rubbed out", but the traces of which being still slightly visible. For Genette, this serves as a metaphor of the eponymous "literature in the second degree", referring to the understanding of writing as continual re-writing. The Yorick of the *Journey* can thus be called a palimpsestic character, constituted not only by the text of Sterne's final work but also by the author's previous texts, not being completely "rubbed out" and showing through the texture of the *Journey*. To make matters even more complicated, what also shows through is the grand text of Sterne's autobiography, related to his novels not only by the fictitious element of his personal writing but also by the author's inclination to fashion his life in the likeness of his literature.

2. Yorick's heterogeneity in *A Sentimental Journey*

Multiplicity of (literary) voices is a quality which, in fact, defines Yorick as a character in *A Sentimental Journey*. In effect, Yorick's self is a heterogeneous construct within which seemingly contradictory qualities find their place. He is not only a conglomeration of all the qualities making up Sterne's Yoricks but also, as the protagonist of Sterne's "*Work of Redemption*", a figure reconciling the author's two masks – that of the frivolous Mr Shandy and the latitudinarian and sentimental Parson Yorick, which were regarded by the author's contemporaries as mutually exclusive.

The complexity of character is a notion Yorick himself addresses in some of his reflections. At one point, accounting for a sudden change of decision, he declares: "I am govern'd by circumstances—I cannot govern them" (*ASJ*, 104); elsewhere, he admits that "THERE is not a more perplexing affair in life to [him], than to set about telling any one who [he is]" (*ASJ*, 112), only to conclude, sometime later, that "there is nothing unmixt in this world" (*ASJ*, 116). Thus, I would argue, Yorick's discourse of the self should be treated as an elucidation of Hume's theory of the "abandonment of personal identity",

---

[4] In fact, as Cash points out, Dessein's inns were well-known in England and enjoyed a good reputation (Cash 1986: 122).

as Perry calls it (Perry 2008: 157), which assumes a transitory and destabilised nature of the self. As Dussinger points out, this destabilisation manifests
itself through the poetics of Sterne's fiction, "present[ing] life as the continually interrupted, inadequate moment of words, gesture, and feeling" (Dussinger 1974: 173).

The idea of polyphony, which shares common assumptions with Hume's
theory of the self as a theatre of diverse perceptions, seems to be quite literally adopted in the *Journey*. Standing in front of the remise door in Calais,
Yorick thus accounts for his doubts concerning the offer of a joint post chaise
travel he is about to make to the encountered lady:

> Every dirty passion, and bad propensity in my nature, took the alarm, as I stat-
> ed the proposition—It will oblige you to have a third horse, said AVARICE, which
> will put twenty livres out of your pocket.—You know not who she is, said CAU-
> TION—or what scrapes the affair may draw you into, whisper'd COWARDICE—
>
> Depend upon it, Yorick! said DISCRETION, 'twill be said you went off with a
> mistress, and came by assignation to Calais for that purpose—
>
> —You can never after, cried HYPOCRISY aloud, show your face in the world—
> or rise, quoth MEANNESS, in the church—or be any thing in it, said PRIDE, but a
> lousy prebendary. (*ASJ*, 28-29)

However ironic the account may be, Yorick clearly indicates that his nature is
constituted by a dialogue of different voices. Some of these, curiously
enough, stand in opposition to the character traits Sterne ascribed to Yorick
in his previous works – avarice, hypocrisy or meanness seem to be difficult to
reconcile with the protagonist's good nature, "the kindliest climate", authenticity or criticism of false gravity and affectation.

The passage above is by no means the only example of internal dialogues
Yorick goes through. Another one is to be found in the chapter entitled "Amiens", in which the protagonist ponders the decency of his possible meeting
with Madame de L*** (the same with whom he engaged in a conversation
near the remise door) in Brussels on his way back from Italy:

> Then I will meet thee, said I, fair spirit! at Brussels—[...]
> There was nothing wrong in the sentiment; and yet I instantly reproached my
> heart with it in the bitterest and most reprobate of expressions. [...]
> —I will not go to Brussels, replied I, interrupting myself—(*ASJ*, 57-58)

Not only does Yorick prove to be governed by contradictory voices in this excerpt but also indicates that the representation of a dialogue ("said I", "replied I, interrupting myself") is the appropriate rhetoric to address the intricacies of one's self. In Humean terms, Yorick's mind may be regarded as a theatre where different ideas successively "make their appearance".

Yorick's heterogeneity in the *Journey* also manifests itself in the protagonist's reliance on the contradictory notions of naturalness and artificiality, as well as sentimentalism and the masquerade. I have already discussed this double-voice, but the masquerade, which is by nature related to the ideas of multiplicity (polyphony) in terms of identity, deserves further scrutiny. So far, I have addressed the masquerade as an antonym of naturalness and sentimentalism – a juxtaposition sanctioned by the epigraph of this part. I elaborated upon this understanding of the phenomenon in my reading of Fielding's novels, in which the masquerading hypocrites were juxtaposed with good-natured protagonists. When analysing Smollett, however, I treated the masquerade as a metaphor of one's potential for change, of one's adaptability and openness to put on new identities. Surprisingly, the picaresque idea that the road offers a chance to play many roles is also taken up by Sterne.

Despite aspiring to renew the tradition of travel writing, *A Sentimental Journey* is by all means indebted to the contemporary forms of journey narratives. Apart from its relation to grand tour accounts, on which I have already commented, the work, just like *Tristram Shandy*, displays affinities with the picaresque tradition. These affinities were noticed already by Sterne's contemporaries, e.g. by Diderot (Asfour 2004: 29), and have been given some attention in Sternean criticism ever since. Among others, Markley identifies in the *Journey* "a marriage of convenience between picaresque imitations of nature and sentimental displays akin to the kind of Christian idealism that Sterne preached on Sunday mornings" (Markley 1987: 228-229); Phelps, in turn, labels the text "a picaresque novel" in which "the traditional string of episodes and encounters is replaced by a series of sentimental ones" (Phelps 1988: 104); whereas Pfister points to "the picaresque tales of adventure" as one of the basic elements of "the intertextual dialogue" Sterne enters into in the *Journey* (Pfister 2001: 84). Apart from the chronotope of the road, what makes *A Sentimental Journey* resemble picaresque narratives is its episodic nature and fragmentation, scenes in inns and post chaises, accidental encounters and, of course, the antithetical arrangement of the main character and his servant. At first glance, however, Yorick bears little, if any, resemblance to a typical picaro – the latter's inherent plasticity and adaptability seem to be impossible to reconcile with the former's explicit self-definition as the senti-mental traveller, being on a "quiet journey of the heart in pursuit of NATURE" (*ASJ*, 111). Yorick's attempt at a substantialist conceptualisation of his iden-tity is at odds with the anti-substantialist understanding of the individual inscribed in the picaresque tradition, which manifests itself in the dominance of the motif of role-playing. However, Yorick's consistency in this approach to his self leaves much to be desired and is, in fact, undermined by the quoted statements testifying to the protagonist's uncertainty with regard to his self-hood. If these statements are confronted with such expressions as "I am posi-tive I have a soul; nor can all the books with which materialists have pester'd the world ever convince me of the contrary" (*ASJ*, 151), the reader cannot help but gain the impression that Yorick refers to both substantialist and anti-substantialist discourses when referring to his person; within the same narra-tive, the protagonist can be both "perplexed" and "positive" when arriving at self-definitions. The voices of Humean and Christian reflection over personal identity interweave.

Consequently, despite being a self-proclaimed enemy to hypocrisy, dis-guise and affectation, Yorick proves to be able to put on false identities on his journey. Curiously enough, the protagonist's masquerading potential is realised in the most literal way possible, when as a result of his conversation with Count de B**** he receives a passport identifying him as "Mr. Yorick, the king's jester" (*ASJ*, 116). Even though the protagonist feels obliged to clarify the matter at first – "I am not the king's jester" (*ASJ*, 115) – he admits shortly after that "the triumph of obtaining the Passport was not a little tar-nish'd by the figure [he] cut in it" (*ASJ*, 116). Thus, similarly to the resilient protean characters of Smollett, Yorick resorts to identity play and puts on a mask of a different character in order to survive when feeling threatened (the Bastille). Furthermore, Yorick's masquerade proves highly beneficial for the protagonist in terms of his social status (just as it did for Roderick). Being generally believed to be the king's jester, the parson becomes a socialite in Parisian salons (the chapter entitled "Paris"), enjoying conversations with "a few people of rank" (*ASJ*, 145).

As I have previously demonstrated, Yorick's absorption in the *beau monde* makes him develop an aversion to the "children of Art" and generally for the high life. The ensuing symbolic death resembles Tom Jones's fall in the wake of the masquerade he attended and his consequent intoxication with the world of hypocrisy and affectation. Just as Tom understood that he had lost his way and languished for his beloved Sophia, symbolising his good-natured and authentic disposition, Yorick grows ashamed and languishes for the children of Nature, against whom he will have the opportunity to re-define himself as the sentimental traveller and an enemy to hypocrisy and affectation. Yorick's renewal takes place when he encounters the insane Maria and the peasant family on his way to Lyon. Both episodes are con-ceived in such a way as would highlight Yorick's sentimentalism; both the insane Maria and the peasants are represented as "objectified" subjects (McGuirk 1980: 508) against which the protagonist's self can be re-established. Curiously enough, however, the episode with the peasants, which aspires ultimately to confirm Yorick's sentimentalism, features the protago-nist wearing a mask of a different character. On entering the house, Yorick is welcomed by the father of the family and is made to "s[i]t down at once like a son of the family" (*ASJ*, 158). Yorick immediately recognises the theatrical potential of the scene and openly admits to making effort "to invest [him]self in the character as speedily as [he] could" (*ASJ*, 158). Through this declara-tion, the protagonist once and for all resolves the boundary between senti-mentalism and the masquerade, naturalness and theatricality.

The Yorick of the *Journey* is also a character reconciling the two strains dominating Sterne's work – bawdiness and benevolent sentimentalism – which were associated with the two masks Sterne would alternately wear during his public performances; that of Mr Shandy and Parson Yorick respec-tively. The first of these masks, from the moment the first volume of *Tris-tram Shandy* was published, scandalised some of Sterne's reviewers and exposed the author to critical commentaries highlighting, for example, his "impropriety of character" or "prurient humour" (Howes 1974: 5). The figure of Yorick, in turn, was seen in an autobiographical light with the publication of Sterne's *Sermons*. Even though the sermonist himself did not raise contro-versies, given the sermons' modest nature and conformity to doctrine (Parnell 2009)[5], what was regarded as most indecent was the fact that subsequent volumes of *Tristram Shandy* and *The Sermons* were published practically simultaneously, and that the eponymous Yorick originated in the immoral *Tristram Shandy*.[6] *A Sentimental Journey* features a protagonist governed by

---

[5] In fact, some reviewers praised Sterne's abandonment of prurient interests (prema-turely as it later appeared) for the sake of ethical and religious ones. For example, the *Critical Review* for May 1760 reads: "It is with pleasure that we behold this son of Comus descending from the chair of mirth and frolick, to inspire sentiments of piety, and read lectures in morality (...)." (quoted in Howes 1974: 76).

[6] For example, the *Monthly Review* for May 1760 finds *The Sermons* "the greatest outrage against Sense and Decency" pointing to its relationship with *Tristram Shandy*:

the two extremes. As becomes apparent in the course of his narrative, he is not only capable of reconciling prurience and ethics but also of combining them into a very peculiar ethical discourse; an ethics of sexual desire. As Brissenden argues, "carnality leads to benevolence" in *A Sentimental Journey* (Brissenden 1974: 219), and "the relationship between the erotic and the moral connotations of 'sentimental'" is one of the key paradigms in the novel (Brissenden 1974: 221). Indeed, Yorick's *double-entendre* fre16quently carries sexual connotations, and his sentimentalism becomes erotically ambiguous. When the traveller defines the objectives of a sentimental travel – "to spy the nakedness of their hearts" – the reader, bearing the bawdiness of *Tristram Shandy* in mind, can only wonder if the nakedness Yorick wishes to discover is truly the metaphorical nakedness of the heart. The ambiguity of Yorick's disposition also comes to the fore in the final scene of the narrative – "The Case of Delicacy" – in which, having broken the artificial "treaty of peace" between himself and the Piedmontese lady, Yorick "stretche[s] out [his] hand" only to "ca[tch] hold of the Fille de Chambre's / END OF VOL.II". The reader is here forced to fill in the gap and answer the question of what Yorick catches hold of. However, the act of reading is in this case quite explicitly governed by the author, or, more precisely, by the paratextual "END" concluding the *Journey*. As Kraft aptly notices, despite the fact that "on the surface *A Sentimental Journey* seems to exchange Tristram's bawdiness for Yorick's acute sensitivity to the feelings of others", such scenes as the final one imply that the languished "communion with another" is by no means "the attribute of the celibate saint but of the desiring sinner" (Kraft 1996: 128).

To recapitulate, Yorick's polyphony, very much in line with the double-voice of the *Journey*'s poetics and the fragmentation of the narrative, is a character quality leaving the reader with the impression that Sterne's novel, in fact, features several protagonists, each with his own intricacies. There is the Yorick from Shakespeare's *Hamlet*, the good-natured parson from *Tristram Shandy*, the author of latitudinarian sermons, sentimental correspond-

---

"every serious and sober Reader must have been offended at the indecency of such an assumed character. For who is this *Yorick*? We have heard of one of that name who was a *Jester* —we have read of a *Yorick* likewise, in an obscene Romance. —But are the solemn dictates of religion fit to be conveyed from the mouths of Buffoons and ludicrous Romancers? Would any man believe that a Preacher was in earnest, who should mount the pulpit in a *Harlequin's coat*?" (quoted in Howes 1974: 77). Quite tellingly, it is not the content of the sermons that comes under criticism but the alleged masquerade of the author.

ence and a journal; there is also the sentimental traveller, fluctuating between naturalness and artificiality, sentimentalism and the masquerade, as well as bawdiness and benevolence; a figure capable of declaring certainty with regard to his self and pondering over its instability and indefiniteness at the same time.

⤚

Sterne's Yorick is a character whose complexity most appropriately concludes the present work. What he shares with Joseph and Tom is his good nature, self-proclaimed authenticity and hostility towards the masquerading world, as well as the need for self-definitions. His affinities with Roderick and Peregrine, in turn, result from them being set against similarly fragmented, and consequently destabilised, narrative realms and include inclination to jest, ease of adaptability and the impossibility of arriving at definite conclusions regarding the self. Sterne's Yorick is thus an epitome of Humean complexity and indefiniteness; a polyphonic construct accurately reflecting the intricacies of the *ancien régime* of identity. He excels at joining contradictions, just as the poetics of the *Journey* is constituted by conflicting voices. In Sterne's realm the masquerade can be both contrasted and combined with sentimentalism, naturalness can be treated as an objective pursued by artificial means, and being in earnest does not make jesting impossible. Finally, just as literature can represent life, one's life – in a peculiar form of masquerade – can be fashioned in the likeness of one's literary creation.

Conclusion

My aim was to demonstrate that the turmoil over the category of self in the eighteenth century, giving rise to Wahrman's notion of the *ancien régime* of identity, finds its reflection in the construction of character in the selected novels from the mid-century. I argued that the masquerade and the journey – that is, those socio-cultural rituals which were by nature related to the quest for identity – can be treated as organising principles of the selected novels of Fielding, Smollett and Sterne, governed by their focus on an individual acquiring experience. Approaching their texts, I put forward the idea of masquerade poetics, understood (analogically to Bakhtin's carnivalisation) as the transposition of the masquerade into the language of the eighteenth-century novel. This understanding of the masquerade assumed that the phenomenon was not limited to masked assemblies themselves but should be regarded as a broad spectrum of behaviours and dispositions based on disguise, fraud, social and personal metamorphosis, and identity play.

The first part of the book focused on Henry Fielding's two most famous travellers – Joseph Andrews and Tom Jones – and argued that their stabilised literary identity reflects Fielding's longing for a time of certitude. Being constructed as descendants of epic and romance heroes, and contrasted with contemporary picaresque rogues and men of stratagem climbing the social ladder, Joseph and Tom find themselves in quest of their origins and thus true and unchanging selves. The masquerade throughout both novels is understood metaphorically and stands for hypocrisy and affectation, dominating the world against which the good-natured protagonists are differentiated. I argued that when Joseph and Tom are absorbed in the world of masquerade, they appear to be passive participants, involved in it contrary to their will. I demonstrated, however, that in contrast to the self-consistent Joseph, Tom is overwhelmed by a moment of weakness in the wake of the masked assembly he attends in London. Drawing on Terry Castle's theory of the masquerade as a disruptor of allegorical consistency, I claimed that the masquerade scene in

Tom Jones poses a threat to the protagonist's so far stable and unchanging self, undermining the ideological implications of the narrative.

Just as Fielding's novels seem to express some concern about the *ancien régime* of identity and an aristocratic longing for social and personal stability, Smollett's *Roderick Random* and *Peregrine Pickle* feature protagonists who make the most of the time they find themselves in. Part II, in which I examined the two novels, argued that in contrast to the pre-defined protagonists of Fielding, Smollett's Roderick and Peregrine are conceived as nobody-characters, the former being a tormented Scot in England, the latter a disowned exile. I pointed out that the only predetermination that can be discerned in the characters concerns their natural disposition for travelling – with the former coming from a nation "addicted to travelling" and the latter bearing a meaningful name. Being, in a sense, forced to travel, the two protagonists find themselves in a picaresque world welcoming, and at times demanding, social and personal transformations. I thus analysed Roderick and Peregrine as protean characters, exploiting throughout the whole narratives their masquerading potential. Consequently, the masquerade scenes present in the texts were not disruptors of a moral argument but further evidence testifying to the protean nature of the two protagonists.

In the final part, analysing Sterne's *A Sentimental Journey*, I aimed at revealing the paradoxes and incongruities of the advocated vindication of sentimentalism at the cost of the masquerade, and a return to naturalness at the cost of artifice. Taking as my starting point Sterne's binary distinction between his sentimental disposition and the world "in Masquerade", I shed light on those aspects of *A Sentimental Journey* which dissolve the boundaries between the seemingly contradictory notions. I argued that this dialogical nature of Sterne's text corresponds with the author's tendency to put on public performances, playing the roles of Mr Shandy or Parson Yorick. I also demonstrated that just as boundaries between the masquerade and sentimentalism are frequently indiscernible, the distinction between the advocated naturalness and the seemingly abandoned artificiality is by no means clear-cut. Finally, I claimed that Sterne's protagonist – Mr Yorick – is a polyphonic figure reconciling the diversity of contradictory voices permeating the texture of *A Sentimental Journey*; a character who shares both the need to discover his true self, as did Joseph and Tom, and the will to exercise, like Roderick and Peregrine, his protean potential.

On the whole, I hope that the book has managed to reveal the complexity of the discourse of the self in eighteenth-century fiction. The novels of the three authors provided versatile material, the analyses of which have thrown light on diverse attitudes towards a time when the ancient precept "know then thyself" seems to have acquired special significance. The attitudes range from Fielding's self-protective attempts at perfecting reality to Smollett's openness or resignation to its chaos and fragmentation. Sterne's reconciliatory strategies situate himself in between the two extremes, which implies that the dynamics of a time constituted by the interweaving trends of the rational and the irrational, of doubt and certitude could have been best understood by an "odd person [...] join[ing] contradictions".

Undoubtedly, the limited scope the book and the need to maintain coherence and clarity of argument must have led to some selections and thus omissions. The three authors and their works offer such an enormous interpretative potential that it could not have been possibly grasped in its entirety in this work. It would be interesting to juxtapose the negatively valued masquerade of Fielding's novels with the way the topos is deployed in the author's dramatic output, where it is possible for masquerading stratagems to be valued positively. For example, in his *Love in Several Masques* the masquerade, inevitably leading to unmasking, is conceptualised as a way of uncovering the truth. As far as Smollett's work is concerned, it might be rewarding to pair the destabilised and fragmented selves of Roderick and Peregrine with self-consistent travellers in the author's *Travels through France and Italy* and *The Expedition of Humphry Clinker*. Smollett's stylistic and narrative development has already been accounted for by his critics; it would be worthwhile, though, to investigate the way the discourse of the self changes along with narrative developments. Finally, the study of Sterne's dialogised poetics of the masquerade and sentimentalism could shift focus towards the author's real stay in France. It would be an enriching endeavour to conduct research not only into the author's correspondence but also into the letters, journals and other testimonies of those whom he met on his way, and who thus witnessed Sterne's public performances and appearances in respected salons; this idea would be certainly in line with the contemporary tendency to dissolve the boundaries between fact and fiction.

The possibilities are practically endless, and the ones I have mentioned seem to logically complement the arguments I put forward in this book. The richness of eighteenth-century fiction as well as its striking up-to-dateness have always given rise to stimulating readings. I can only hope that my readings have managed to contribute to the field and provided fresh insight into the eighteenth-century novel.

Bibliography

Primary sources

Aristotle. 2000. *Poetics* in *Classical Literary Criticism* (tr. Penelope Murray and T.S. Dorsch). London: Penguin: 57-97.

Barrow, Isaac. 1798. *Twenty Two Sermons on Various Subjects*. Oxford: Clarendon Press.

Boswell, James. 1929. *On the Profession of a Player. Three Essays. Now first reprinted from The London Magazine for August, September, and October, 1770*. London: Elkin Mathews & Marrot.

——. 1991. *London Journal, 1762-1763*. Edinburgh: Edinburgh University Press.

Butler, Joseph. 2008. 'Of Personal Identity' in Perry (2008): 99-105.

Defoe, Daniel. 1991. *A Tour Through the Whole Island of Great Britain* (ed. P.N. Furbank, W.R. Owens and A.J. Coulson). New Haven and London: Yale University Press.

Fielding, Henry. 1967. *Joseph Andrews* (ed. Martin C. Battestin) (The Wesleyan Edition of the Works of Henry Fielding). Oxford: Clarendon Press.

——. 1972a. 'An Essay on the Knowledge of the Characters of Men' in Henry Fielding *Miscellanies by Henry Fielding, Esq. Volume One* (ed. Henry Knight Miller) (The Wesleyan Edition of the Works of Henry Fielding). Oxford: Clarendon Press: 153-178.

——. 1972b. 'Of Good-Nature' in Henry Fielding *Miscellanies by Henry Fielding, Esq. Volume One* (ed. Henry Knight Miller) (The Wesleyan Edition of the Works of Henry Fielding). Oxford: Clarendon Press: 30-35.

——. 1974. *Tom Jones*. (eds Martin C. Battestin and Fredson Bowers) (The Wesleyan Edition of the Works of Henry Fielding). Oxford: Clarendon Press.

——. 1983. *Amelia* (ed. Martin C. Battestin) (The Wesleyan Edition of the Works of Henry Fielding). Oxford: Clarendon Press.

——. 1988a. 'A Charge Delivered to the Grand Jury, &c' in Henry Fielding *An Enquiry into the Causes of the late Increase of Robbers and Related Writings* (ed. Malvin R. Zirker) (The Wesleyan Edition of the Works of Henry Fielding). Oxford: Clarendon Press: 1-30.

——. 1988b. *An Enquiry into the Causes of the Late Increase of Robbers, &c.* in Henry Fielding *An Enquiry into the Causes of the late Increase of Robbers and Related Writings* (ed. Malvin R. Zirker) (The Wesleyan Edition of the Works of Henry Fielding). Oxford: Clarendon Press: 61-174.

——. 1993. *A Journey from This World to the Next* in Henry Fielding *Miscellanies by Henry Fielding, Esq. Volume Two* (eds Bertrand A. Goldgar and Hugh Amory) (The Wesleyan Edition of the Works of Henry Fielding). Oxford: Clarendon Press: 1-128.

——. 2003. *Contributions to The Champion and Related Writings* (ed. W.B. Coley) (The Wesleyan Edition of the Works of Henry Fielding). Oxford: Clarendon Press.

——. 2008. *The Masquerade, A Poem Inscribed to C---T H--D--G—R* in Henry Fielding *Journal of a Voyage to Lisbon, Shamela, and Occasional Writings* (ed. Martin C. Battestin) (The Wesleyan Edition of the Works of Henry Fielding). Oxford: Clarendon Press: 11-27.

——. 2011. *Miss Lucy in Town. A Sequel to the Virgin Unmasked. A Farce* in Henry Fielding *Plays. Volume Three: 1734-1742* (ed. Thomas Lockwood) (The Wesleyan Edition of the Works of Henry Fielding). Oxford: Clarendon Press: 473-502.

Hoadly, Benjamin. 1755. *Twenty Sermons.* London: John and Paul Knapton.

Horace. 2000. *The Art of Poetry* in *Classical Literary Criticism* (tr. Penelope Murray and T.S. Dorsch). London: Penguin: 98-112.

Hume, David. 1975. *A Treatise of Human Nature* (ed. L.A. Selby-Bigge). Oxford: Clarendon Press.

Locke, John. 1975. *An Essay Concerning Human Understanding* (ed. Peter H. Nidditch). Oxford: Clarendon Press.

Montaigne, Michel de. 1958. *The Complete Essays of Montaigne.* Stanford: Stanford University Press.

Rousseau, Jean Jacques. 2000. *Confessions* (tr. Angela Scholar). Oxford: Oxford University Press.

Shaftesbury, Anthony Ashley Cooper. 1999. *Characteristics of Men, Manners, Opinions, Times* (ed. Lawrence E. Klein). Cambridge: Cambridge University Press.

Shakespeare, William. 2006. *Hamlet. The Texts of 1603 and 1623* (eds Ann Thompson and Neil Taylor) (The Arden Shakespeare. Third Series). London: Arden Shakespeare.

Short Remarks upon the Original and Pernicious Consequences of Masquerades. 1721 in *The Conduct of the Stage Consider'd.* London: Printed for Eman. Matthews: 35-43.

Smollett, Tobias. 1979. *Travels Through France and Italy* (ed. Frank Felsenstein). Oxford: Oxford University Press.

——. 1988. *The Adventures of Ferdinand Count Fathom* (eds Jerry C. Beasley and OM Brack Jr.) (The Works of Tobias Smollett). Athens and London: The University of Georgia Press.

——. 2012. *The Adventures of Roderick Random* (eds James G. Basker, Paul-Gabriel Boucé and Nicole A. Seary) (The Works of Tobias Smollett). Athens and London: The University of Georgia Press.

——. 2014. *The Adventures of Peregrine Pickle* (eds John P. Zomchick and George S. Rousseau). (The Works of Tobias Smollett). Athens and London: The University of Georgia Press.

Sterne, Laurence. 1978. *The Life and Opinions of Tristram Shandy, Gentleman* (eds Melvyn New and Joan New) (The Florida Edition of the Works of Laurence Sterne). Gainesville: University Press of Florida.

——. 1996. *The Sermons of Laurence Sterne* (ed. Melvyn New) (The Florida Edition of the Works of Laurence Sterne). Gainesville: University Press of Florida.

——. 2002. *A Sentimental Journey through France and Italy and Continuation of the Bramine's Journal* (eds Melvyn New and W.G. Day) (The Florida Edition of the Works of Laurence Sterne). Gainesville: University Press of Florida.

——. 2009. *The Letters* (eds Malvyn New and Peter de Voogd) (The Florida Edition of the Works of Laurence Sterne). Gainesville: University Press of Florida.

The Gentleman's Magazine and Historical Chronicle. Volume XL. 1770. London: Printed for D. Henry.

The Monthly Review, or Literary Journal. Volume XXII. 1760. London: Printed for R. Griffiths.

Secondary sources

Abramowska, Janina. 1978. 'Peregrynacja' in Michał Głowiński and Aleksandra Okopień-Sławińska (eds) *Przestrzeń i Literatura*. Wrocław: Ossolineum: 125-158.

Abrams, Meyer Howard. 1994. 'Spiritual Travelers in Western Literature' in Bruno Magliocchetti and Anthony Verna (eds) *The Motif of the Journey in Nineteenth-Century Italian Literature*. Gainesville: University Press of Florida: 1-20.

Adams, Percy G. 1983. *Travel Literature and the Evolution of the Novel*. Lexington: The University Press of Kentucky.

Ardila, J.A.G. 2009. 'Henry Fielding: From Quixotic Satire to the Cervantean Novel' in J.A.G. Ardila (ed.) *The Cervantean Heritage: Reception and Influence of Cervantes in Britain*. London: Legenda: 124-141.

Asfour, Lana. 2004. 'Movements of Sensibility and Sentiment: Sterne in Eighteenth-Century France' in Peter de Voogd and John Neubauer (eds). *The Reception of Laurence Sterne in Europe*. London and New York: Continuum: 9-31.

Baker, Sheridan. 1960. 'Henry Fielding's Comic Romances' in *Papers of the Michigan Academy of Science, Arts, and Letters* 45: 411-419.

Bakhtin, Mikhail. 1981. *The Dialogic Imagination: Four Essays* (tr. Caryl Emerson and Michael Holquist). Austin: University of Texas Press.

——. 1984a. *Problems of Dostoevsky's Poetics* (tr. Caryl Emerson). Minneapolis: University of Minnesota Press.

——. 1984b. *Rabelais and His World* (tr. Hélène Iswolsky). Bloomington and Minneapolis: Indiana University Press.

Barresi, John and Raymond Martin. 2004. *Naturalization of the Soul. Self and Personal Identity in the Eighteenth Century*. London: Routledge.

Bartolomeo, Joseph F. 1991. 'Interpolated Tales as Allegories of Reading: *Joseph Andrews*' in *Studies in the Novel* 23: 405-415.

Batten, Charles L. Jr. 1978. *Pleasurable Instruction: Form and Convention in Eighteenth-Century Travel Literature*. Berkeley, Los Angeles, London: University of California Press.

Battestin, Martin C. 1959. *The Moral Basis of Fielding's Art: A Study of Joseph Andrews*. Middletown: Wesleyan University Press.

——. 1989. *The Providence of Wit: Aspects of Form in Augustan Literature and the Arts*. Virginia: The University Press of Virginia.

——. 1994. '*A Sentimental Journey*: Sterne's "Work of Redemption"' in *XVII-XVIII. Bulletin de la société d'études anglo-américaines des XVIIe et XVIIIe siècles* 38: 189-204.

Beasley, Jerry C. 1998. *Tobias Smollett: Novelist*. Athens and London: The University of Georgia Press.

Bell, Michael. 2000. *Sentimentalism, Ethics, and the Culture of Feeling*. Houndmills: Palgrave Macmillan.

Benedict, Barbara M. 1995. 'Reading Faces: Physiognomy and Epistemology in Late Eighteenth-Century Sentimental Novels' in *Studies in Philology* 92: 311-328.

Berger, Peter L., Brigitte Berger and Hansfried Kellner. 1973. *The Homeless Mind: Modernization and Consciousness*. New York: Random House.

Białas, Zbigniew. 2010. 'The Mobile Body: Prolegomena to the Corporeality of Travel' in Grzegorz Moroz and Jolanta Sztachelska (eds) *Metamorphoses of Travel Writing: Across Theories, Genres, Centuries and Literary Tradition*. Newcastle: Cambridge Scholars Publishing: 10-20.

Black, Jeremy. 1992. *The British Abroad: The Grand Tour in the Eighteenth Century*. Stroud: Alan Sutton Publishing.

Blackwell, Mark. 2011. 'Disjecta Membra: Smollett and the Novel in Pieces' in *The Eighteenth Century* 52(3-4): 423-442.

Bohls, Elizabeth. 2009. 'Age of Peregrination: Travel Writing and the Eighteenth-Century Novel' in Paula R. Backscheider and Catherine Ingrassia (eds) *A Companion to the Eighteenth-Century English Novel and Culture*. Oxford: Blackwell: 97-116.

Boucé, Paul-Gabriel. 1972. 'Smollett's Pseudo-Picaresque: A Response to Rousseau's "Smollett and the Picaresque"' in *Studies in Burke and His Time: A Journal Devoted to British, American, and Continental Culture, 1750-1800* 14: 73-79.

——. 1976. *The Novels of Tobias Smollett* (tr. Antonia White). London and New York: Longman.

Briggs, Peter M. 2006. 'Laurence Sterne and Literary Celebrity in 1760' in Thomas Keymer (ed.) *Laurence Sterne's* Tristram Shandy*: A Casebook*. New York: Oxford University Press: 79-107. First published in 1991 in *Age of Johnson* 4: 251-280.

Brissenden, R.F. 1974. *Virtue in Distress: Studies in the Novel of Sentiment from Richardson to Sade*. London: Macmillan.

Brownlee, Marina S. 1994. 'Discursive Parameters of the Picaresque' in Carmen Benito-Vessels and Michael Zappala (eds) *The Picaresque: A*

Symposium on the Rogue's Tale. Cranbury: Associated University Presses: 25-35.

Buzard, James. 2002. 'The Grand Tour and after (1660-1840)' in Peter Hulme and Tim Youngs (eds) *The Cambridge Companion to Travel Writing*. Cambridge: Cambridge University Press: 37-52.

Bystydzieńska, Grażyna. 1993. *W Labiryncie Prawdy. Studia o Twórczości Laurence'a Sterne'a*. Lublin: Wydawnictwo Uniwersytetu Marii Curie-Skłodowskiej.

——. 1996. 'Laurence Sterne and the Art of Gestures' in Leszek Kolek (ed.) *Approaches to Fiction 2*. Lublin: Folium: 39-48.

Campbell, Jill. 1995. *Natural Masques: Gender and Identity in Fielding's Plays and Novels*. Stanford: Stanford University Press.

Carter, Sophie. 2004. *Purchasing Power: Representing Prostitution in Eighteenth-Century English Popular Print Culture*. Aldershot: Ashgate.

Casellas, Jesús López-Peláez, David Malcolm and Pilar Sánchez Calle (eds). 2004. *Masquerades: Disguise in Literature in English from the Middle Ages to the Present*. Gdańsk: Wydawnictwo Uniwersytetu Gdańskiego.

Cash, Arthur H. 1986. *Laurence Sterne: The Later Years*. London: Methuen.

Castle, Terry. 1986. *Masquerade and Civilization: The Carnivalesque in Eighteenth-Century English Culture and Fiction*. London: Methuen.

——. 1987. 'The Culture of Travesty: Sexuality and Masquerade in Eighteenth-Century England' in G.S. Rousseau and Roy Porter (eds) *Sexual Underworlds of the Enlightenment*. Manchester: Manchester University Press: 156-180.

Cauthen, I.B. 1956. 'Fielding's Digressions in *Joseph Andrews*' in *College English* 17: 379-382.

Chadwick, Joseph. 1978-9. 'Infinite Jest: Interpretation in Sterne's *A Sentimental Journey*' in *Eighteenth-Century Studies* 12: 190-205.

Chard, Chloe. 1999. *Pleasure and Guilt on the Grand Tour. Travel Writing and Imaginative Geography, 1600-1830*. Manchester: Manchester University Press.

Cirlot, Juan Eduardo. 2002. *A Dictionary of Symbols* (tr. Jack Sage). Mineola: Dover Publications.

Coolidge, John S. 1962. 'Fielding and "Conservation of Character"' in Ronald Paulson (ed.) *Fielding: A Collection of Critical Essays*. Englewood Cliffs: Prentice Hall: 158-176. First published in 1960 in *Modern Philology* 62: 245-259.

Courtine, Jean-Jacques and Claudine Haroche. 2007. *Historia Twarzy. Wyrażanie i Ukrywanie Emocji od XVI do Początku XIX Wieku* (tr. Tomasz Swoboda). Gdańsk: słowo/obraz terytoria.

Cox, Stephen D. 1980. *"The Stranger Within Thee": Concepts of the Self in Late Eighteenth-Century Literature*. Pittsburgh: University of Pittsburgh Press.

Craft-Fairchild, Catherine. 1993. *Masquerade and Gender: Disguise and Female Identity in Eighteenth-Century Fictions by Women*. University Park: The Pennsylvania State University Press.

Crane, Ronald. 2006. 'The Concept of Plot and the Plot of *Tom Jones*' in Dorothy J. Hale (ed.) *The Novel: An Anthology of Criticism and Theory, 1900-2000*. Malden: Blackwell Publishing: 119-139. First published in 1950 in *Journal of General Education* 4: 112-130.

Craveri, Benedetta. 2005. *The Age of Conversation* (tr. Teresa Waugh). New York: New York Review of Books.

Cuddon, John Anthony. 1999. *The Penguin Dictionary of Literary Terms and Literary Theory*. London: Penguin.

Culler, Jonathan. 1975. *Structuralist Poetics. Structuralism Linguistics and the Study of Literature*. London and Henley: Routledge and Kegan Paul.

Curley, Thomas M. 1990. 'Sterne's *A Sentimental Journey* and the Tradition of Travel Literature' in John McVeagh (1990): 203-216.

Curtius, Ernst Robert. 1990. *European Literature and the Latin Middle Ages* (tr. Willard R. Task). Princeton: Princeton University Press.

Dentith, Simon. 1995. *Bakhtinian Thought: An Introductory Reader*. London: Routledge.

Dilworth, Ernest Nevin. 1948. *The Unsentimental Journey of Laurence Sterne*. New York: Morningside Heights.

Douglas, Aileen. 1995. *Uneasy Sensations: Smollett and the Body*. Chicago and London: The University of Chicago Press.

Dussinger, John. 1974. *The Discourse of the Mind in Eighteenth-Century Fiction*. The Hague and Paris: Mouton.

Ehrenpreis, Irvin. 1964. *Fielding: Tom Jones*. London: Edward Arnold.

Erickson, Robert A. 2005. 'Milton and the Poetics of Ecstasy in Restoration and Eighteenth-Century Fiction' in Paula R. Backscheider and Catherine Ingrassia (eds) *A Companion to the Eighteenth-Century English Novel and Culture*. Oxford: Blackwell: 117-139.

Erikson, Erik H. 1959. *Identity and the Life Cycle*. New York: International Universities Press.

Feldman, Doris. 1997. 'Economic and/as Aesthetic Constructions of British-ness in the Eighteenth-Century Domestic Travel Writing' in *Journal for the Study of British Cultures* 4: 31-45.

Fox, Christopher. 1988. *Locke and the Scriblerians: Identity and Consciousness in Early Eighteenth-Century Britain*. Berkeley: University of California Press.

Freeman, Lisa A. 2002. *Character's Theater: Genre and Identity on the Eighteenth-Century English Stage*. Philadelphia: University of Pennsylvania Press.

Frye, Northrop. 1957. *Anatomy of Criticism: Four Essays*. Princeton: Princeton University Press.

——. 1976. *The Secular Scripture: A Study of the Structure of Romance*. Cambridge: Harvard University Press.

Genette, Gerard. 1997. *Palimpsests. Literature in the Second Degree* (tr. Channa Newman and Claude Doubinsky). Lincoln: University of Nebraska Press.

Gerard, W.B. 2006. *Laurence Sterne and the Visual Imagination*. Aldershot: Ashgate.

Gibson, William. 2007. 'Tobias Smollett and Cat-for-Hare: The Anatomy of a Picaresque Joke' in *Eighteenth-Century Studies* 40(4): 571-586.

Gilson, Étienne. 1936. *The Spirit of Medieval Philosophy* (tr. Alfred H.C. Downes). New York: C. Scribner's sons.

Goffman, Erving. 1956. *The Presentation of Self in Everyday Life*. Edinburgh: University of Edinburgh.

Goring, Paul. 2005. *The Rhetoric of Sensibility in Eighteenth-Century Culture*. Cambridge: Cambridge University Press.

Grant, Damian. 1977. *Tobias Smollett: A Study in Style*. Manchester: Manchester University Press.

Grimal, Pierre. 1990. *The Concise Dictionary of Classical Mythology* (tr. A.R. Maxwell-Hyslop). Oxford: Basil Blackwell.

Grimes, Ronald L. 1975. 'Masking: Toward a Phenomenology of Exteriorization' in *Journal of the American Academy of Religion* 43: 508-516.

Haller, William. 1957. *The Rise of Puritanism; or, The Way to the New Jerusalem as Set Forth in Pulpit and Press from Thomas Cartwright to John Lilburne and John Milton, 1570-1643*. New York: Harper.

Haynes, Clare. 2010. '"A Trial for the Patience of Reason"? Grand Tourists and Anti-Catholicism after 1745' in *Journal for Eighteenth-Century Studies* 33(2): 195-208.

Heyl, Christoph. 2001. 'The Metamorphosis of the Mask in Seventeenth- and Eighteenth-Century London' in Efrat Tseëlon (2001): 114-134.

Hourihan, Margery. 1997. *Deconstructing the Hero: Literary Theory and Children's Literature*. London: Routledge.

Howes, Alan B. 1974. *Sterne: The Critical Heritage*. London and Boston: Routledge and Kegan Paul.

Hulme, Peter and Tim Youngs. 2002. 'Introduction' in Peter Hulme and Tim Youngs (eds) *The Cambridge Companion to Travel Writing*. Cambridge: Cambridge University Press: 1-16.

Hundert, E.J. 1997. 'The European Enlightenment and the History of the Self' in Roy Porter (ed.) *Rewriting the Self: Histories from the Renaissance to the Present*. London and New York: Routledge: 72-83.

Hunter, J. Paul. 1990. *Before Novels. The Cultural Contexts of Eighteenth-Century Fiction*. New York and London: W.W. Norton.

Jung, Carl Gustav. 2003. *Four Archetypes: Mother, Rebirth, Spirit, Trickster* (tr. R.F.C. Hull). London: Routledge.

Karremann, Isabel. 2011. 'Introduction: Mediating Identities in Eighteenth-Century England' in Isabel Karremanna and Anja Müller (eds) *Mediating Identities in Eighteenth-Century England: Public Negotiations, Literary Discourses, Topography*. Farnham: Ashgate: 1-15.

Keymer, Thomas. 2009. '*A Sentimental Journey* and the Failure of Feeling' in Thomas Keymer (ed.) *The Cambridge Companion to Laurence Sterne*. Cambridge: Cambridge University Press: 79-94.

Kraft, Elizabeth. 1992. *Character and Consciousness in Eighteenth-Century Comic Fiction*. Athens and London: The University of Georgia Press.

——. 1996. *Laurence Sterne Revisited*. New York: Twayne.

Kukkonen, Karin. 2013. 'The Minds Behind the Mask: Reading for Character in the Masquerade' in *Neophilologus* 98: 161-176.

Laden, Marie-Paule. 1987. *Self-Imitation in the Eighteenth-Century Novel*. Princeton: Princeton University Press.

Leed, Eric J. 1991. *The Mind of the Traveler: From Gilgamesh to Global Tourism*. New York: Basic Books.

Lifton, Robert Jay. 1970. 'Protean Man' in *History and Human Survival*. New York: Radnom House: 311-331.

——. 1993. *The Protean Self: Human Resilience in an Age of Fragmentation*. Chicago and London: The University of Chicago Press.

Lipski, Jakub. 2010. 'Moral Implications of the Journey to the Other World: Henry Fielding's *A Journey from This World to the Next*' in Grzegorz

Moroz and Jolanta Sztachelska (eds) *Metamorphoses of Travel Writing: Accross Theories, Genres, Centuries and Literary Tradition*. Newcastle: Cambridge Scholars: 156-164.

———. 2011. 'Crossing the Boundaries of the Self: The Masquerade Scene in *Tom Jones*' in *The New Review: An International Journal of British Studies* 3: 39-47.

———. 2012. 'The Face as Mask in Fielding's *Joseph Andrews* and *Tom Jones*' in Grażyna Bystydzieńska and Emma Harris (eds) *From Queen Anne to Queen Victoria: Readings in 18th and 19th Century British Literature and Culture*. Warszawa: Uniwersytet Warszawski, Ośrodek Studiów Brytyjskich: 309-315.

Lotman, Yuri M. 1990. *Universe of the Mind: A Semiotic Theory of Culture* (tr. Ann Shukman). Bloomington and Indianapolis: Indiana University Press.

Lutz, Alfred. 2001. 'Representing Scotland in *Roderick Random* and *Humphry Clinker*: Smollett's Development as a Novelist' in *Studies in the Novel* 33(1): 1-17.

Mace, Nancy A. 1996. *Henry Fielding's Novels and the Classical Tradition*. Newark: University of Delaware Press.

Mancing, Howard. 1979. 'The Picaresque Novel: A Protean Form' in *College English* 6: 182-204.

Manning, Susan. 2004. 'Sensibility' in Thomas Keymer and Jon Mee (eds) *The Cambridge Companion to English Literature, 1740-1830*. Cambridge: Cambridge University Press: 80-99.

Maresca, Thomas E. 1974. *Epic to Novel*. Columbus: Ohio State University Press.

Markley, Robert. 1987. 'Sentimentality as Performance: Shaftesbury, Sterne, and the Theatrics of Virtue' in Felicity Nussbaum and Laura Brown (eds) *The New Eighteenth Century: Theory, Politics, English Literature*. London: Methuen: 210-230.

Mauss, Marcel. 1985. 'A Category of the Human Mind: The Notion of Person, the Notion of Self' (tr. W.B. Halls) in Michael Carrithers, Steven Collins and Steven Lukes (eds) *The Category of the Person. Anthropology, Philosophy, History*. Cambridge: Cambridge University Press: 1-25.

McGuirk, Carol. 1980. 'Sentimental Encounter in Sterne, Mackenzie, and Burns' in *Studies in English Literature* 20: 505-515.

McKeon, Michael. 2002. *The Origins of the English Novel, 1600-1740*. Baltimore and London: The Johns Hopkins University Press.

McMaster, Juliet. 2004. *Reading the Body in the Eighteenth-Century Novel*. Houndmills: Palgrave Macmillan.

McVeagh, John (ed.). 1990. *All Before Them, 1660-1780*. London and Atlantic Highlands: The Ashfield Press.

Miller, Henry Knight. 1976. *Henry Fielding's* Tom Jones *and the Romance Tradition*. Victoria: University of Victoria.

Miller, Stuart. 1967. *The Picaresque Novel*. Cleveland and London: The Press of Case Western Reserve University.

Monkman, Kenneth. 1971. 'Sterne, Hamlet, and Yorick: Some New Material' in Arthur Hill Cash and John M. Stedmond (eds) *The Winged Skull: Papers from the Laurence Sterne Bicentenary Conference*. London: Methuen: 112-123.

Moore, Robert Etheridge. 1948. *Hogarth's Literary Relationships*. Minneapolis: University of Minnesota Press.

Müller, Patrick. 2009. *Latitudinarianism and Didacticism in Eighteenth-Century Literature: Moral Theology in Fielding, Sterne, and Goldsmith*. Frankfurt am Main: Peter Lang.

New, Malvyn and W.G. Day. 2002. 'Notes to *A Sentimental Journey*' in Laurence Sterne *A Sentimental Journey through France and Italy* and *Continuation of the Bramine's Journal* (eds Melvyn New and W.G. Day) (The Florida Edition of the Works of Laurence Sterne). Gainesville: University Press of Florida: 230-383.

Niehus, Edward L. 1985. 'Quixote Figures in the Novels of Sterne' in *Essays in Literature* 12(1): 41-60.

Nietzsche, Friedrich. 1986. *Human, All Too Human: A Book for Free Spirits* (tr. R.J. Hollingdale). Cambridge: Cambridge University Press.

Nixon, Cheryl L. 2011. *The Orphan in Eighteenth-Century Law and Literature: Estate, Blood, and Body*. Farnham: Ashgate.

Novak, Maximillian E. 1977. 'Introduction" in Maximillian E. Novak (ed.) *English Literature in the Age of Disguise*. Berkeley, Los Angeles, London: University of California Press: 1-14.

Nowicki, Wojciech. 1986. *The Picaresque Hero in a Sordid World. A Study of the Early Novels of Tobias Smollett*. Lublin: Uniwersytet Marii Curie Skłodowskiej, Wydział Humanistyczny.

———. 1994. *"Models" and "Countermodels": Literariness in Fielding's "Joseph Andrews"*. Gdańsk: Wydawnictwo Gdańskie.

———. 2008. *Awatary Szaleństwa: O Zjawisku Donkiszotyzmu w Powieści Angielskiej XVIII Wieku*. Lublin: Wydawnictwo Uniwersytetu Marii Curie-Skłodowskiej.

Parnell, Paul E. 1963. 'The Sentimental Mask' in *PMLA* 78(5): 529-535.

Parnell, Tim. 2009. '*The Sermons of Mr. Yorick*: The Commonplace and the Rhetoric of the Heart' in Thomas Keymer (ed.) *The Cambridge Companion to Laurence Sterne*. Cambridge: Cambridge University Press: 64-77.

Paulson, Ronald. 1976. 'Life as Journey and as Theater: Two Eighteenth-Century Narrative Structures' in *New Literary History* 8: 43-58.

———. 1998. *Don Quixote in England: The Aesthetics of Laughter*. Baltimore and London: The Johns Hopkins University Press.

Perry, John (ed.). 2008. *Personal Identity*. Berkley and Los Angeles: University of California Press.

Pfister, Manfred. 2001. *Laurence Sterne*. London: Nortcote House/British Council.

Phelps, Gilbert. 1988. *A Short Guide to the World Novel: From Myth to Modernism*. London: Routledge.

Pomper, Philip. 1985. *The Structure of Mind in History: Five Major Figures in Psychohistory*. New York and Guildford: Columbia University Press.

Porter, Roy. 1985. 'Making Faces: Physiognomy and Fashion in Eighteenth Century England' in *Etudes Anglaises* 38(4): 385-396.

——— (ed.). 1997. *Rewriting the Self: Histories from the Renaissance to the Present*. London: Routledge.

Preus, J. Samuel. 1991. 'Secularizing Divination: Spiritual Biography and the Invention of the Novel' in *Journal of the American Academy of Religion* 59(3): 441-466.

Putney, Rufus. 1940. 'The Evolution of *A Sentimental Journey*' in *Philological Quarterly* 19: 349-369.

Rademacher, Jőrg W. 1996. 'Totalized (Auto-)Biography as Fragmented Intertextuality: Shakespeare, Sterne, Joyce' in David Pierce and Peter de Voogd (eds) *Laurence Sterne in Modernism and Postmodernism*. Amsterdam and Atlanta: Rodopi: 81-86.

Rawson, Claude J. 1972. *Henry Fielding and the Augustan Ideal under Stress: "Nature's Dance of Death" and Other Studies*. London and Boston: Routledge and Kegan Paul.

Ribeiro, Aileen. 1984. *The Dress Worn at Masquerades in England, 1730-1790, and Its Relation to Fancy Dress in Portraiture*. New York: Garland Publishing.

Richetti, John. 1999. *The English Novel in History 1700-1780*. London: Routledge.

Riley, Philip. 2007. *Language, Culture and Identity*. London: Continuum.

Ross, Ian Campbell. 2001. *Laurence Sterne: A Life*. Oxford: Oxford University Press.

———. 2009. 'Laurence Sterne's Life, Milieu, and Literary Career' in Thomas Keymer (ed.) *The Cambridge Companion to Laurence Sterne*. Cambridge: Cambridge University Press: 5-20.

Rousseau, G.S. 1971. 'Smollett and the Picaresque: Some Questions About a Label' in *Studies in Burke and His Time* 12: 1886-1904.

Ryba, Janusz. 1998. *Maskarady Oświeconych. Próba Opisu Zjawiska*. Katowice: Wydawnictwo Uniwersytetu Śląskiego.

———. 2009. *Oświeceniowe Tutti Frutti: Maskarady – Konwersacja – Literatura*. Katowice: Wydawnictwo Uniwersytetu Śląskiego.

———. 2011. 'Rozkosze Światowców: Konwersacja' in Teresa Kostkiewiczowa (ed.) *Przyjemność w Kulturze Epoki Rozumu*. Warszawa: DiG: 45-52.

Sacks, Sheldon. 1964. *Fiction and the Shape of Belief: A Study of Henry Fielding with Glances at Swift, Johnson and Richardson*. Berkeley and Los Angeles: University of California Press.

Schofield, Mary Anne. 1990. *Masking and Unmasking the Female Mind: Disguising Romances in Feminine Fiction, 1713-1799*. Cranbury: Associated University Presses.

Schonhorn, Manuel. 1968. 'Fielding's Digressive-Parodic Artistry: *Tom Jones* and the Man of the Hill' in *Texas Studies in Language and Literature* 10: 207-214.

Sherburn, George. 1959. 'Fielding's Social Outlook' in James L. Clifford (ed.) *Eighteenth-Century English Literature*. New York: Oxford University Press: 251-273. First published in 1956 in *Philological Quarterly* 25: 1-23.

Sherman, Stuart. 2005. 'Diary and Autobiography' in John J. Richetti (ed.) *The Cambridge History of English Literature, 1660-1780*. Cambridge: Cambridge University Press, pp. 649-672.

Shesgreen, Sean. 1972. *Literary Portraits in the Novels of Henry Fielding*. DeKalb: Northern Illinois University Press.

Simpson, Kenneth. 1988. *The Protean Scot: The Crisis of Identity in Eighteenth-Century Scottish Literature*. Aberdeen: Aberdeen University Press.

Sinko, Zofia. 1973. 'Wstęp' in Laurence Sterne *Podróż Sentymentalna przez Francję i Włochy* (tr. Agnieszka Gliczanka). Wrocław: Zakład Narodowy im. Ossolińskich: III-LXXXIII.

Skinner, John. 1996. *Constructions of Smollett: A Study of Genre and Gender*. Newark: University of Delaware Press.

Spacks, Patricia Mayer. 1976. *Imagining a Self: Autobiography and Novel in Eighteenth-Century England*. Cambridge: Harvard University Press.

——. 2003. *Privacy: Concealing the Eighteenth-Century Self*. Chicago and London: The University of Chicago Press.

Stafford, Barbara. 1996. 'The Eighteenth Century at the End of Modernity' in *Good Looking: Essays on the Virtue of Images*. Cambridge: MIT Press: 54-67.

Steward, Carol. 2010. *The Eighteenth-Century Novel and the Secularization of Ethics*. Farnham: Ashgate.

Stovel, Bruce. 1989. '*Tom Jones* and the *Odyssey*' in *Eighteenth-Century Fiction* 1: 263-279.

Tadié, Alexis. 2003. *Sterne's Whimsical Theatres of Language: Orality, Gesture, Literacy*. Farnham: Ashgate.

Tennant, R.C. 1982. 'The Anglican Response to Locke's Theory of Personal Identity' in *Journal of the History of Ideas* 43(1): 73-90.

Thompson, Carl. 2011. *Travel Writing*. London: Routledge.

Thornbury, Ethel Margaret. 1931. *Henry Fielding's Theory of the Comic Prose Epic*. Madison: University of Wisconsin.

Tileagă, Cristian and Jovan Byford (eds). 2014. *Psychology and History: Interdisciplinary Explorations*. Cambridge: Cambridge University Press.

Todd, Janet. 1986. *Sensibility: An Introduction*. London: Methuen.

Todorov, Tzvetan. 1995. *The Morals of History* (tr. Alyson Waters). Minneapolis: The University of Minnesota Press.

Tseëlon, Efrat (ed.). 2001. *Masquerade and Identities: Essays on Gender, Sexuality, and Marginality*. London and New York: Routledge.

Van Sant, Ann Jessie. 1993. *Eighteenth-Century Sensibility and the Novel: The Senses in Social Context*. Cambridge: Cambridge University Press.

Varey, Simon. 1990. *Space and the Eighteenth-Century English Novel*. Cambridge: Cambridge University Press.

Viviès, Jean. 2002. *English Travel Narratives in the Eighteenth Century: Exploring Genres* (tr. Claire Davison). Aldershot: Ashgate.

Voogd, Peter Jan de. 1981. *Henry Fielding and William Hogarth: The Correspondences of the Arts*. Amsterdam: Rodopi.

Wahrman, Dror. 2004. *The Making of the Modern Self: Identity and Culture in Eighteenth-Century England*. Yale: Yale University Press.

Watt, Ian. 1949. 'The Naming of Characters in Defoe. Richardson and Fielding' in *Review of English Studies* 25: 322-338.

———. 2001. *The Rise of the Novel: Studies in Defoe, Richardson and Fielding*. Berkley and Los Angeles: University of California Press.

Westen, Drew. 1985. *Self and Society: Narcissism, Collectivism, and the Development of Morals*. Cambridge: Cambridge University Press.

Wicks, Ulrich. 1974. 'The Nature of Picaresque Narrative: A Modal Approach' in *PMLA* 89: 240-249.

Wieczorkiewicz, Anna. 1996. *Wędrowcy Fikcyjnych Światów. Pielgrzym, Rycerz i Włóczęga*. Gdańsk: słowo/obraz terytoria.

Wikander, Matthew H. 2002. *Fangs of Malice: Hypocrisy, Sincerity, and Acting*. Iowa City: The University of Iowa Press.

Wright, Andrew. 1966. *Henry Fielding: Mask and Feast*. Berkeley and Los Angeles: University of California Press.

Zunshine, Lisa. 2005. *Bastards and Foundlings: Illegitimacy in Eighteenth-Century England*. Columbus: Ohio State University Press.

Index